# Rivets, Trivets &
# Galvanised Buckets

# Rivets, Trivets & Galvanised Buckets

## Life in the village hardware shop

## TOM FORT

HEADLINE

First published in 2023 by
HEADLINE PUBLISHING GROUP

1

Please refer to page 288 for image credits.

Cataloguing in Publication Data is available from the British Library

Hardback ISBN: 978 1 4722 9196 7

Designed and typeset by EM&EN
Printed and bound in Great Britain by Clays Ltd, Elcograf S.p.A.

Headline's policy is to use papers that are natural, renewable and recyclable
products and made from wood grown in well-managed forests and other
controlled sources. The logging and manufacturing processes are expected
to conform to the environmental regulations of the country of origin.

HEADLINE PUBLISHING GROUP
An Hachette UK Company
Carmelite House
50 Victoria Embankment
London EC4Y 0DZ

www.headline.co.uk
www.hachette.co.uk

*To Caroline Dawnay*

# Contents

Prologue *ix*

One: Everyone Needs Something *1*

Two: The Handyman Cometh *18*

Three: Doing It Her Way *31*

Four: Hardware in the Time of Lockdown *47*

Five: The Wild Place *62*

Six: He Did It Barry's Way *78*

Seven: Butcher's Hooks and Ideal Homes *89*

Eight: A Man and His Toolbox *102*

Nine: 'Without Tools, He is Nothing' *110*

Ten: A Man and his Workshop *127*

Eleven: The Death of DIY? *143*

Twelve: Rivets, Trivets . . . *151*

Thirteen: . . . and Galvanised Buckets *168*

Fourteen: Lockpickers, Nail-makers and Fruit-bottlers *181*

Fifteen: Let There Be Light (and Sandpaper,
Masking Tape and Rawlplugs) *198*

Sixteen: If I Had a Plunger (and a Hammer) *214*

Seventeen: If I Had a Screwdriver (or a Spirit Level) *223*

Eighteen: The Indispensables *232*

Nineteen: The Cabinet of Death *249*

Twenty: 'Would You By Any Chance . . . ?' *264*

Postscript *285*

*Acknowledgements 287*

*Bibliography 289*

*Index 299*

# Prologue

THE SHOP STANDS BACK from the road as if reluctant to advertise itself too obviously. It doesn't have to. Almost everyone in the village knows Heath & Watkins and what its business is.

In front is the forecourt, an expanse of tarmac where customers park their cars with varying degrees of care and consideration for others. The surface has been patched and repaired many times, but as soon as one hole is filled, it seems that another appears. When there has been a lot of rain, there are puddles great and small to be avoided. People grumble, but it doesn't deter them from coming.

Between the forecourt and the road is a long, rectangular raised bed made of sturdy railway sleepers. It contains a section of holly hedge merging into laurel, a yucca, a solitary flowering cherry – its partner died – and assorted shrubs. The bed, and others, are weeded and kept orderly by a group of worthy volunteers known as the Village Gardeners – mainly in their sixties or older, mainly female but with a couple of blokes. They assemble one Thursday morning and one Sunday morning each month in their green gilets with barrows and tools to do their bit to make the village presentable.

The shop occupies half of the ground floor of a substantial building dating from the 1920s. It has no pretensions to architectural distinction. But with its steep, tiled roof, high chimneys, decorative vertical beams set into pebbledash under the eaves, and its wide first-floor bay windows, it has a certain solid dignity, verging on handsomeness. When I came to live in the village in the 1990s, the other half of the ground floor was a newsagent's, where I bought my paper. I used to observe and relish the palpable tension between the couple who ran it: a quiet, reserved and harassed husband, and his more vivacious wife, who smoked a great deal and always wore short dark skirts, usually flecked with cigarette ash. In time, their lease expired and they moved away, and for several years the premises has been a dry-cleaner's.

The retail mix along the forecourt is completed by a small, square single-storey building of extreme functionality. This is a pet shop, dispensing food, treats, toys, bedding, crates and cages, dietary supplements and the full range of other items required by the village's army of pet owners to keep their animals healthy and contented. There is another, much larger, pet shop on the far side of the village, not more than half a mile away; that this place can sustain two such competing businesses is testimony to the size and purchasing power of the pet-owning community.

Above and behind our shop and the dry-cleaner's are two separate maisonettes. Aesthetically, the appeal of the whole building is unarguably let down by the single-storey extension added at the side of the shop and the yard next to it, which is covered by corrugated plastic sheets laid at a very slight angle over a wooden frame. The yard is separated from the forecourt by a roll-up garage door, a side door and some wooden panelling. During business hours, the garage door is normally kept open to allow access to the stock stored in the yard, and to the battered wooden workshop at the back, which were the premises of Heath & Watkins in its original incarnation in pre-war days.

The name is a masterpiece of the commonplace. When I was a boy, I was much intrigued by posters in my home town of Reading advertising the services of a company called Vanderpump, Wellbelove, Wellesley-Smith and Co. The Dickensian resonance of this triumvirate was striking, and suggested to my youthful mind an enterprise of great but mysterious importance (in fact, they were and remain a firm of chartered surveyors, although the Wellesley-Smith was dropped from the name some years ago). In contrast, the conjunction of Heath with Watkins suggests nothing of note – no mystery, no importance, just a somewhat colourless respectability. Mr Heath and Mr Watkins: they could be anyone, engaged in anything.

The profound and reassuring ordinariness of the name fits perfectly with the location and appearance of the shop. The road in front is a very ordinary road, which leads in one direction to a bend and another very ordinary road, and in the other to what is known as the village centre, where the majority of the shops and the village hall are located. I say 'known as the village centre' because, in terms of its shape and physical composition, our village does not have a centre in the traditional sense. There is no green, no place for the villagers to gather for recreation or protest or to put up a maypole, no old church with ancient yews and lychgate and bells to mark the time and summon the faithful to prayers. Our village has no old history, nor any accidental historical associations; it hardly even warrants a footnote in the annals of times past. It came into existence piecemeal during the course of the last century, creeping, dwelling by dwelling, along what had previously been rural lanes and cart tracks, spreading offshoots which were in turn built on. It grew steadily, but was not recognised as an administrative entity in its own right until – more than halfway through the century, and with a population of more than 1,500 – it became the parish of Sonning Common.

IT IS EASTER SATURDAY. The clouds have parted, and there is a precious warmth from the sun, and a softness in the air that speaks of spring and nudges minds towards summer. It is a time to think about plants and projects.

Outside the shop stand trolleys stacked with trays set out to greet the new season in the garden: pots of pansies, primroses, violas and sweet peas ready for planting out. On stacks of pallets, the veg and fruit are displayed: leeks slenderer than pencils, sprigs of lettuce, delicate runner beans and cucumbers, clumps of strawberries, fronds of carrot leaves. The foliage bends to the breeze. Everything looks small and vulnerable, but green with promise.

A car arrives and a couple get out. They are both beyond retirement age but fit enough. There is a purposeful air about the way they approach the shop. They are here to buy, not just to browse and dither. But the browsing is part of it, and they divide either side of the first trolley of bedding plants to examine the contents and exchange comments. They remove a couple of trays and place them on a convenient pallet for the moment.

They move on to the veg display. One remarks that late March or early April is very early to be putting out runner beans or leeks or anything else. But they agree that a place might be found in the greenhouse for the infant seedlings to be protected until the soil has warmed enough for them to face the rigours of the English summer, so several strips are added to the intended basket.

In the window behind the vegetables is displayed an array of essentials for garden wellbeing. There is a discussion about seed potatoes and onion sets and bulbs, then another about the respective merits of pelleted chicken manure and other plant foods. A need for a new pair of knee pads is identified. The case for buying the gleaming partnership of ash-handled spade and fork is made, but eventually not accepted.

It so happens that she likes to bake and he likes to make, and in the other window of the shop can be found the where-withal for the pursuit of both interests. Her eyes range over the cake tins and pastry shapers and equipment for piping icing. She is well aware that she has everything she needs at home, but that is all old and familiar, and it is pleasant to let the mind roam over the possibilities suggested and sharp-ened by the gleaming new.

As she has her store of baking paraphernalia, so he has a box overflowing with screwdrivers, chisels, spanners and the rest; and hooks and big nails in the cross-struts of his shed, from which hang saws and drills and other larger tools. Like her, he does not need a new saw in the sense that there is an actual deficiency. But what about his saw? It is flecked with rust and the teeth are worn. With that new one in the window – its unsullied silver blade glinting, its teeth so sharply defined – he could go through lengths of two-by-four like the proverbial hot knife through butter.

And what is that hanging temptingly just to the right of the saw? He presses his nose to the glass to get a closer view. A rivet gun with pop rivets. Now *that* he does not have. Nor does he have a clear idea of what he would do with it, except he knows that, with rivets, you can achieve results impossible with bolts and nuts and screws. In his mind's eye, he sees himself finally replacing the sagging shed guttering with something fit for purpose; or attaching an elegant brass plate inscribed with the name or number of their house to the gatepost; or . . . His imagination wanders in various directions.

The shop is a nurturer of dreams. It reveals paths and invites customers to follow them. It provides for basic every-day requirements, such as lightbulbs, batteries, matches, washing-up liquid and the like, but also promotes higher ambitions. With a bag of screws, a strip of Rawlplugs and some brackets, you can, at last, begin installing the book-shelves for which your living room has been silently yearning for years. Add paint and new brushes, and you can breathe life and colour into those tired walls. A packet or two of veg seeds or trays of the infant plants, and you picture your raised beds bursting with produce – wigwams of climbing beans, dense ranks of carrot tops, thickets of peas, their pods heavy and fat. A tub of tile grouting, and the shower surround, with its distressing streaks of black mould along the joints, is transformed into ceramic perfection. A box of grass seed and another of fertiliser and moss killer combined, and the lawn – in which the grass has fought and lost the war with plantains, clover, daisies and moss – becomes a lush carpet hardly distinguishable in terms of quality from Centre Court at the start of Wimbledon fortnight.

In their imaginations, the customers of the shop glimpse visions of homes and gardens reborn. Of course, a harsh reality lurks in the chasm between hope and outcome. But in the context of the relationship between shop and customer, it doesn't matter that the shelves in the living room sag a little when the books are put on them, or that the smartness of the newly painted walls fades; it doesn't matter that the cakes don't always rise, or that most of the carrots fail to germinate and the lettuces are ravaged by slugs, and the moss raked out of the lawn so effortfully is back by the following winter. These trials and tribulations may be and are discussed in the shop – but they belong elsewhere. The contract between shop and customer is founded firmly on aspiration and hope rather than on Proust's 'dust of realities'.

THE NAME OF the shop is written in plain white capitals on the pale green fascia that runs its length, with the street number at either end. It has been like that for as long as anyone can remember, and is a significant element of the image that the shop presents to the world. It is not self-consciously old-fashioned, but there is something potently timeless about it. You feel that it could have belonged in any decade from the 1930s onwards, and would be entirely appropriate in a post-war black-and-white Ealing comedy.

Imaginatively, you would not be surprised to see Margaret Rutherford pedal past on a Rudge's touring bike with a woven basket attached to the handlebars, or Stanley Holloway pull up in a Riley RMB, or the youthful Dickie Attenborough emerge and light a fag, his trilby at a jaunty angle.

This is our shop.

## CHAPTER ONE

# Everyone Needs Something

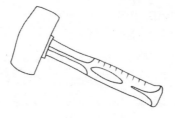

I AM NOW on the wrong side of seventy. I have lived in the village for more than twenty-five years. I am used to it and find it still suits me, so I suspect I will see out my days here. When I came, I knew no one. It was just a place with a small house I could afford to buy, within easy distance of the railway station at Reading so I could get to my job at the BBC in London. I was bruised by a recent divorce, and battered spiritually and financially by the attendant upheaval. I was also somewhat daunted by the challenge of doing the best I could for my three children, then aged between eight and fifteen.

In the first years, I got to know my immediate neighbours – an elderly couple on one side who were very kind to me, and a young couple on the other – and no one else. I cannot recollect when I became aware of the hardware shop. I must have registered its presence as I developed the habit of getting my newspaper from the newsagent's next door, and sooner or later, in need of a light bulb or a ball of garden twine, I would have encountered Mick behind the counter. If you lived in the village and regularly needed household or garden items, that meant getting to know him to a degree. It was impossible not to.

His name was Mick Wells. He was sometimes referred to by regulars as Uncle Mick, which he liked, because – I suspect – it accorded with his preferred self-image as a gruff, friendly, no-nonsense, feet-on-the-ground sort of chap, who knew the world and its ways and was regarded as a reliable dispenser of advice and opinions on practical matters, whether or not the means to address them were available in the shop. He was generally to be found perched on a stool behind the counter, on whose worn and shiny laminate surface he would spread his big hands, clenching a fist or jabbing a finger to emphasise his point.

His physique was not particularly impressive, perhaps diminished by various brushes with cancer. But his head and features – which were what you saw most of – were imposing. He had a fine nose and a distinctive white beard that matched his strong, forceful voice. Like all of us, Mick was more complicated than he seemed. But in the one-dimensional relationship between shopkeeper and customer, to know him was generally to warm to him. The transaction might extend no further than a new nail brush or a packet of lettuce seeds, but he always had time to explore whatever issue of the day had caught his attention, or discuss the weather as it related to the health of the plants and vegetables he grew. As a degree of intimacy was established, he became more confidential, relaying titbits about the meanness, ignorance and eccentricities of his other customers.

He would talk with anyone, but favoured the company of men, with whom he felt comfortable in calling a spade a fucking spade and indulging a fondness for colourful invective that deviated somewhat from his easy-going Uncle Mick persona. His domestic situation was not straightforward. He had been married long before his Heath & Watkins days, and had two daughters from that marriage. But for many years he had lived with Jo, who had been his neighbour as well as working for him in his business. She had looked after him after their respective marriages foundered and he first got cancer, and the cohabiting arrangement had endured. They were, or appeared to be, a companionable couple. For several years, one of Jo's daughters, Emma, worked in the shop on a regular basis, until Mick – providing a glimpse of another, less genial side – decided he could no longer afford her wages and summarily dispensed with her services.

His previous business, whose accounts Jo was employed to keep in some sort of order, had involved the wholesale purchase and distribution of vegetables from a base near Slough. It had developed from an earlier enterprise centred on potatoes, a vegetable that Mick retained a keen interest in long after he had ceased trading in it in bulk. He was extremely knowledgeable about the merits and failings of different varieties, and was happy to drive many miles in his Range Rover in pursuit of a particular favourite seed potato to add to the range available at the shop. When I ventured into growing spuds, it became a bond between us, and he would sing the praises of Lady Christl, a 'first early' variety notable for smoothness of skin and pure whiteness of flesh, which Mick esteemed most highly of all.

In time, Mick had wearied of the veg business (or it may be that his affairs became too tangled to prosper – he was always distinctly vague about that phase in his life). He hankered for pastures new and began looking for a fresh challenge. It was thus that he became the owner and face of Heath & Watkins.

In 1938, two men – Jack Heath and Ted Watkins – who had both worked at a wireless company a few miles from our village, got together and opened a small workshop across the road from the current premises. They specialised in the sale and repair of radios and bicycles, and sold spare parts and other useful items as well. They did a decent trade, but then the war intervened. Jack Heath joined the RAF and Ted Watkins the Royal Navy, and the business was left in the care of a friend, Jack Sweetman. They both survived and returned to Sonning Common to take up the reins again. In 1958, they migrated across the road to 41a Wood Lane, taking the workshop with them. The shop premises and the maisonette above and behind it were owned by the village butcher, who – having invested cannily and extensively in acquiring local commercial premises – decided to move the meat side of his business to a bigger outlet opposite the post office.

Heath & Watkins became a hardware shop, with cycle repairs carried out in the old green workshop at the back of the yard. After Jack Heath's death, Ted Watkins assumed sole charge, and in time he handed over to his son James, who ran it successfully for more than twenty years up to 1990. A couple took it over for a while before selling it to Mick Wells.

Mick told me he paid £50,000 for the business. The ownership of the shop, the maisonette and the land behind had passed from the village butcher to his daughter (who owns it still). Mick paid rent to her, and initially he and Jo lived in the maisonette. Subsequently, as a result of some nimble wheeler-dealing, he managed to take on the lease of the other half of the building, which was under entirely separate ownership. He and Jo moved across to the other maisonette, and he then sublet both the second shop and his previous living quarters.

Mick relished such manoeuvring. It confirmed his view of himself as an astute operator; and if opaqueness is a measure of astuteness, he was right. A regular reader of the *Daily Mail*, he had acquired a deep-seated suspicion of 'them' – the powers-that-be, the regulatory authorities, the institutions appointed to ensure that citizens paid their dues. Mick paid his dues when he had to. But he was, by nature, a cutter of corners, who regarded rules on health and safety, workers' rights, planning and anything else that threatened his freedom of operation with contempt.

The shop's motto was 'Everyone Needs Something From Heath & Watkins'. It had prospered and continued to prosper modestly because proper attention was paid to meeting those needs. Very few villages in southern England (and not that many small towns) can boast a hardware shop. As the longest-established retail outlet in the village, Heath & Watkins remained an essential port of call, its position aided by the unusually rich and diverse mix of shops close by.

As time went on, Mick was in the shop less and less. After the abrupt departure of Jo's daughter, the serving slack was taken up by two male retirees who were acquaintances of Mick's. Mick himself had further health issues. When well, he liked to go on extended winter cruises with Jo, or attend to his pet project, a disused quarry he'd bought in rural Devon, where he had installed a caravan and some sheep.

The shop entered a phase of gentle decline. Mick was well aware of it, but preferred to blame competition from Amazon and the big DIY stores rather than address the root cause. People might need something at Heath & Watkins, but they had increasing difficulty in getting it.

THE TERM 'HARDWARE' is older than it might seem. It is sometimes assumed to have originated in the United States, and to have made its way across the Atlantic to elbow aside the good old-fashioned English 'ironmonger'. In fact, the *Oxford English Dictionary* dates the first written reference to 'hardware' to the sixteenth century, so it must have been current well before that. It was applied to a range of specific items, mainly metalware, that were contained under the broader umbrella of ironmongery. The dealer in such goods was the ironmonger, and the shop – when there was a shop – could be referred to as an ironmonger, an ironmongers or even an ironmonger's.

It is the way of language and the constant process of linguistic change that meanings shift and gain and lose currency in mysterious ways that are very difficult to record. It is not possible to say why hardware should have come to eclipse ironmonger as the favoured general term for the trade; although I do wonder if it might have had something to do with a perceived awkwardness in the naming of a shop and the provision and placing (or not) of an apostrophe, and the problem of pluralising it satisfactorily. The old designation has not disappeared entirely – I recently came across Dawsons Ironmongers (without any apostrophes) in the splendid covered market in Todmorden in west Yorkshire, and a fine hardware shop it is.

The word 'ironmonger' is Anglo-Saxon in origin. As a surname for those practising the trade and as a name applied to locations where such traders were concentrated – such as Ironmonger Row and Ironmonger Lane – it was widely recorded in the thirteenth century. A detailed inventory dating from 1356 of the stock in an ironmonger's shop in Cornhill, London, reveals an impressive range of metalware being offered for sale: iron gauntlets and braces, brass pots and plates, a trivet and sledgehammer, iron punches, fire forks, door latches, spits, hinges, axes, pincers, grates, chisels, locks, an anvil and much else. The shop, owned by John Leche, also sold non-metal items, such as cushions, bench-covers, tablecloths, a tapestry and even a wooden bedstead (valued at two shillings).

John Leche's establishment – which may well have comprised as many as three shops – was evidently a notable early standard-bearer in a tradition that reached its apogee in the splendour of the Victorian ironmonger. By 1850, many of the familiar staples of the good hardware shop of today were readily available in the ironmongers that had sprung up in towns and cities all over Britain. The first sensation that would have struck you as you entered a well-run, well-stocked ironmongery emporium in, say, 1864 (the year Dickens's last novel, *Our Mutual Friend*, was published) would probably have been olfactory: a rich and subtle aroma composed of paraffin, glues, oils, varnishes, polishes, waxes and a thousand other elements.

Behind the counter, in cap and heavy black apron, would be the proprietor or his assistant. First, you might inspect the lighting section: lamps, globes, mantles, glass chimneys, candles of wax and Russian tallow, bottles of linseed, cod and sperm whale oil, paraffin. Heating belongs next to lighting: fire grates, bellows, fire irons, fenders, coal scuttles, stoves powered by various oils. The kitchenware shelves are packed with tinplate pots and pans, enamelled dishes and utensils, kettles and coffee pots, breadboards and knife boxes. You glimpse mangles and ringers, gridirons and goffering irons, umbrella stands and coffin handles. A japanned bird cage hangs from the ceiling just above your head. Around the corner is drysaltery: Zebra black grate polish, Nixey's black lead, assorted dyes and bleaches, glycerine, treacles, varnishes and vinegar cleaners.

Edging your way forward to the tools section, there are ranks of spades: London spades, Scotch spades, Gloucester, Norfolk and Lancashire spades, rabbiting spades, draining spades, spades with T-shaped handles, D-shaped handles, Y-shaped handles. There are Warrington hammers, Exeter hammers, Canterbury claw hammers, mallets, pincers, pliers, vices, clamps. There are saws, planes, chisels, gouges, brad-awls, gimlets, bevels, spirit levels. There are nails. There are screws, now – mercifully – made with standardised threads.

Through the door at the back filters the racket of hammering and the roar of the furnace, coming from the workshop where many of the items in the shop are made. It is spacious enough for carriages to be wheeled in for repair. There is a machine for fixing metal rims to cartwheels, rolls of wire and coils of rope, prams and pushchairs, stacks of custom-built kitchen ranges and grates.

A catalogue printed in 1881 for the Norwich ironmonger Piper, Theobald & Co. illustrates the great range of essentials and extras that the middle-class Victorian household might aspire to possess. The goffering irons – for making ruffles and frills – were eight pence a pair. Parrot cages were between twelve and sixpence and thirty shillings, presumably depending on the size of the bird as well as the degree of ornamentation. A nine-inch chop cover was listed at one and ninepence; a bronchitis kettle (distinguished from other kettles by its immensely elongated spout with a flattened end for inhaling the steam), four and sixpence. An adjustable brass trivet was seven and ninepence; an Athenian hip bath, twenty-eight shillings and sixpence. The single most expensive item on offer was the Piper & Theobald patent refrigerator, with improved ventilation, at ten pounds fifteen shillings.

By then, however, the ironmongery landscape was changing. Factory mass production had already transformed the supply of basics, such as nails, screws and standard tools. It soon embraced a host of other essentials – kettles, saucepans, buckets, fire irons, lamps, pots, pans and the like. Choice widened immensely, restrained only by the space available in the individual ironmonger's premises. Chains of retail outlets developed. One of the best-known was under the name of George Mence Smith of Bexleyheath in south-east London, who advertised himself as 'an Italian warehouseman'. He began trading in Bexleyheath itself and expanded steadily until he had twenty shops in London and seventy altogether across south-east England. (Although Smith himself died in 1896, the businesses carried on under his name until the 1940s, when they were taken over by Timothy Whites.)

Broadly speaking, by 1900, shops selling ironmongery and household items – whether calling themselves Italian warehouses, hardware shops or ironmongers – were acting principally as distributors of goods made elsewhere. Some retained their workshops to do repairs and maintenance, but the old tradition of manufacture on the premises had largely died out. Tools, accessories and other articles poured out of the noisome and grimy factories that had sprouted in the industrial towns and cities over the previous half-century. The customer base was comprised of professionals making up the service industry – farmers, carpenters, tinmen, whitesmiths, blacksmiths, tanners, shoemakers, builders, carriers and the rest.

The notion that consumers might do some of this kind of work for themselves – might even wish to – had not yet taken shape.

BEHIND HEATH & WATKINS is a plot of land extending the width of the shop and perhaps fifty yards in length. The portion nearest the shop is concreted and used to store the pallets of compost, bark, topsoil and other bulky garden products in plastic sacks. One of Mick's favourite tasks was to move pallets around on an elderly forklift truck that he had picked up for a song from some other dodgy dealer. It had decidedly defective brakes, and characteristically, he never bothered to obtain the licence legally required for him to operate it.

Over the years, the rest of the plot became a graveyard of abandoned projects, littered with installations and objects associated with them. Behind the original green workshop was a large wooden store that had once been covered in roofing felt. This material had, over time, proved inadequate to resist rain and wind and occasional falls of snow, and had rotted and collapsed, its downfall accelerated by an invading force of brambles rooted in the gap between it and the perimeter fence. The surviving misshapen sheets of felt hung from the joists to which they had been nailed, leaving everything that Mick had stored there – including two upright fridge-freezers, a metal storage cupboard, various old tools and a stack of pots of Hammerite metal paint either forgotten or too damaged to be sold – exposed to the elements.

The green workshop itself was originally used by Mick to repair bicycles when the mood took him, which it did erratically. He subsequently agreed to rent it to Greg, a former groundsman who was looking to establish a one-man mechanical repair business focused on motor mowers. Greg's wife was (and is) the same Emma who once worked for Mick in the shop. Despite the strains created by her departure, Greg continues to operate there to this day. He is a man with a great talent for keeping mowers going, but even he is not always successful, and over the years a considerable number of his discards – abandoned either because they were beyond salvation, or because they had been forgotten by owners who had moved away or become too decrepit to do the mowing or had died – had been exiled to the store at the back to join the casualties of Mick's enterprises, where, like everything else, they rusted and decayed.

There were other ruins scattered about. There was a shed whose roof had long since fallen in, leaving its contents to degrade to the point at which it was no longer possible to determine what their original intended function had been. Lying on their sides or at curious angles were several of the trolleys once used to transport and display bedding plants, their wheels now broken or jammed. The cage on wheels in which the retailer of Calor gas was legally required to store the canisters – Mick could not be bothered with that kind of palaver – had been left at the foot of a large mound of rubble and broken bricks, with bindweed and brambles twisting their way through the mesh until it was held in a smothering embrace.

The melancholic effect of these relics was deepened by the gloom that prevailed over most of the plot most of the time. Two sides were enclosed by a high wooden fence, which Mick had had topped with strands of barbed wire to deter intruders. Along the bottom end and the boundary with the garden next door – Mick's since he and Jo had moved – someone had, long ago, planted a beech hedge. This had been left to make its own way in life, and had responded by growing from a hedge into a towering barrier of thirty-foot-high trees that blocked out most of the available sunlight.

The most prominent feature of this desolate scene was the skeleton of a large polytunnel that Mick had installed in the days of his first enthusiasm for the business. This will play a crucial part in the story I am telling, but first I need to introduce that story's chief protagonist, and – if a narrative about a shop can have one – its hero.

She is the long-term partner of the eldest of my five children. His name is Hugh. Hers is Sharona, taken from the hit song of 1979 (The Knack's 'My Sharona'), which her mother sang along to during the pregnancy. It has been shortened by Hugh to 'Shro'. I will not try to itemise Shro's many qualities here, as I hope they will become apparent as the story unfolds. Suffice for the moment to say that she has a great passion for making things and growing things, fortunately combined with a rare talent for both.

At the time of which I speak, she had a fairly low-level administrative job at the Ministry of Defence. She had once said that one of her many ambitions was to have a piece of land on which she could put up a polytunnel. She and Hugh had bought a small house in a suburb of Reading, where every available space, inside and out, was occupied by plants and herbs and flowers and vegetables. The garden was fine, she said, but think what you could do with a polytunnel. Her face shone with longing, nourished by visions of melons, grapes, sagging tresses of tomatoes and exotic blooms, burgeoning and ripening in the warm moisture promoted under plastic.

At that time, I was ready to expand my own gardening horizons, but in a much more mundane way. I had got married again, to Helen, and we had moved from the little house I had bought at the edge of the village to a bigger one in the centre, with a bigger garden. I had made raised beds to grow vegetables and a cage for soft fruits, and was ready to strike out in new directions – particularly that of potatoes, which I had never tried. Shro's polytunnel aspiration nudged open a door in my mind.

Mick's polytunnel had flourished for a while, until he began to lose interest. Then a bonfire was allowed to get out of hand, igniting the polytunnel's plastic covering and destroying it. That put paid to any lingering ambitions Mick may have had to play the part of nurseryman, and the frame was left to rust, with torn sheets and gobbets of burned plastic flapping mournfully from the struts whenever the wind blew.

By then, I was on friendly terms with Mick and I asked him if Shro and I could refurbish the polytunnel and restore it to its intended use. He gave us a free hand; he was more than happy to see it functioning as it should, providing he didn't have to do it himself or pay for it. Shro was exultant. She went straight to YouTube and studied videos showing how the re-covering should be done. She bought the plastic, and I was set to work digging the trench around the base of the polytunnel in which the plastic was to be fixed. Then, over the course of one long and arduous day, Shro, Helen, Hugh and I stretched the plastic over the frame, anchored and tightened it, and brought the polytunnel back to life. Shro took charge. It was my first experience of her leadership qualities. She was decisive, unfailingly good-humoured, ingenious in overcoming the many difficulties that arose and – as long as she was nourished by a regular intake of strong tea – tireless.

The resurrection of the polytunnel initiated a new phase in my relationship with Mick. By now he was in his late seventies, and his health and interest in the shop were flagging. He rarely served behind the counter any more, leaving it to his two assistants. He preferred to spend his time either tending to his sheep in Devon, or sitting on the sofa in his living room, watching daytime TV and working his way through the columns of the *Daily Mail*, always ready to pontificate on the state of the world for the benefit of anyone prepared to linger. He concerned himself closely with my selection of seed potatoes for the first planting in the raised beds I'd constructed in the polytunnel, and was almost as thrilled as I was when I presented him and Jo with the first fruits, a colander one third full of pale, fat, smooth Lady Christl tubers.

He gave me a key so I could use the side door to attend to the polytunnel's needs whenever I wanted to. I became a regular visitor and got into the habit of dropping in on him for a cup of tea and a dose of salty common sense. Shro came over two or three times a week from her home in Reading to tend to the flowers and plants on her side of the poly, as we called it (we had contrived an amicable division of space). Mick got used to seeing her around.

Mick was diagnosed with cancer for a third time. It was in his lung, and as he subjected himself resolutely to a new but familiar regime of chemotherapy and drugs, I do not think he ever really expected it to be third time lucky (and in fact he died on the last day of February 2019). One day, as we held our mugs of tea, he told me he had decided to pack in the shop. He asked me, more in hope than expectation, if I might be interested in taking it over. The alternative was the closure for good of a village institution.

I naturally asked if he couldn't advertise it as a going concern. He was not a man for self-deception. He admitted openly that trade had diminished to such an extent that the term no longer applied. But he was also insistent that, with new blood, new energy, new enthusiasm, it could be turned around. Might Sharona be interested, he asked tentatively?

I walked slowly back to our house with my mind swirling. I was an ex-BBC journalist and writer of books in my late sixties, and Helen was still a senior editor with the Corporation. It was inconceivable that either of us would embark on a new career in shopkeeping at our time of life. But Shro? I had a strong presentiment that she would leap at the chance. It matched many of her dreams, and I never doubted that she was brave enough and resourceful enough to meet such a challenge. I talked it over with Helen, and we then talked it over with Shro. Helen was sceptical; Shro – after she recovered from the initial shock – cautiously interested.

Mick and I talked more. He outlined the terms of a deal under which his lease on the shop and the maisonette – which had three years to run – would be transferred. We would pay a modest sum for the stock and a nominal sum for the business, which he conceded was, in effect, valueless. We decided that it might work if Shro was in charge. She was prepared to give up her job to take it on. We declared an interest in principle.

There ensued a lengthy period of negotiation, in the latter stages of which the lawyers became involved. The chief stumbling block was the condition of the building. Characteristically, Mick had entirely failed to fulfil the condition in his lease requiring him to maintain it in good repair. There was a leak in the roof over the shop, multiple leaks in the plastic covering over the yard, and the state of the maisonette was little short of ruinous. He had sublet it (cash in hand, of course) to a reclusive couple who shared it with their four dogs. The roof was damp because of a leak beside the chimney, two of the window frames were entirely rotten, and the guttering was falling off in various places.

For the owner to agree to the lease transfer, all this had to be put right. This was mental agony for Mick, because it meant he had to put his hand in his pocket in a major way, something he habitually avoided. His mood was not improved when the lawyers I had engaged said we should commission a full structural survey, as well as having the electrics and damp courses checked. At times, my relationship with Mick cooled, and came close to breaking point. He wriggled and ducked and dived, and complained bitterly that I didn't seem to trust him to get the work done – which I didn't. I took refuge behind the lawyers, and in the end he bit the bullet and forced himself to address the situation.

What had begun as a nice idea belonging in the realm of fantasy became an imminent and increasingly daunting reality. I do not remember feeling that anxious, but sub-consciously I must have felt it because – as the legal bills mounted – my hair began to fall out in patches.

Shro handed in her notice at the MoD. The couple living in the maisonette initially resisted Mick's demand for them to leave, and then – under some kind of pressure from him into which I preferred not to enquire – departed suddenly with their quartet of snappy dogs. They left the place filthy and stinking, and we had a testing few days cleaning and airing it, and removing the reeking carpets and other detritus. It became just about habitable, and Hugh and Shro arranged to let their house in Reading and move in.

On 1 October 2018, Shro became the lessee of 41a Wood Lane, and the owner of the business registered as Heath & Watkins, hardware shop.

## Chapter Two

# The Handyman Cometh

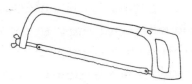

TWO MONTHS LATER, on a mild December day, we put on what we called the Grand Reopening, although it was neither grand nor a reopening, as the shop never actually closed. We invited our families and friends and the village. We provided beer and mulled wine and hot dogs, and laid them out on tables in the covered yard. The nearest we could get to a celebrity to officiate was my brother Matthew, a long-serving judge on the BBC Two series *The Great British Menu*. We had draped a ribbon across the yard for him to cut, and set out a pair of antique shears for the cutting.

He mounted a stepladder and burbled eloquently about the shop's glowing future. But, despite several energetic efforts, the ribbon refused to yield to the shears, which, on closer examination, proved to be blunt and badly warped. The shop scissors were sent for and the cutting was done amid much hilarity. Photographs were taken and the guests mingled amid the aromas of bangers and spiced wine. The till kept up a cheerful refrain as visitors did their bit to support the contention that Everyone Needs Something at Heath & Watkins.

A considerable number of the regular customers came as well, and to a man and woman, they said how glad they were that the shop had survived. But the event still felt uncomfortably reminiscent of those quayside farewells for mariners embarking on hazardous voyages, where the cheers and smiles and waving hands mask a nagging anxiety. We all knew that it would take a lot more than goodwill to keep the shop afloat, and that there was much to be done if the goodwill was to be turned into cash regularly earned. 'Everywhere I looked,' Shro said later, 'there was something that needed sorting. The shop was full of Mick's crud.' But a start had been made. The whole shop had been cleaned for the first time in years, and the windows filled with bright, clean, new stock.

Mick himself, sitting unseen on his sofa beyond the dividing wall between the properties, had expressed the hope that she would seek and follow his advice – after all, he had had twenty years' experience of running the shop and she had none. Much of his counsel, which he endeavoured to relay through me, involved avoiding costs and keeping the turnover below the threshold for paying VAT, a tax for which he retained a lively hostility. I suspect that secretly he hoped she would struggle and have to come to ask for his guiding hand. If so, he was disappointed. Shro surprised me with her lack of sentimental feeling towards him, which amounted to a polite ruthlessness. 'It's my shop now,' she said, 'not his, and I'll run it my way.' As for his offer to do a few shifts to smooth the transition and reassure regulars that everything was going to be the same, she was adamant she did not want him around. 'And it's not going to be the same,' she added. 'It's going to be a lot better, because it has to be.'

A feature of the layout that she particularly disliked was the island of chipboard shelving towards the far end of the shop, which rose almost to the ceiling, creating an awkward passage around it and obscuring any view of what was displayed on the walls beyond. It carried items of aged Tupperware, a hairdryer or two in boxes faded by prolonged exposure to light, and – an object of her particular scorn – an electric bun toaster ('Who would want a bloody bun toaster?' she snorted). She sentenced the shelving to banishment, dismantling and then reassembling it in the covered yard to display watering cans, rolls of wire mesh and other damp-resistant stock for which there was no room inside. The island was replaced by two hip-high shelving units on wheels, which Shro joined together by fixing a sheet of hardboard over them. Initially, she covered it in brown papier-mâché to smarten it, then decided instead to paint the whole thing in what she determined should be the Heath & Watkins livery, Urban Slate Grey.

Mick's island had stood on an expanse of dingy and damaged lino floor tiles, once sky-blue, but now grubby and worn. Beneath one curled edge, Shro and Helen caught a glimpse of terracotta. They lifted the square and realised that the lino had been laid over a floor of burned clay tiles, presumably put in when it was a butcher's. They and Hugh went to work with scrapers and solvents, and eventually revealed the full floor in all its rich, warm redness. It looked stylish but also old-fashioned in the right way, conveying continuity with the past and the impression that someone cared for it. Shro was very pleased.

In every way, she was fired by a sense of mission. She served behind the counter all week, bar two afternoons when one of Mick's old assistants stood in. She continued his practice of opening on Sunday mornings (although not his little tax dodge of making it till-free and cash only). Whenever there were no customers, she busied herself cleaning, moving, rearranging, and experimenting with different ways of displaying her wares. And in the evenings and on Sunday afternoons, she tackled the bigger projects, armed with her favourite companions, her electric saw and her Bosch cordless drill/screwdriver.

Shro is a born DIYer: nimble-fingered, meticulous in preparation, conceptually clear-sighted, infinitely painstaking, never satisfied with a job half-done or imperfectly finished. As a schoolgirl, she had excelled at design technology, and in her teenage years had repainted much of the family home, as well as stripping and refurbishing a dining table. She liked to roam around Homebase and B&Q, and was a devotee of home-improvement TV shows, particularly *Changing Rooms* with smiley Carol Smillie, languid Laurence Llewelyn-Bowen and the cheeky carpenter 'Handy' Andy Kane. She grew into adulthood believing that if anything around the house or garden needed fixing, she – with a little help from YouTube – should be the first to try to fix it.

If I had ever suggested to her (which I never did) that DIY was really an occupation for men, she would have looked at me and my son – both male, both DIY incompetents – and laughed incredulously. But, as in so many fields of endeavour, gender parity in DIY has taken time, and has not been easily won.

THE NOVEL PROPOSITIONS that women might be as capable as men, and that society should recognise this and allow women a full place within it, achieved significant traction in the United States long before the cause was taken up in Britain. A prime mover was an exceptionally high-minded woman, Catharine Beecher, who – following the death of her fiancé in a shipwreck – devoted the rest of her life to teaching, lecturing, campaigning on educational and social issues (including arguing for the abolition of slavery and for more humane treatment of Native Americans), and writing weighty volumes telling her fellow Americans how to live more fulfilling lives.

Born in 1800, Beecher was inspired by the example of her father, Lyman Beecher, a dynamic Presbyterian evangelist minister celebrated for his fiery denunciations of the wickedness of Roman Catholicism. Her moral vision was centred on the role of women in society, as mothers, wives and homemakers – even though her personal experience encompassed none of these. 'It is in America alone,' she wrote in her *Treatise on Domestic Economy*, published in 1843, 'that women are raised to an equality with the other sex; and that both in theory and practice their interests are regarded as of equal value.'

Such a contention would have been met with hilarious incomprehension in educated British society of the time, and regarded as dangerously revolutionary. But Catharine Beecher was no political radical. Unlike her siblings – who included the famous author of *Uncle Tom's Cabin*, Harriet Beecher Stowe – she argued against women being allowed to vote, on the grounds that they should not be tarnished by involvement in the rough and sordid world of politics. She asserted that, in morals and manners and education, women were actually superior to men, and that a healthy and vigorous democracy – to be found in the United States and nowhere else – should utilise that superiority fully.

In 1869, she and Harriet Beecher Stowe produced an epic work of instruction entitled *The American Woman's Home*. Its tone was set by its dedication to 'the women of America, in whose hands rest the real destinies of the Republic as moulded by the early training and preserved amid the mature influences of home'. The task of the American woman, the sisters declared, was to be 'the chief minister of the family estate', while that of the man was to be 'the outdoor laborer and provider'. Their theme was how best to minister to the family estate, covering everything from the deodorising of earth closets and the cleaning of chimneys to the benefits of fasting in Lent, drinking hot chocolate, early rising and refraining from speaking in angry tones, to the injurious effects on young women of dancing indoors in tight dresses.

In their introduction, the sisters nostalgically harked back to the pioneer past, when their female forebears, of necessity, swept, cleaned, cooked, baked, sewed, mended, and filled their days with wholesome hard work. But they recognised that the world had changed and society had developed. These menial chores were now most likely to be carried out not by women of education, but by their servants – most of them woefully untrained and ignorant. The thrust of the Beecher code of instruction was how to manage, not how to do. Women of leisure needed to learn how to enhance the performance of their servants, and, to achieve that, they required intimate knowledge of the household processes. 'Many would be willing to perform labor,' the sisters observed sadly, 'but are not willing to place themselves in a situation where their self-respect is hourly wounded by the implication of a degree of inferiority.'

Manual work of any kind was considered beneath the dignity of American women in polite society, and absolutely unthinkable in the British equivalent. But there was a class of activity that was not included in that prohibition, and was considered appropriately female on both sides of the Atlantic. That was decorative work with the hands: embroidery, needlework, appliqué, quilting, rug-making, japanning and the like. These activities, decorously pursued in the boudoir or drawing room, were acceptable in the same way that other accomplishments – drawing, the painting of pleasing watercolours, singing and playing the piano – were acceptable. They fitted with the more general view of the woman's place in the home, defined by John Ruskin as 'her power [. . .] for sweet ordering, management and decision'.

The Beecher sisters did not subscribe fully to this suffocating condescension. In a radical section about furnishing the ideal American home, they exhorted the American woman to set aside her needle and crochet work and be ready to 'drive a nail here and there' when refurbishing a broken-down armchair and transforming it into an elegant, chintz-covered easy chair for the parlour. This suggests a familiarity with hammer and nails that Ruskin and his fellow arbiters of taste in London would have considered most inappropriate. They would have been similarly taken aback by the suggestion a little earlier that 'your menfolk' should be amenable to a request for them to 'knock up for you out of rough unplaned boards some ottoman frames' – also implying the presence in their homes of tools and a familiarity with basic furniture-making techniques.

Radicalism was evidently on the march. In 1878, the fashionable and influential New York architect Henry Hudson Holly published a book entitled *Modern Dwellings in Town and Country*, in which he recounted how a 'gentleman' of his acquaintance, 'having considerable leisure amused himself an hour or two each day in an amateur workshop [where] he produced a number of very artistic pieces of furniture'. Another gentleman, having commissioned an 'artistic cottage', astonished his friends by furnishing one of the rooms himself with artefacts from his workshop. Moreover, his wife – blessed with what Holly termed 'a kindred talent for artistic work' – decorated the walls of the cottage with her paintings of flowers and leaves, installed decorative panels of glass, made the curtains, and designed a wooden scroll to support the curtain rods, 'which she herself cut with a bracket saw'.

At about the same time that Henry Hudson Holly was promoting woodwork and carpentry as suitable leisure pursuits for the idle rich, a contributor to the periodical *Godey's Lady's Book* – published in Philadelphia – urged women to try making their own furniture, which could be done 'by any lady who can manage a hammer and nails', adding that the 'little rough work that is needed is within the power of any schoolboy or manservant'. It is likely that the demarcation lines between what were and were not considered proper pastimes for gentlefolk were not as rigid as social historians would like to think. The embracing of the joys of suburban living came earlier in the United States than in Britain – Frederick Law Olmsted and Calvert Vaux completed the celebrated suburban community of Riverside, outside Chicago, in 1869. And it may well be that this fostered a more relaxed attitude to previously rigid social norms.

In America, adventurous would-be woodworkers might well have subscribed to *The Craftsman*, the periodical founded in 1901 by the Arts and Crafts pioneer Gustav Stickley. The early issues were mostly written by Irene Sargent, lecturer in aesthetics and Italian art history at Syracuse University. It was a distinctly elevated production, designed – as the foreword to the first issue stated – 'to promote and extend the principles' of 'the great decorator and socialist William Morris'. As such, it did not trouble itself with advice on the actual making of the beautiful furniture it featured. But, in other publications, Stickley did come down from his high pulpit to provide practical instruction, intended, in his words, to 'be utilized by any boy or man who wishes to do something with his own hands and head, and to learn how to do things right'. In a pamphlet entitled *Home Training in Cabinet Work*, Stickley advised readers on the purchase of a toolbox (ten dollars) and a work bench (eight dollars), and how to go about constructing a dog kennel, a bird house, a small chair, an armchair and various useful cabinets.

In Britain, the leading publisher of improving books and educational periodicals, Cassell, sought to exploit and expand a space in the market by launching, in 1889, *Work: An Illustrated Magazine of Practice and Theory* (later altered to *Work: An Illustrated Journal for Mechanics*). The first editorial declared: 'Never, forsooth, at any time has the necessity for sound technical education for the workman been so thoroughly impressed upon the minds of men as now; and never has it been so eagerly desired and demanded by all grades and classes of the people.' The founders sought to have their clarion call heard on both sides of the divide between professional and amateur workmen. 'If the professional works to live,' they demanded eloquently, if opaquely, 'does not the amateur in an equal degree live to work?'

Between 1893 and 1909, *Work* was edited by an Australian-born journalist, Paul Noonacre Hasluck, about whom disappointingly little is recorded beyond that he was born in 1854, came to England as a young man, lived in Brixton and died in 1931. His influence in the first flowering of handicrafts for ordinary people was immense. As well as editing *Work* and a sister publication, *Building World*, Hasluck complied around forty books of technical instruction, among them *Lathe-making: a Practical Treatise*; *Beehives and Beekeepers' Appliances*; *Sewing Machines: their Construction, Adjustment and Repair*; *Knotting and Splicing Ropes and Cordage*; and *The Clock Jobber's Handybook*. Other volumes cover making and repairing bicycles, bookbinding, making model boats and even the basics of sanitary conveniences and drainage – all culled from the columns contributed to the magazines he edited, which he reworked.

His magnum opus was *The Handyman's Enquire Within* (subtitled *Making, Mending, Renovating*), which Cassell published in 1908 and which was, in effect, an encyclopaedia covering the whole gamut of working with the hands. It was arranged alphabetically, beginning with acetylene – how to make the gas and use it in bicycle lamps – and extending to zinc and its role in making alloys and mixing paints. Much of the instruction was clearly not intended for amateurs. Some parts would have been extremely laborious to implement, for instance the recipe for glue – 'best made from waste pieces and parings from hide soaked in milk of lime for several days then drained and exposed to the air to dry, then soaked again in milk of lime, heated with water and alum added, filtered, run into moulds, made into cakes which are warmed over wire netting . . .' Some might well have proved hazardous, for instance mixing hog's lard with phosphorous, whisky, sugared flour and aniseed to make rat poison ('The most effective way,' Hasluck suggests drily, 'is to employ a professional rat-catcher.')

But there are plenty of straightforward tips for the Edwardian home-improver of any standard, on such essentials as what hammer or saw to buy, which hinges to choose, how to select appropriate nails, making wallpaper paste, combatting woodworm, and so on. It is all severely practical, and the prose and the drawings are as plain and functional as a bradawl. In contrast to *The Craftsman, Work* was far removed from the high ideals and artistic pretensions of the Arts and Crafts movement. It flourished by telling the archetypal handyman how to become handier, and by helping promote a growing fellowship of home-improvers.

In 1910, Ira S. Griffith, a professional teacher of woodworking, declared in an article for the American magazine *Suburban Life* that 'every person should have some interest apart from his daily work if he would maintain that balance and poise – physical and mental – which is so essential to right living [. . .] nothing has greater fascination or gives more satisfactory returns to the sincere participant than woodworking.' Two years later, the same publication carried an article about home decoration in which the term Do-It-Yourself – hyphenated and capitalised – was used. The American historian of DIY, Steven Gelber, believes this was its first appearance in print. The fellowship had acquired a name.

*

BY CHRISTMAS, our shop had begun to look like a patient on the mend after a long and debilitating illness. New stock had brought life and colour to the shelves. Shro had moved a window divider to create spaces of equal size. She filled one with gardening tools and accessories previously left in damp obscurity in the yard. Green wellington boots thrust their toe-ends out on the top shelf, attended by balls of twine below. Packets of bulbs promising bursts of garden colour when their season came hung from hooks on peg boards. Secateurs and trowels and hand forks with handsome ash handles posed seductively. Boxes of blood-fish-and-bone and sulphates of potash and ammonia stood shoulder to shoulder.

Although it had been gently but firmly made clear to me that I belonged in the same unwanted class as Mick in terms of serving behind the counter, I was allowed to assist with menial manual tasks, such as shifting pallets of compost or tackling unsightly legacies of the Mick era. Having liberated the metal cage in which the gas canisters were supposed to be stored from the clasp of brambles and bindweed, I set about restoring it to useful life. This involved hours of attack on the rust with a succession of wire brushes, followed by repainting it using pots of Hammerite metal paint rescued from the heap abandoned in the roofless outside store. It was a dirty, time-consuming, satisfying job, and I felt proud and fulfilled when the cage was wheeled into position in its restored blue colour, loaded with the heavy orange, blue and green gas containers, and secured by Shro with a padlock.

In the shop, customers were becoming used to the 'new management' advertised in the window. Shro listened to them, commiserated with them, and laughed with them as she sent them on their way with a cheery 'take care' or 'come back soon'. If they complained about the prices, she invited them politely to use Amazon or go to B&Q.

She put up a Christmas tree in the far window and decorated it with baubles, wooden spoons, spatulas, honey drizzlers, balls of string and gleaming tea strainers. For the fairy on top of the tree, she adopted a suggestion from my son and stuck on an upended empty bottle of retro Fairy Liquid (discontinued in 2000 and later reintroduced as a novelty). People loved it. Someone offered a carload of wooden reindeer figures they had cut from pine wood. They came with painted golf balls for noses, which Shro thought could be improved on, so she commissioned our daughter Rosie to prise them off and replace them with authentic baubles.

Next door, Mick beamed his approval. Heath & Watkins was back in business.

# CHAPTER THREE

# Doing It Her Way

THERE ARE SCORES of books about life in English villages. I added one of my own a few years ago called *The Village News*, and in the course of researching it, I became something of an authority on the genre. A great many – particularly those that involve looking back to childhood – are permeated with that facile sentimentality so often, and so offputtingly, associated with nostalgia for the past. But they are all – even those that concentrate studiously on data about poverty, violence, exclusion, prejudice and dreadful living conditions – inevitably partial. Any attempt to present a full picture of the village as an organism is certain to fail, because so much is necessarily hidden and therefore absent.

For twelve years, until shortly before beginning to write this book, I served on my village's parish council, and partici-pated in and helped organise several consultation exercises designed to elucidate what residents felt and feel about the place. Comments such as 'It has real community spirit', and 'People smile here', and 'It's a proper village', tend to predominate in the feedback, and these responses undoubtedly do reflect what some of the villagers feel about it some of the time. But the resulting picture is distorted, because it is those who feel that way who take the trouble to participate – and they do so *because* they feel that way. Those who do not share those sentiments rarely participate, and so their views are not taken into account.

The wholesome image of the village that smiles and cares is promoted forcefully by our village magazine, which is delivered every two months to every household. Scanning its pages, you would be forgiven for thinking that village life consisted of one endless round of giving, volunteering, fundraising for good causes, ethical campaigning, organic planting, worshipping, playing team sports, joining health walks, listening to enlightening talks, cleaning up rubbish, helping out at the schools, visiting the aged lonely, and everyone generally putting themselves out for the community.

A jacket-potato lunch is held to raise funds for the First Responders who attend medical emergencies. At the Horticultural Society's annual show, there is an award for exceptional runner beans and another for outstanding dahlias. Sixty pensioners attend the Christmas lunch at the village hall, and enjoy turkey with all the trimmings and a glass of Buck's Fizz, and are given chocolates and miniature gingerbread men. The Friends of the Library donate £1,300 for new books. Sixty-six volunteers fill sixty-eight sacks with rubbish in the annual spring clean. Five hundred cyclists join the 'On Your Bike Ride', raising £4,000 for good causes. Volunteers organise nine days of fun for children in the Memorial Park, with den-building, a mud kitchen and butterfly-spotting. A couple are featured for fostering their eighty-first baby. One of the churches puts on an artisan bread-making workshop. The choir celebrates ten years of staging public concerts.

Very occasionally, the magazine carries a hint of a darker side to village life. A scandalous episode in which a stolen car was driven through the woods and onto the football pitches, where it was used to smash goalposts and gouge tyre tracks over the grass before being set on fire, is reported with sadness. The decision of the health centre to stop offering ear syringing is mentioned. Those grieving for loved ones are invited to coffee and cakes by the Bereavement Group.

But, overwhelmingly, the sun rises on a busy and warm-hearted community at peace with itself and the outside world.

A rather more nuanced version of village life is encountered through the meetings and work of the parish council. Much of this is utterly mundane: street-cleaning, grass-cutting, maintaining the allotments, the pond and the children's playgrounds, addressing blocked drains, confronting invasions of Japanese knotweed, and so on. But the opening of the parish office on Monday mornings, and the open invitation to the public to attend council meetings, both provide opportunities for the tensions that simmer away beneath the surface to burst into infrequent flame. Over-hanging branches, untrimmed hedges, deposits of dog shit on pavements and footpaths, atrocious parking across pavements and at junctions, the throwing of beer cans and discarded balloons used for inhaling gas, fireworks, noisy parties – these can all arouse powerful emotions.

The powers of the parish council to intervene are very limited. It cannot, for example, impose speed limits, paint yellow lines to deter inconsiderate parking, take possession of derelict homes used for illicit drugs parties, or command the arrest of youths who climb onto the roof of our Co-op supermarket to lob missiles at passers-by. And it is often trapped in the conflict between what residents want and the requirements emanating from higher up the administrative hierarchy. The most contentious issue is the incendiary matter of building new homes. In general, people do not want new housing, because they think there is enough of it already, and they particularly do not want it close to their own dwellings. Yet the parish council is legally obliged to allow for new housing and has a significant role in determining where it should go. Those charged with trying to resolve the conflict – I was one of them for several years – sooner or later find themselves being verbally bludgeoned over hard decisions necessarily made, and the scars from such battles can take a long time to heal.

Nor has it always been sweetness and light on the council itself. When I first joined, the chairman was a formidable woman who regarded it as her personal fiefdom and brooked no dissent. It is the fate of tyrants, however, that, sooner or later, dissent is born and their power is challenged. So it was with ours, and her undermining and eventual overthrow were accompanied by extreme levels of bitterness and anger. At length, she went away to lick her wounds and growl threateningly from the margins. This ushered in an era of harmony and cooperation, which – with a few minor hiccups – lasted throughout the rest of my twelve-year period of service.

The work of the council was certainly better done as a result of the revolution, but it was less interesting, and I occasionally found myself nostalgically thinking back to the fire-and-brimstone of earlier days, when the raising of certain issues – the state of the flower beds in the village centre, for instance, or the extravagant spending on the ornamental duck house on the village pond (known whimsically as Duckingham Palace), or the defective state of our standing orders – would precipitate an immediate explosion of wrath.

The village is shaped like a wedge, with the broad end to the north-west and the tapered end to the south-east. It stands in a pleasant but undramatically undulating landscape of hedged fields and woods and copses. A mile or so to the south is the large town of Reading, which is on the confluence of the Thames and its largest tributary, the Kennet. To the north-east is the much smaller town of Henley-on-Thames. Smaller settlements are scattered around the district, for which our village acts as a service hub.

By English standards, the village is laid out on a spacious scale. Building took place in phases along the roads and lanes, with the spaces within the wedge being filled in by estates of new homes from the 1960s onwards. There are no individual houses of any architectural or historic distinction, but the village has a pleasingly leafy texture. The houses all have gardens, and the older ones extensive gardens, although quite a few have been eaten up by more houses. It is largely middle-class and predominately white-skinned. A sizeable and growing proportion of the population is defined as elderly (sixty-five plus), which concerns the would-be social engineers, but since most of the volunteers and do-gooders come from that demographic, there are advantages. The village has a secondary school and a primary school, so there is a significant flow of younger blood, which would be stronger still were it not for the prohibitive cost of housing.

Of course, there is misery in the village. There is violence, domestic abuse, alcoholism, cruelty, depression, drug-dependency, hatred, boredom, alienation, disillusion. There is loneliness, isolation, pain, sickness, mental illness, dementia. It is like anywhere else. But it would take a writer of fiction to tease out that dark, hidden dimension, and I am not a writer of fiction. Like everyone, I have had my blacker moments. I acknowledge that the cheerful picture presented by the magazine scratches no more than skin deep. But at the same time, I have never regretted the accident that brought me here; in most ways, this has been the happiest period of my life, that happiness embedded in the solid structure of life that supports the scratched surface.

IN THE VERSION OF American domestic life promoted so industriously by Catharine Beecher and her sister Harriet, women were kept away from full participation in the workings of society but – almost in exchange – controlled the home. The role of men was less clearly defined. Apart from being on hand occasionally to knock up an ottoman frame, they were largely absent. It can be assumed that they might be in the office making money, or at their club, or attending a meeting of other males bound together in a shared interest. If they did happen to be at home, they were probably sitting with legs crossed in an easy chair, reading the newspaper and checking on their investments.

Marital harmony required that the partners occupied what Professor Steven Gelber neatly identified as 'non-overlapping spheres of influence'. They would come together in the evenings to renew acquaintance with their children (otherwise looked after by servants) or to go out to dinner, the theatre or the opera, or entertain. Such occasions saw gender-mixing but also highlighted separateness – after eating, the women would gather in a drawing room while the men passed the port and cigars and discussed business. Sessions of male bonding might well extend into games of billiards.

But by the end of the nineteenth century, the demarcation lines were blurring. Middle-class women were joining mothers' groups and shopping together in the new department stores; some were beginning to agitate for a political say. The migration of the well-to-do from the cities to the cleaner air and manufactured greenness of the suburbs accelerated the process. Men were at home more and were being urged by the opinion-shapers in magazines and newspapers to pay more attention to their wives, and even to be prepared to help out around the house. The birth and growth of DIY can be seen as a measure of the profound societal changes taking place on both sides of the Atlantic.

The concept and practice of DIY was born before the First World War, went through childhood and adolescence between the World Wars, and came of age post-1945. Perhaps the key factor was the promotion and embracing of the ideal of home-ownership (although in Britain, generally speaking, this came later and more falteringly). Another, particularly in the Unites States, was the mass production and easy availability of automobiles. Car ownership encouraged the development of land for housing way beyond the reach of bus and rail services, enabling people to drive previously unthinkable distances to their places of work. Men were spending more time at home in the evenings and at weekends. They were with their wives and children more, around the house more, and, inevitably, they sought and created opportunities to spend that time usefully. DIY fitted their newfound ambitions perfectly.

In America (where it still tends to be known as 'do it yourself'), DIY was taken up with equal enthusiasm by white-collar and blue-collar workers, who often had the advantage of familiarity with tools and techniques. Many who splashed out on Henry Ford's Model T drove it home and then built a garage or shelter for it. Home improvement was seen as a way of saving money and of getting the job done when it needed to be done, rather than when a professional might get round to doing it. There was a moral element as well. Having a useful hobby was good for the soul, particularly if it involved enhancing that domestic temple, the home.

Respect and even reverence for the implements that made the hobby possible were eagerly fostered. 'Tools, like weapons,' wrote Arthur Wakeling, editor of the magazine *Popular Science*, in 1930, 'are very wonderful things when you get to know them well.' He encouraged the handyman to develop an almost sacred sense of duty towards tools, and in a book called *Things to Make in Your Workshop*, he provided a list of essential tools for the amateur woodworker and general DIYer that ran to well over 100 items, requiring a fair-sized workshop to house.

The spread of the hardware store fed this new enthusiasm. In 1929, Carl W. Dipman, editor of the journal *Good Hardware*, produced a book called *The Good Hardware Store*, in which he celebrated 'the rugged character and business acumen' of the new breed of retailer. In the face of competition from mail-order firms and syndicate stores, they had adapted and modernised to meet consumption that was now 'the largest per capita in the world' and still increasing 'by leaps and bounds'.

They were not just selling mass-produced tools. Home-owners could add extra interior walls using drywall panels made of gypsum, in which plaster was sandwiched between layers of paper. Linoleum, or lino (invented in England as long ago as the 1850s), became the kitchen floor covering of choice because it was so easy to lay and keep clean, and so durable. Bathroom walls shone with ceramic tiles, and amateur plumbers learned how to fit gleaming white basins, toilets and baths.

The target market remained overwhelmingly male, but women began to get a look-in. An advert in *Suburban Life* in 1911 stated baldly that 'women do not paint' but added that they 'should know something about the paint their painters use'. However, according to Carl Dipman twenty years later, the American female 'had become quite a painter', which was reason enough for hardware retailers to 'cash in on her peculiarities, her wants and fantasies'. Other avenues of usefulness were opening up. An article in a 1936 issue of *American Home* was daringly headlined 'Some Tips for Mrs Fixit', and asserted that women would derive satisfaction from being able to 'put new washers in leaky faucets and replace burned-out fuses without calling for male assistance'.

Britain soon followed where America led, and, here as there, what we would now call lifestyle magazines were immensely influential in shaping tastes and trends. The social historian Fiona Hackney analysed a clutch of new titles that appeared in the 1920s and 1930s, aimed at women and their roles as home makers. Home crafts – embroidery, crochet, flower-arranging, rug-making and the like – were presented as allowing opportunities for self-expression and self-reliance. The modern woman was encouraged to combine her creative side with 'economy renovations' – which, crucially, were expanded to include elements of DIY. An article in *Modern Woman* in 1935 urged readers to 'be your own decorator and save money', and gave practical advice on wallpapering, distempering and floor staining. An advert for Hall's Distemper declared: 'She rather than her pipe-smoking husband takes the important decisions.'

In an early issue of *Woman* – which first appeared in 1937 and is still going today – the long-serving home editor, Edith Blair, exhorted her readership to take up a toolbox and get stuck in. Under the headline 'I Did It Myself', she described how she had taken a plain trolley, sanded it, then sized and lacquered and painted it, turning it into a 'tea waggon'. The dilemma for women was how to venture into these exciting new fields of endeavour while retaining their traditional image. The writer Margaret Lane, in an editorial for the very first issue of *Woman*, summed it up thus: 'We are trying to blend our old world with our new. Trying to be citizens and women at the same time. Wage-earners and sweethearts [. . .]'

This meant not challenging the male domain. Edith Blair admitted that her 'magnificent triumph' with the tea waggon was initiated by her husband suggesting that instead of talking about the project, she should put on overalls and tackle it herself. DIY remained overwhelmingly male territory. In the introduction to *The Practical Man's Book of Things to Make and Do*, a 640-page compendium of DIY instruction published in 1940, the editor, James E. Wheeler, stated: 'The man with a hobby is generally happier, more resourceful and better able to think things out for himself than one who has no interest in anything other than his usual routine of work, meals and sleep.' DIY fitted this prescription perfectly, and the photograph at the front of the book shows the archetypal handyman thinking for himself and being resourceful while engaged in making a cabinet: sleeves well rolled up, waistcoat and sensible trousers, pencil behind ear, screwdriver in hand, an expression of intense but tranquil concentration on his bespectacled face.

It was important, James Wheeler declared, for the would-be practical man to start with the right attitude. 'If you are faced with a difficult task, do not let it get the better of you but make up your mind to master it.' Proper preparation was the key to success – 'be methodical, otherwise your efforts may become a bore rather than an interesting and pleasant pastime'.

With the right approach, a dazzling world of possibilities was opened up. Make a nest of dwarf tables, 'useful in any house'. Build yourself an aquarium, but remember that 'the glass should be sufficiently thick to withstand the weight of the water'. Fit a trapdoor into the ceiling – 'can be effected cheaply and efficiently' – or a pump for the bath, 'neither costly nor difficult'. Make a summerhouse or a gramophone; put a bridge over your garden pond ('considerably enhances the appearance of the pool'). Assemble a reflectorscope, 'a simply constructed apparatus which will give endless pleasure to the younger members of the family'.

The central theme is that, armed with the basic set of tools – saws, jack plane, smoothing plane, brace, chisels, gouge, screwdrivers, Warrington hammer, pincers, oilstone, mallet, bradawl, a two-foot rule and a few other items – the amateur handyman can expect to transform home and garden into a palace and pleasure ground of comfort, convenience and beauty. Unlike the DIY manuals of the more safety-conscious post-1945 era, *The Practical Man's Book of Things to Make and Do* wholeheartedly embraces a 'give-it-a-go' approach to electrical jobs. Fitting a new fuse board is simple. Electro-plating is well within the amateur's range, as is making a battery charger or a burglar alarm. There is advice on providing lighting for amateur theatricals (where a breakdown 'might be fatal to the performance') and on how 'an excellent floodlight can be made out of a large square biscuit tin'.

But there was a limit to gung-ho, even for James Wheeler. 'Never touch any electrical equipment while having a bath,' he counsels wisely.

Two months after Shro took charge at Heath & Watkins, a grand old hardware business in nearby Reading, Drews Ironmongers, shut its doors for good after eighty-seven years of serving the town. It was sad because it was very much a feature of the Reading retail landscape, and a tremendously useful shop, spread over two floors, that employed twenty-five people. But its closure undoubtedly gave a boost to our business. One of the Drews brothers who ran it came into Heath & Watkins and suggested to Shro that it might be worth her while coming over for the stock clearance then in progress. She came back with two magnificently seasoned tin cabinets in military green with multiple little drawers for holding washers, sink and bath plugs, wood screws, casters, jubilee clips, nuts and bolts, anchor bolts and a host of other items that self-respecting hardware shops are expected to stock even if their contribution to turnover is on the negligible side.

The two drawer cabinets fitted the image, the feel, of our shop perfectly. Apart from being extremely useful, they brought with them a sense of their own past; that they belonged in a tradition that had been of value to previous generations and unknown numbers of customers now departed. Shannon Mattern, a professor of anthropology at the New School University in New York, wrote perceptively about this aspect of the role of hardware shops (or stores) in an article entitled 'Community Plumbing'. She defined the good hardware store – she had grown up with her family hardware business in Pennsylvania – as an episteme, a repository of knowledge.

It must also be a place of safety and reassurance. 'In a world of uncertainty,' the Canadian writer and broadcaster Stuart McLean mused in a radio essay, 'hardware stores stand out as islands of confidence. Theologians despair, psychiatrists and social workers shuffle their opinions as often as their feet, politicians shrug their numbed shoulders in despair, but the clerks in my hardware store field problems with the coolness of a left-fielder in a grass outfield. No matter what your problems are, you should take them to the nearest hardware store.'

Shro and Helen have become used to fulfilling this role. They know where things are (including the contents of more than a hundred tin drawers) and they also have specialised knowledge. This may or may not extend to how to do standard DIY jobs; Shro is stronger than Helen on DIY, while Helen probably has the edge in plant knowledge. Then the customers, or some of them, bring aspects of their own knowledge with them. The process of the transaction, beginning with the question 'Do you by any chance have . . . ?', quite often teases out some of their expertise: a past experience directly or indirectly connected with the item asked for; a memory, a tip. It is shared, added to the invisible store available to the community at no extra cost.

Shro was finding that she was more than just a shop-keeper. She was the custodian of the shop's past: its look, its long-established function, its place in the shared consciousness. She realised that her customers were looking for more than just the light bulb or the bedding plants that had been their conscious reason for coming. They needed to feel that they were in a familiar and welcoming place where they might, if the mood took them, be comfortable in communicating something about themselves or learning something they did not know before.

It so happened that Shro's personality and way of talking were very well suited to this aspect of the shop's role in the village. She has a rare talent for the kind of superficially banal verbal exchange that oils the wheels of the ensuing transaction. Behind the shop, out of sight and earshot, she might be anxious, cross, tense, sipping her tea and confiding how irritated she had been by someone in search of a particular light bulb whose specifications they could not remember. Then the bell activated by the shop door opening would jingle, and she would put down her mug and hasten back inside with a cheery smile and a 'Hello, darling – how are we today?'

She was resolved to make the shop better than it had ever been by enhancing its traditional side while also embracing new ideas. One day, a woman came in and asked if Heath & Watkins did refillables – washing-up liquid, detergent, fabric conditioner, hand-cleaner and similar products, dispensed from bulk containers into bottles that can be brought back and used again and again. At the time, Shro didn't – but she soon did. She had read about the idea online and realised that it would catch on among consumers getting concerned about sustainability and ethical issues. She contacted a business in Oxford that had been developing the 'cleaner greener' market for some years and began by offering washing-up liquid and hand-cleaner. They proved popular and she quickly extended the range, eliminating the throwaway equivalents. People liked the change; it made them feel a little better about their carbon footprints without seriously threatening their cleaning efficiency.

Key-cutting is key business for the hardware shop. Mick had long ago bought two cutting machines – one for cutting cylinder keys, the other for mortice keys – which we acquired with the rest of his stock. The mortice key-cutter resided in Greg's workshop and was erratic in its performance. Sometimes the keys Mick cut turned the lock, sometimes they didn't. Shro quickly realised that people did not care for the hit-and-miss approach. She got rid of both Mick's machines and leased a single dual-purpose cutter for £60 a month, which came with a man to show her how to operate it. She practised until she felt confident enough to resume the service, and she then converted a small table she had bought from the charity shop across the road into a neat unit to house the machine and reduce the noise from it.

The first year of trading passed, and a second Christmas came and went. The shop looked as if it had undergone a miracle rejuvenation cure. We painted part of the frontage in the Urban Slate livery. The windows gleamed and glittered with temptation, and the shelves and surfaces and pegboards were filled and covered with stuff. Instead of Mick driving down to the warehouse near Bristol to load up with new stock when the mood took him, Shro organised regular deliveries. Takings were on a steady upward graph, and it was clear that the business was sound and would provide a decent living.

Then, on 31 December 2019, in an industrial city in central China that very few people outside the country had ever heard of before, the medical authorities released a statement about cases of 'a viral pneumonia of unknown cause'.

## Chapter Four

# Hardware in the Time of Lockdown

Like almost everyone, we watched the prime minister announce the first national lockdown on 23 March 2020. And, like almost everyone, we experienced a chill of anxiety amounting to fear. This was the most sudden and extreme upheaval in daily life in post-war history. Listening to Boris Johnson's words, it was difficult not to be swept by a sense of dread about what the future might hold.

We assumed that 'the immediate closure' of all non-essential shops would cover our shop. Shro mentally prepared to approach the landlady to ask for a rent suspension and get herself ready for a lengthy break in which she would hone and extend her crafting skills. Then the list of essential shops was published, and we were pleasantly astonished to find that hardware shops were on it, together with pet shops, bicycle shops and laundrettes (but not bookshops).

Shro readied herself for the new world order, realising that she would be entirely on her own. Barry, who had worked for Mick and had continued to do a couple of afternoons a week, was in the vulnerable age group and packed it in for good. Because of the narrowness of the shop and the need for social distancing, Shro imposed a restriction of one customer inside at a time. Other customers were asked to queue outside, two metres apart, and to be patient, although in the new national mood of care and consideration for others, the call for patience was hardly needed.

Initially, the response to lockdown was shaped largely by the need for people to understand the great number of things they could no longer do. Getting used to the idea that you could no longer go to work, go to the pub, buy books in bookshops, play team sports, go fishing and all the rest of it demanded a drastic overhaul of mental processes. But fairly soon, the majority got a grip on what they could not do and began to consider what they could do to keep themselves sane. Confined to their homes and finding that competition for their time and energy was much reduced, people looked at their immediate surroundings with a degree of close attention that felt quite unfamiliar and stimulating. The overlooked, the long-forgotten and the pushed-to-one-side were examined and assessed and added to a list.

People had time to paint windows. They discovered or resuscitated carpentry skills they didn't know they had. They pulled out lengths of two-by-four and planking discarded years before and brushed off the cobwebs. They got the bikes out of the shed, dusted the helmets, blew up the tyres and wobbled off along the lanes on family bike rides. Teenagers who, a few months before, would have no more contemplated a walk for pleasure than they would have volunteered to stop using their phones, pulled on boots and tramped the foot-paths with siblings and parents. Lifelong commuters denied the daily journey to the treadmill mixed cement to fashion patios and construct raised beds, inviting family members to admire the first seedlings.

The experience of lockdown revealed to a great many people aspects of themselves and the way they lived that they had not closely considered before. It reminded them why they had chosen to live where they did; what it was about their homes and gardens that had first attracted them; and of the unfulfilled plans they had once had to improve and enhance these spaces. DIY in its broader sense – embracing the garden as well as the home itself – was, for many, a way to deal with and mitigate the impact of the virus.

DIY OCCUPIES a somewhat indeterminate position in the hierarchy of leisure pursuits. It is clearly associated with the crafts category but is distinct from it because of the absence of (or minimal part played by) the creative impulse. It is likely that the crafter is capable of accomplished DIY if required to do it, but it is essentially beneath them. And the converse does not apply at all – the skilled and experienced DIYer may never stray into the realm of crafts.

The crafter works with raw materials, like clay and wood, to fashion objects that express his or her individuality, whereas the DIYer relies on semi-finished products available in retail outlets, such as panels, paints, textiles or tiles, to get done a job that needs doing. The DIY project is rarely undertaken purely for pleasure, but generally to improve the property or even to enhance its financial value (hence the well-documented trend of increased DIY activity when a home is being put up for sale). Craft is often subtly politicised, implying an anti-consumerist stand against mass-produced uniformity. DIY is more mundane. Much of it – painting, decorating, putting up shelves, replacing floor tiles, applying filler to unsightly holes – amounts to little more than basic maintenance.

The marketing analysts Mintel, surveying the DIY industry nationally, defined it as 'repairs or additions to the home or garden [. . .] covering anything from installing a new bathroom or kitchen to putting up shelves, fixing the fence or building a barbecue.' In an article for the *Journal of Consumer Culture* entitled 'Product, Competence, Project and Practice', two British academics, Matthew Watson and Elizabeth Shove, shone a revealing light on the motivation for DIY derived from interviews with fourteen DIYers, seven men and seven women. They identified four broad categories: the confident enthusiast with experience and expertise; the pragmatist, getting the job done with the minimum fuss and expenditure of time; the newcomer, often a first-time homeowner full of bright ideas drawn from TV makeover shows but lacking experience and expertise; and the careful practitioner, leaning more towards craft ideas and more concerned with process than outcome.

They found the nature of DIY to be inherently exploratory. Removing the wallpaper and replacing it or painting the walls often generated dissatisfaction with the carpet. One project led to another, because almost nothing was entirely satisfactory. Sometimes DIYers overreached themselves, attempting projects beyond their capabilities, which ended in failure and disillusionment. In the case of homeowners, moving into a new house usually triggered an initial burst of DIY enthusiasm, followed by fallow periods punctuated by new surges of activity arising from such events as the birth of a child or children leaving home (and leaving their tatty bedrooms behind) or retirement ('Now, at last. I have the time to . . .')

Paul Atkinson, Professor of Design and Design History at Sheffield Hallam University, sees DIY as removing 'the stigma of manual labour' and thereby challenging or undermining class division. He acknowledges the blurring of boundaries between types of DIY – maintenance, decorating, interior design, garden design, self-build, vehicle repair and so on – and also in the motivation for it, in which a decision to deal with a real and pressing situation is mixed with the pursuit of fulfilment. Atkinson also identifies four categories of practitioner, but in slightly different terms to Watson and Shove: the proactive, with ideas about design, looking for projects in the pursuit of fulfilment; the reactive, dependent on kits and manufactured components; the essential, undertaking maintenance because of economic pressure or the unavailability of professional labour; and lifestyle, undertaken from choice rather than need.

DIY is founded on the principle of self-reliance and does allow opportunities for self-expression, even if, broadly speaking, it does not belong in the arena of genuine creativity. When our two daughters were small, I decided to make them a play cottage in the garden. As well as being at the lower end of DIY accomplishment, I have no design capability, so I relied on Helen to work out how it should be built. But once I got her concept into my head, I went ahead and realised it, using planks and poles bought from the local timber yard, which I sawed to size and nailed together. That the resulting construction is evidently rough and ready (the girls never actually played in it and it became a woodstore, which is still its function today) is beside the point. I know there must have been many moments of rage and frustration and even despair in the making of it, but they are erased from memory. What survives is the faint glow of satisfaction when I go to retrieve wood from the shelter, the residue of the pleasure and absorption I derived from those many hours of working with my hands.

It is possible that at times during the making of the cottage, I surrendered to what the Hungarian-born psychologist Mihaly Csikszentmihalyi famously labelled 'flow': that I was carried by a current in which 'action follows upon action according to an internal logic that seems to require no conscious intervention by the actor'. Csikszentmihalyi had observed artists entering 'an almost trance-like state' when their work was going well, and extended his study to leisure activities such as rock-climbing and chess, where he found the same tendency at work. The key elements were the sense of control experienced by the practitioner, the intensity of concentration, which precluded attention being given to anything else, and a sense of time either profoundly altered or suspended altogether. The point of the activity – whatever it might be – is the doing itself and not the achievement of the goal, which might be reaching the summit of the mountain or achieving checkmate – or, in my case, completing an ill-made structure of no obvious use to anyone.

I cannot claim to have experienced that intense sense of flow often in my periodic engagements with DIY over many years, for obvious reasons. But I have experienced it many times when pursuing my lifelong passion, which is angling. To be standing in waders in the current as dusk deepens on a still summer's evening, staring fixedly upstream at a strand of moving water between two beds of weed, searching for the break at the surface as a trout takes a hatching insect, and to flex your rod as you lengthen the line until instinct and experience tell you it is the moment to release the fly to land at the top of the strand of water, is to be enveloped in Csikszentmihalyi's flow. Compared with that genuinely trance-like condition, the actual capture of the fish – should you succeed – seems almost banal. And after that, time suddenly reasserts itself. You look around and find that, unnoticed, it has become almost dark; or glance at your watch and recall the promise to be back in time for dinner. You lumber off along the bank back to the car, where all the familiar concerns that dominate the rest of your life crowd in on you once more.

In DIY, the outcome does matter, even if it is the process that sets flow in motion. They are separate components in its appeal, assuming you find it appealing. To have deployed competence, judgement, dexterity, even ingenuity in making something that was damaged or neglected whole again, or making something that didn't exist before, can be profoundly fulfilling. Autonomy is crucial. You are not part of a bigger process initiated and completed by others. You are in charge, from start to finish. Marx saw the absence of that autonomy as causing the sense of alienation felt by industrial workers. 'What makes us human,' he wrote, 'is our ability to generate a kind of creative surplus over what is materially necessary.'

IN 1946, BLACK & DECKER of Towson, Maryland, introduced a new line of power tools that the company called Home Utility, intended for use at home by the new breed of DIY enthusiast. Company history records that this masterstroke of an idea came from Alonzo Decker Jr, the son of one of the founders of the company. Black & Decker had begun making electric-powered drills in 1916, but the early models were heavy, cumbersome and costly, and were aimed at the professional market. Alonzo Jr had begun working for his father and his father's partner, Duncan Black, at the age of fourteen. Later in his long life, he would recall with a chuckle how, during the war, he had discovered that a number of Black & Decker employees were regularly borrowing drills and taking them home to do domestic projects, and how he had persuaded the partners that there was an untapped market out there.

Within five years, Black & Decker had sold a million quarter-inch and half-inch Home Utility power drills. Other manufacturers leaped aboard the bandwagon, and, by 1954, an estimated fifteen million drills were in use in the United States. It was known as 'America's favourite tool' and was instrumental in shaping what the magazine *Business Week* dubbed 'the age of do-it-yourself'.

This coming-of-age was invested with an overtly moral element. As early as 1941, the author of a book called *Fifty Things to Make for the Home*, Julian Starr, had laid emphasis on the healing power of the basement workshop as 'a place of refuge, a source of rejuvenation for a spirit bewildered or worn by the vicissitudes of daily life'.

Starr's intended audience was clearly male, and his implication was that the man of the house should be able to retreat to his workshop when he felt like it and be alone with his tools and raw materials. In other words, the wife and children from whom he was escaping were presumably to be numbered among the 'vicissitudes'. But even then, the gender balance was poised to shift. Once the US joined the war against Germany, the war effort required that women replaced their fighting men in the factories. They were taught how to change fuses, tackle painting and plumbing, and repair furniture. They were allowed access to tools previously regarded as the preserve of their husbands. Norman Rockwell's celebrated poster depicting Rosie the Riveter – in goggles and oil-streaked overalls, cradling her rivet gun on her lap beneath muscular arms, with her feet on a copy of Hitler's *Mein Kampf* – cemented an image of the American woman breaking down the barriers and storming the male domain.

Across the US, the end of the conflict set off a tremendous boom in home-building and family-making. The 'cult of domesticity' that had been so vigorously promoted by the Beecher sisters a century before staged a triumphant return. But its rules had changed completely. In the new settlements – of which Levittown on Long Island was the most celebrated – husband, wife and children came together in a unified cellular social structure (or, at least, that is how the propaganda portrayed it). Conventionally, the workshop and its store of tools remained a principally male preserve, but the dividing lines elsewhere were becoming fainter by the year.

In the winter of 1951–52, New York's Museum of Modern Art used its People's Art Centre for a range of arts and crafts classes, including a woodworking course aimed specifically at fathers and sons so they could 'work together making toys and simple woodworking projects'. In March 1953, the first DIY trade show was staged in New York. Although the majority of the 6,000 daily attendees were men, a minor and ill-defined role was allowed for women. The female half of a couple from Iowa who visited the show was featured as 'Miss Do-It-Yourself' in a magazine after she told the reporter that back home she had laid tiles and lino and painted walls. She was hired by the organisers to pose in jeans and a plaid shirt with a selection of heavy tools – although at no stage was she seen actually using any of them.

The message of the DIY movement in America in its early stages was not that husbands and wives – or fathers and children – should come together in a shared leisure pursuit, but that there should be a space in the home where the man could be active, useful and contented while keeping at bay any nagging suspicion that he was being unmanned by the arrangement. DIY sat comfortably beside cleaning the car, mowing the lawn, slipping the steaks on and off the barbecue and throwing a curveball at the boy in the range of home-based activities appropriate to the self-respecting suburban male.

New materials joined forces with the new power tools to drive the boom forward. Armed with his power drill and portable band saw (introduced by Porter-Cable in 1953), the DIYer was ready to work wonders with plywood panels. 'You Can Be Your Own Cabinet-Maker' urged a headline in *Better Homes and Gardens* in 1952. You could also, if you felt so inclined, thrust your Kem Roller Coater into a tray full of one of the new water-based paints and spread warm colours across your plywood panels, or paper them with pre-cut lengths of wallpaper, or fit vinyl tiles on the floor. On a Saturday, the family could pile into the newly washed car outside their new suburban home and get down to the new DIY store to obtain the wherewithal.

And the hands on the paint roller or the fingers on the scissors cutting the wallpaper could be – and often were – female.

An issue of *Time* magazine in August 1954 examined the new 'billion-dollar hobby' that had gripped America. Linking it with social identity and wellbeing, the text presented DIY as having therapeutic benefits extending well beyond the mere money-saving aspect: 'Anyone from president down to file clerk can take satisfaction from the fine table, chair or cabinet taking shape under his own hands – and bulge with pride again as he shows them off to his friends.' DIY allowed people to initiate, execute and finish projects, and observe and enjoy the contribution made to the household. The *Time* cover depicted a young male in a check shirt smoking a pipe, typically American in his clean-cut good looks – apart from the six arms and hands with which he was simultaneously operating saw, drill and plane, while putting up wallpaper, attending to his workbench and navigating the sit-on mower.

The embracing of DIY in Britain also followed a steady upward graph, but the context was significantly different. Home-ownership did increase in the immediate post-war period, but nowhere near as dramatically as in the US, where in a single year, 1950, the construction of two million homes began. Acute labour shortages meant that many people – home renters as well as owners – were forced to do repairs and refurbishments themselves because they could not secure the services of a professional handyman. Materials and tools were also in short supply; it was a matter of doing the best you could with whatever you could get rather than nipping down to the DIY store to load your car boot with panels of plywood, the new Black & Decker drill and the Shopsmith combination table saw, lathe and sander.

The more straitened circumstances facing the British DIYer are clearly illustrated on the dust jacket of a popular manual, *Man About the House*, published in 1946 and written by a conscientious objector and the one-time secretary of the H.G. Wells Society, Peter Hunot. In contrast to the smiling, pipe-puffing, super-well-fed six-armed freak depicted in *Time* magazine, the man of *Man About the House* is a weedy-looking bloke in grey flannels and sleeveless pullover with a fag in his mouth, who is applying what looks suspiciously like distemper from a battered, streaked bucket to the wall of a presumably Victorian house. The other wall visible in the illustration is stained and cracked and in need of urgent attention. The floor is bare wood and the paint on the sash window is in a deplorable condition.

Strikingly, the man with the brush is accompanied by two female assistants – assumed to be his wife and daughter. The elder is half-kneeling to paint the fire surround a sober grey. The other is bending over a tin basin, washing down the skirting board. Compared with their American counterparts, they all look pallid and underfed. The scene is imbued with a powerful sense of post-war austerity and is devoid of the aspirational optimism of the US model. This is a family compelled by necessity to do their best to make their battered, possibly bomb-damaged home habitable. There is nothing new or smart in the house; it is a matter of repairing, mending and patching up.

The section in the book about furnishings reinforces the making-do impression. A touch of modernity – more like an illusion – can be introduced by cutting the legs off a chest of drawers so that it rests on its base and replacing the round handles on the drawers with slim strips of wood. That's as stylish as it gets. The house is old, the furniture and furnishings are old, and the tools in the illustrative black-and-white photographs are old. Some of the nails shown in the 'useful nails, screws and fixing devices' picture are palpably rusty.

Britain's DIY revolution moved more slowly, and from a narrower base. But quite soon it began to pick up pace – witness the wide range of tools and products advertised in a 1950 issue of *The Ironmonger* magazine. If you had the money, you could splash out on a Black & Decker portable drill made under licence at Harmondsworth in Middlesex ('He's five times the man with a Black & Decker'). You could get an electric sander made by Matthew Wylye Ltd of Glasgow ('99% efficiency claimed'). Aluminium ladders and steps were a huge advance on the traditional, rickety, wormy wooden ones ('Lightness, immense strength, absolute safety, durability, impossibility of rotting, warping or rusting'). A spanner set from Macrome Ltd of Wolverhampton – 'extra tough, extra light, extra long, extra thin' – would set you back thirty-five shillings. If your kitchen was afflicted by odour issues, a bottle of Airwick at three-and-sixpence was clearly called for, because 'it is bought regularly by eleven million Americans'.

On both sides of the Atlantic, DIY had come of age. In a post-war world in which hope and aspiration were nudging aside fear and deprivation, it was ready for lift-off.

As LOCKDOWN GRIPPED, our village became a very different place. Most obvious was the quiet resulting from the absence of motor traffic and airliners overhead. Queues formed daily outside the butcher's, the pharmacy, the Co-op supermarket and our shop. Everyone followed the rules. They were patient, quiet, slightly cowed, feeling their way in deeply unsettling circumstances.

As if to offer some comfort, the weather was glorious and unseasonably warm. It was a pleasure to lounge in the garden, to take walks and bike rides alone or with the family. And all over the village, wood was being sawn, screws were being turned and nails were being hammered. Drills whizzed. Paint brushes and pots were retrieved from sheds and examined. Projects were hatched.

One resident returned from a holiday in South America just before the restrictions were imposed – she told me it felt like 'falling from a great height into a dark hole'. Unable because of her age to go out for food, she commissioned her grandson to get in supplies and set about redecorating the bedroom and assembling furniture from Ikea flatpacks. In the garden, she had a eureka moment and began digging a wildlife pond. She got the pond liner from Amazon, fitted and filled it, installed a solar-powered pump to oxygenate it, and watched it become colonised by plants and creatures. Dragonflies appeared. Her grandson found a small frog. Birds and hedgehogs drank from it. These were small things at a time when small things had suddenly assumed great importance.

Another local, retired and stuck at home and clearly at the upper level of DIY accomplishment, stripped out the floor and skirting in the downstairs study and replaced it with laminate, then redid the lighting. He moved on to the utility room. Out came the old cupboards and the old sink and taps. New ones were delivered and the house was filled with the percussive music of DIY in progress, softened by cheerful whistling.

I too was infected to a degree by the home-improvement bug. For at least two years, I had been looking at the exterior of our downstairs windows and thinking that we must find someone to repaint them, and doing nothing about it. Now there was no excuse for inaction. The sun was shining, drying conditions were good, I had no other calls on my time. I put on my filthiest old clothes, got sheets of sandpaper, a scraper, a new paint-stripping heat gun and white gloss from our shop, and set to work. It took a couple of weeks and I would not claim that it was done to the highest professional standard, because – even with painting – I am down the scale of proficiency. It was quite boring, and I do not think that at any stage I surrendered to Mihaly Csikszentmihalyi's concept of flow, although I did listen to a good deal of familiar and unfamiliar classical music on BBC Radio 3.

But it was OK, and I felt quite pleased when it was done. And even now – as with the play cottage/woodstore – I pause every now and then and look at the windowsills and frames and experience a small glow of satisfaction. That is what lockdown did for you.

## CHAPTER FIVE

# The Wild Place

AS THE LOCKDOWN restrictions bit, the village did its best to help those in need and spread whatever good cheer was available. A network of volunteers was recruited to take food and medical supplies to those forced to isolate at home. A food bank was established to feed hard-pressed families. The secondary school, now closed, lent its bus to deliver supplies. Keep-fit and dance classes were organised in the street by instructors stuck at home. A girl made fairy cakes and left two on the doorstep of every home on her road, and followed that with a bar of soap, a story, a picture and a decorated stone.

In the shop, Shro worked harder than at any time in her life. With summer beckoning – and almost all the big garden centres closed – the demand for plants, trays of vegetable plugs, seeds, bulbs and compost was insatiable. Customers waited patiently in line outside, and, when their turn came, filled their car boots with whatever they could get. Takings soared to unprecedented levels – on some days she recorded more than Mick had in a good week. But she was too run off her feet to bask in any feeling of satisfaction. Helen started helping out behind the counter when her own job permitted, but the pace was relentless. To preserve herself from complete exhaustion, Shro introduced a one-hour closure at lunchtime, which – more often than not – she spent replenishing depleted shelves, or on the phone urgently seeking deliveries of more stock.

Time and an absence of hurry are crucial components of life in a successful hardware shop. But in the early phase of lockdown, time was in very short supply. With only one customer in the shop at a time, and an eager queue very visible outside, the transaction had to be brisk, and any accompanying conversation compressed. In any case, people were not feeling chatty in the normal way – and there was only one subject and everyone soon wearied of that.

The behaviour of customers changed significantly. Instead of pondering and dithering and discussing their requirements at leisure, they came in resolved on what they wanted. That resolution had been fixed in the period spent waiting outside, during which a quiet desperation had often developed. People watched with growing concern as the trolleys of plants outside the shop emptied and the stacks of compost diminished. Those in front of them emerged with more trays of plants and veg than they could comfortably carry. Excess fed excess, so that when their turn came, they tended to throw restraint to the winds, accelerating the depletion. Those who had arrived intending to buy two bags of compost and a tray of runner beans, peas and courgettes decided while they were standing outside that this might be their last chance and ended up buying as much as they could get in the boots of their cars. Compost was a particular issue – you can never have too much of it, and it will always come in handy. Shro soon had to limit purchases, and then announce, to general dismay, that there was none left until the next delivery, whenever that might be.

She felt the change keenly. She was taking more money than she had ever envisaged, but the unreality of the situation infected everything. Her pleasure was not in gloating over the balance sheet, but in listening to her customers and doing her utmost to meet their requirements. But she also knew that people were buying things they did not need – and in some cases would never make use of – for reasons that had little to do with the service she wanted to provide. She hated running out of stock and hated not knowing when replacement stock would come. She hated disappointing people, and there was plenty of disappointment around. And she hated not having a moment to make a cup of tea, go to the loo, and have a proper chat.

I was of little use to her except at those unpredictable moments when the call would come to say the big lorry bearing pallets of compost, bark, topsoil and other horticultural accessories was on its way. The pallets, each loaded with up to seventy forty-litre bags, were dumped on the forecourt and had to be moved to the storage area at the back of the shop. On safety grounds, Shro had disposed of Mick's much-cherished forklift in favour of a manual pump-truck. It took three people – Shro pulling and steering, two others with their shoulders pushing against the stack – to manoeuvre each pallet across the uneven tarmac and patches of dodgy concrete to its resting place. On a dry day, when the contents of the bags were not permeated with moisture, it was hard, quick work. But one day, Shro and I and my daughter Katie, then aged eighteen, shifted twenty-six pallets in drenching rain. By the end, my shoulders were sore and my legs were trembling with weariness.

'THE HOME IS the only place of liberty,' G. K. Chesterton wrote, 'the only spot on earth where a man can alter arrangements suddenly, make an experiment or indulge in a whim. The home is not the one tame place in a world of adventure. It is the one wild place in a world of rules and set tasks.'

In post-war Britain and the United States, the flowering of DIY enabled millions to escape the rules and set tasks and explore the wild places of their homes. In October 1955, James Dean's last film, *Rebel Without a Cause*, was released in America; the BBC began transmitting TV programmes in colour for a selected sample of viewers; and Buckingham Palace announced that Princess Margaret would not be getting married to the love of her life, Group Captain Peter Townsend. Somewhat overlooked in the national and international news headlines was the launch by the magazine company George Newnes Ltd of a new monthly called *Practical Householder*.

Flagged as 'the new Do-It-Yourself magazine', it was devised and edited by F. J. Camm – Frederick J. Camm – a pioneer of how-to-do journalism and responsible for a stable of similar publications, including *Practical Motoring*, *Practical Television*, *Practical Engineering* and *Practical Wireless*. Camm, who remained at the helm until his death in 1959, evidently knew his business and his market, for the first issue of *Practical Householder* flew off the magazine racks as soon as it appeared. So great was the demand that the second issue was a reprint of the first, with a different cover – evidence, the editor purred complacently, of 'the DIY movement in this country'.

The cover of that first issue is a glorious period piece. Two men are doing it themselves in a new kitchen with a red-and-white chequerboard lino floor. They are both wearing crisply creased blue trousers and brown shoes. The elder, to judge from his features, is in a blue shirt, the younger in red. All sleeves are tightly and neatly rolled up above the elbow. The younger man, brimming with youthful ardour, is sanding (or possibly cleaning) the green door of a new kitchen cabinet. The elder is concentrating on sawing lengthways down a piece of wood that he has jammed under his knee across a chair (why no workbench, you may ask?). On the table are carelessly scattered an electric drill, two screwdrivers, a clamp, a plane, a mallet and a tub of what could be grouting. Some of the kitchen units have been fitted, but others are still in pieces. Through the window can be glimpsed a lawn in a garden leading towards open countryside and poplar trees – not that either of the DIYers has any time for gazing outside.

For the cover of November's reprint, our two heroes are replaced by one – clean-cut, dimple-chinned, in pale pink shirt and tie, fawn waistcoat and sensible blue trousers. He has a useful pen in his breast pocket and is poised for action in a modern suburban living room: settee, cushioned table, spare functional chairs; all clean lines and shiny surfaces. On the trestle table are drill, hammer, screwdriver and a box of nails or screws. He is holding an elongated green box, which looks as if it could contain a portable missile launcher, but which we assume contains the blind he is about to put in place above the window.

As promised by F. J. Camm, the editorial pages are 'packed with facts and illustrations'. The by-lines of the contributors are restricted to initials and surnames in the severely non-binary style of the time, but it can be assumed that almost all of them, if not all of them, were male. D. Tapner provided advice on Making an Efficient Water Softener, T. Bugle on Assembling an Electric Alarm, J. L. Walls on Checking on Your Vacuum Cleaner. J. Naylor demonstrated How to Make a Modern Clock-case. F. W. Cousins had tips on Making an Ironing Board. Legal Notes were contributed by W. J. Weston, drawn in wig, gown and bowtie, who quotes the 'old writer' reflecting that 'property turns sand into gold'.

The abundance of advertising suggests a very considerable market was now being tapped. The Coronet Tool Co. of Mansfield Road, Derby, introduces the 'Minor' ten-inch Universal Woodworker with high-speed electric motor from £12 ('Eminently suitable for schools and craftsmen, amateurs and professionals'). Calco proudly presents its Synthetic Resin Glue ('If Samson could have tried his strength on a Calco-glued joint, he would have torn his hair out in desperation'). Rawlplugs are the answer to the rhetorical question Do You Want to Fix a Shelf? ('Will hold the screws in any masonry with a tenacious grip'). The back-page ad urges the DIYer to try the new vinyl wall covering Congowall ('It looks like tile! It cleans like tile! But you put it up by the yard and it costs less than one shilling a foot').

The articles and illustrations in *Practical Householder* are clearly the work of men, intended for men. But a few of the advertisements are daringly gender inclusive. The drawing for Ashley Wallpapers shows the wife in her apron with paste brush and roll of paper in hand, poised for action, while the husband kneels to apply the smoothing brush to paper already hung. The archetypal woman of the house reappears holding a roll of Linovent underlay, and again singing the praises of Polycell Cellulose Adhesive ('Can we manage the paperhanging? Nothing easier. Anyone can hang paper'). But, with tools, she keeps her distance. The ad for the Wolf Club drill – 'The Family Favourite' – shows him with the device itself, pipe clenched in mouth, expression of resolve on face, while she stands to the side, smiling supportively and offering words of encouragement and admiration.

The inclusiveness shown by some of the companies advertising in *Practical Householder* perhaps made an impression on Mr Camm. The cover for the Christmas edition of 1955 portrays the man of the house making a stand for the Christmas tree while his spouse arranges the decorations. By the following October, she is actively engaged in fitting curtains around a cabinet; he is up a stepladder installing a door frame. By Christmas 1956, he is seen unwrapping his new drill, she is seated with what appears to be the business end of a carpet-sweeper on her lap, and the offspring of this union is chortling with delight over his shiny new saw, with the rest of his junior tool kit still in its drawer.

For a time, *Practical Householder* had the field to itself. But DIY was a growing and lucrative sector; rivals were bound to appear. In February 1957, *Do It Yourself* was launched by the Exchange & Mart group. *Do It Yourself* was a direct challenger to *Practical Householder*, but its editor and founder, David Johnson, adopted a subtly yet significantly different approach. He presented the magazine as an agent of democracy, championing the non-professional – empowered by new tools and materials – against the professional. The latter were portrayed as obstacles to progress, jealously guarding their special interests; it was alleged that they were lobbying for legislation to stop the amateur doing anything resembling skilled work.

Whereas *Practical Householder* was, in essence, a repair, maintenance and basic construction manual, *Do It Yourself* ventured boldly into the seductive world of design. Its design agenda was founded on a rejection of the past – particularly the Victorian past – and an embracing of the contemporary. Victorian clutter and ornamentation were out; clean lines were in. A favourite target was panelled doors. *Do It Yourself* readers were urged to board over the panels with plywood to give a sleek, shiny look, and to liberate the housewife from the tedious task of dusting the panel edges.

Although its cover proclaimed it to be for 'The Practical Man About the House', *Do It Yourself* actively promoted DIY as a partnership between husband and wife. In May 1957, the cover shows him up a ladder cleaning the gutter, while she is leaning out of the window below him, rubbing down the sill with an electric sander and smiling happily up at him, while a second male at ground level creates a garden feature by edging a circular patch of turf with angled bricks. In June, husband and wife are seen assembling a shed together. In July, she is up the ladder against an outbuilding, holding out a hammer to a fresh-faced youth – presumably the son – who has been laying green roofing felt and is almost ready to bang in the clouts, while the husband is on the ground, hanging the doors on their hinges. In August, mother and son are putting together the frame of the greenhouse; the father/husband is holding a pane of the glass, ready to fit it.

In October, he is boarding over the banisters, while she sits companionably on the stairs next to him, painting the wall. The lad is absent, probably doing a woodworking course at college.

These vividly coloured pieces of artwork purport to show the standard suburban family working together to bring the standard suburban home up to the appropriate suburban standard. In fact, of course, they are as stylised, idealised and divorced from reality as an early Renaissance altar painting of the Virgin Mary with Child. The men are invariably strong-jawed, chiselled, lean, clean-shaven, with full heads of glossy hair, perfectly brushed. Their wives are all just back from the hairdresser, clothed in blouses and cardigans of pastel shades and elegantly cut skirts and slacks and polished shoes. The offspring – when required – is the mirror image of his dad grinning with the pleasure of helping out on such a fulfilling and enjoyable project.

There is no mess anywhere: no splashes of paint or blobs of plaster or scrunched-up bits of masking tape. There are no screws dropped carelessly on the floor. Tools and accessories are exactly where they should be. Most absurdly of all, no one wears overalls or dirty clothes or has a spot of paint on their chin or needs to clean their hands with Swarfega. They all look as if they have prepared for the arrival of a professional photographer to compose a family portrait rather than being engaged in an actual job of work. It is pure make-believe masquerading as a typical weekend at home.

That is the fantasy promoted by the covers. But the text of the articles generally belonged firmly in the real world. In *Do It Yourself*, the by-lines of contributors used their first names, allowing the shadowy suggestion of a personality.

Gordon Allen advised on 'getting that contemporary look with this unit bookcase'. James Hill instructed on 'wood finishing without tears'. The star columnist, Frank Preston – 'ten-point plan for decorating the exterior of your house' – even had a photograph, which showed him in a white shirt, with black spectacles and a toothbrush moustache.

Within a couple of years of its launch, *Do It Yourself* boasted a readership of three million. The market appeared to have ample room for more journalistic exploitation, and in March 1959, Odhams launched *Homemaker* – 'The Practical How-to-Do-It Monthly'. Its editor, poached from *Do It Yourself*, was Frank Preston, and he – like David Johnson – had ideas on how to make his product distinctive. The couple on the cover, for instance, were invested with a dose of film-star glamour. For the first issue he – bronzed and muscled, with luxuriant and oiled blond hair brushed back from a flawless brow, his lips parted to display dazzling white teeth – is halfway up a stepladder, paint brush in hand. She – slim, beautiful, adoring and similarly blessed in the dental department – is showing him a colour chart in such a way as to suggest that it could be the one piece previously missing from the perfection of their union.

One novelty in *Homemaker* – possibly missed by subscribers – was that the DIY supercouple on the cover are retained for subsequent appearances, changing only the colour schemes of their clothes for different assignments. Another novelty that was more obvious was to have female contributors sharing the billing with men. Along with Edward Capper ('Panelling the Staircase') and Edgar Lucas ('Condensation can be Fixed') could be found Barbara Anne Taylor providing 'The Personal Touch' and Jacqueline Kennish offering advice on 'Good Buys for the Kitchen'. In what was surely a first in DIY journalism, John and Josette Anderson collaborated in giving instruction on 'How to Make a Baby's Cradle'.

IN AMERICA, the emerging and soon booming DIY movement fitted quite comfortably in the embrace of *Better Homes and Gardens*, founded in 1924 and an immeasurable influence on the shaping of American domestic life and taste ever since. DIY had to compete for space in the glossy pages with other *Better Homes and Gardens* staples, including design, cooking, furnishings and gardening, but evidently earned its corn in the eyes of the advertising department.

In 1951, the *Better Homes and Gardens Handyman's Book* was published. Six years later, a second edition, updated and much expanded, appeared. It was bigger and better, but still overwhelmingly masculine in its ethos. 'Handyman projects,' declared the introduction, 'are a whale of a lot of fun [. . .] you are your own boss with no one to satisfy but yourself.' The 'yourself' is a man, through and through. The hands laying the floor tiles are male, the hands fitting the laminate are male, and even with wallpapering – where women might have been allowed a part – it is a man who is measuring up, and hairy male hands that are applying the paste.

In the deeply conservative world of *Better Homes and Gardens*, women were confined to the kitchen, where they dealt with the washing up and did all the cooking; the bedroom, where they chose the furnishings and made the beds; and the living room, where they were responsible for the colour scheme and operated the one power tool to which they had access, the vacuum cleaner. Childcare and the washing were theirs to do; outside in the garden, their delicate, manicured hands might engage with nurturing blooms, taking cuttings, and, at a pinch, dividing an iris, but nothing that could cause calluses or leave soil underneath the fingernails. The magazine reflected and helped perpetuate an America in which the 'non-overlapping spheres of influence' – in Steven Gelber's phrase – were accepted almost unthinkingly.

*The Family Handyman* ('the magazine that tells you in language you can understand') was a specialist DIY publication that first appeared in 1951 and is still going today. The gender bias of the title generally reflected the content, and the covers usually featured rugged blokes in checked shirts – occasionally assisted by a spitting-image son – engaged in heavy outdoors work, or a slightly less rugged bloke fitting tiles or coping indoors. But not always – the cover of the spring issue of 1951 shows a couple working as one, both in caps, checked shirts and blue jeans with the bottoms rolled up. He has laid a section of piping for the underground lawn-sprinkling system; she is poised with a square of turf impaled on her fork, ready to place it over the trench.

'The do-it-yourself movement,' the American anthropologist Margaret Mead wrote in 1957, 'is not just a hobby, it is often a pleasant and meaningful contribution to family life.' A comparative analysis of the way DIY was presented in the US and Britain suggests that, while the Americans were more technical and had more advanced tools, the British were ahead in embracing its gender-inclusive potential as a family activity. The primary message in the US, as Steven Gelber has shown, was that DIY could accommodate masculinity within the domestic setting; that a man was no less a man because he chose to spend his weekend building a brick barbecue rather than crawling around in the woods intent on shooting a deer.

Gelber references an article published in *Popular Mechanics* in 1959, headlined 'Do It Yourself . . . Hollywood Does', which he sees as having helped legitimise DIY as an appropriately male hobby. The writer asks the six-old-old daughter of the film star Dick Powell what her daddy does and is told 'he fixes things'. Other members of Hollywood's 'thriving do-it-yourself colony' are said to be Jerry Lewis, Robert Ryan and Glenn Ford. The main focus of the article is the actor George Montgomery, who was a film and TV regular in the 1950s and 60s and was married to the big-band singer Dinah Shore. Montgomery is said to have designed and helped build three of his own homes and several others, as well as setting up a furniture-making business. 'He gets into blue jeans,' *Popular Mechanics* reports approvingly, 'literally rolls up his sleeves and actually lays bricks, does carpentry and physically aids and abets the realisation of his building concepts.'

There is a photograph in the *Popular Mechanics* article in which Dick Powell is shown in his workshop, cutting a strip of pine to make a picture frame. For obvious reasons, no such picture exists of me. But I do occasionally have my moments.

As the strange summer of 2020 advanced, the quiet frenzy of buying in the shop eased, although it continued to be extremely busy. A simulacrum of normality returned. I was able to resume going to the newsagent's each morning to get my newspaper. I was also permitted to go fishing again, and I went often because it was easier to escape the national feeling of disquiet on the riverbank than anywhere else. There was a lot of hot weather that summer, and Helen and our two girls, and the girls with their friends, spent days beside or in the Thames. In July, Helen left her job at the BBC after more than thirty years and began working two days a week in the shop.

There was a heatwave in August and another spell of glorious sunshine in September. Shro decided that this was the time to tackle the big storage shed at the back, which had fallen into a state of ruin in Mick's time. She tried unavailingly to find a professional builder who would put a new roof on it, then closely studied relevant footage on YouTube and consulted various websites before announcing that we would do it ourselves.

I volunteered to do preliminary clearance and destruction. I hacked down the brambles that had squeezed through the gaps and wrapped themselves around the joists, colonising the empty spaces, and smashed out their roots with my mattock. I ascended the ladder and spent hours prising out the sheeting nails and ripping off the rotten bitumen sheets, dropping them to the ground. Salvageable items were cleared and stored elsewhere, and Greg's precious cylinder grinder for sharpening mower blades – tipping the scales at one and a half tonnes – was shifted into the back of his workshop on rollers in the manner of the bluestones of Stonehenge. Helen and Shro combined to demolish a smaller shed and a lean-to that had long since ceased to serve any useful purpose. All the rubbish and junk was dumped in a skip for removal to the landfill site.

The scene was set for reconstruction. A lorry load of eight-by-four feet sheets of OSB (oriented strand board – a variant of plywood) was delivered, along with huge and heavy rolls of roofing felt and cans of inky bituminous adhesive. The joists were sound, and we began by fitting the boards, one by one, sliding tongues into groves, and nailing them to the joists. It was slightly reminiscent of the scene in the movie *Witness*, in which the youthful and athletic Harrison Ford joins the Amish community to build a new barn in a day. It took us longer, as it does in real life, and we encountered a few setbacks, which does not happen in Hollywood. The main one was the unwelcome appearance of a gap along the apex as we progressed fitting the boards – it was the result of the joists not being completely regular in alignment. Shro berated herself for not having thought of it, but she devised a solution in the form of bitumen ridge tiles that fitted snugly over the gap.

I made a small but, I like to think, vital contribution to strategic thinking. Once the boards were fixed, we had to unroll lengths of roofing felt to fit over them. The rolls were extremely heavy and unwieldy, and the stuff itself was distressingly liable to tear under any strain. How much easier, I thought, if the roll did not have to be lifted and turned by hand. My solution – mine and no one else's – was to put a broom handle through the roll and jam the ends onto raised pallets, so that it could revolve easily as a length of felt was pulled off. It was a small breakthrough, but – as I reminded my workmates until they were tired of hearing it – a pretty damn significant one.

Helen was the only one of us who was light enough and nimble enough to do the necessary work along the apex of the roof. Shro called her the Roof Monkey and fitted hooks onto the end of an aluminium ladder to grip the angle so she could get up and down. She straddled the ridge, banging in nails, sliding felt into position, placing and adjusting the ridge tiles and slapping on the adhesive. The roof was in full view of the health-centre car park, and there was a steady passage of passers-by who would pause and comment on the progress of the project. Some of the blokes felt obliged to assess the standard of work and the methods employed, offering snippets of reminiscence of comparable undertakings, while the women tended to express concern for Helen's safety and admiration for her tenacity.

By the end, her work clothes were sticky with the bituminous adhesive, which had soaked through to her skin. Shro took a picture of her outlined against the bluest of September skies, one knee either side of the ridge, bent in concentration as she fixed another tile. I am standing at ground level beside the ladder, doing nothing, just looking up. It is a neat reversal of the standard image from a cover of *Practical Householder*, *Do It Yourself* or *Homemaker* – although, of course, no one, male or female, who was so filthy and who suggested so strongly the reek of bitumen would have been permitted to tarnish the image of perfection presented by these publications.

The fine weather lasted until the job was done. A couple of weeks later came the wind and the rain. The rain lashed the roof and ran down it and pooled on the ground, and not a drop came through. Two years later, it remains sound.

We had done it ourselves!

# CHAPTER SIX

# He Did It Barry's Way

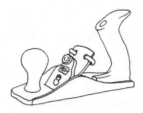

IT IS 1960, just before 6pm on a Tuesday evening, and the man of the house is settling down in his favourite chair to watch his favourite programme on his new TV. To the accompaniment of a chugging, upbeat tune on brass and electric organ, the opening credits feature cut-out photographs of standard DIY tools – hammer, drill, scraper, paint roller, vice and so on – which give way to strips of paper spelling *Do It Yourself*, the 'It' slapped on with a paint brush. The words 'introduced by' appear in lower case, then the name Barry, then a paintbrush, then Bucknell.

The man of the house lights a cigarette. His wife comes in with a cup of tea for him. She settles on the sofa, because she likes the face that now appears on the screen almost as much as he likes the substance of the show. 'Hello again,' the face says with a cheery smile. 'This week on *Do It Yourself*, I'm going to show you how to tackle one of the trickier jobs around the house . . .' With his jutting nose, broad forehead and brushed-back, Brylcreemed hair, silvering a touch over the ears, the presenter is by no means a matinee idol in looks.

He wears grey flannels, a nylon shirt with sleeves rolled up neatly, and a striped tie pinned in place. You could walk past him in the street or sit opposite him on the tube and not spare him a second glance. He is Mr Ordinary, a family man, anyone's dad or uncle or husband.

Except that he is not. As he looks at the camera, his eyes are warm, glinting with humour and sympathetic understanding, his facial expression etched in friendly lines. His voice is as warm as his eyes, the articulation polished, the accent distinctly not posh. His words come easily, as if he was in the room with you, having a chat, ready to say yes to his own cup of tea, instead of being confined remotely behind the screen against the wall.

He is one of a very rare breed: the TV natural. What makes a TV natural? It is one of those mysteries, like what makes a best-selling book? Some of the facets can be described, but the key one is really hard to put into words. You just know it when you see it. Dee Wells, an American columnist and commentator who lived in London and was married to the philosopher A. J. 'Freddie' Ayer, asked herself on behalf of the *Daily Herald* what it was about Barry Bucknell that she found so irresistible. She didn't answer the question directly but gave good guidance: 'People like a modest, simple man or one who appears to be. People don't like being lectured at.'

Barry Bucknell's modesty and simplicity – whether real or affected – were utterly convincing. He never lectured but drew the viewer into a kind of partnership with him as the wise friend, never impatient or in a hurry, always ready with a smile and a quiet word of encouragement as he showed you how to fit a Rawlplug or hold your saw at the right angle. When he said, 'This week, I want to talk about pelmets', he talked about pelmets and made them matter. Women liked him because he did not condescend to them or exclude them from the pelmet conversation. Indeed, his TV break-through came in the 1950s, when he was brought on to the long-running magazine programme *About the Home* to show the presenter Joan Gilbert how to put up shelves.

Barry's career – somehow it seems appropriate to call him by his first name – blossomed with the blossoming of DIY. His half-hour BBC show *Do It Yourself* attracted up to seven million viewers a week. He was an asset that cried out for a bigger stage, and someone at the Corporation – possibly his celebrated producer, Stanley Hyland – had a brainwave.

The Grove, Ealing, was a street like hundreds of other streets in West London: quiet, leafy, lined with mainly mid-Victorian detached and semi-detached houses. But number 79 was a major blot on the street scene. It looked as if some curse had been laid upon it. Ceilings had partially fallen in. Walls were cracked and stained with damp. Floorboards were rotten. There was dry rot and wet rot, and the joists had woodworm. Outside, the gutters were collapsing, the stairs up to the front door were crumbling and letting the water seep into the cellar, and the brickwork was eroded. Worst of all, a previous owner had decided that the appearance of the exterior would be improved by fixing concrete beams painted black in eccentric patterns across front and back.

'This monstrosity' – as the *Daily Herald* called it – became Bucknell's House. Over thirty-nine weeks in 1962, he set about taming the monstrosity and civilising it into two self-contained flats, appointed and furnished to meet the tastes and aspirations of his time – with the TV cameras recording his every move.

He began at the beginning, introducing the ruined house and advising on such matters as applying for grants and getting local authority permission to do the work. Then Barry began to address the practicalities, the first of which was the workbench. No project, great or small, could be methodically tackled without a workbench and bench vice. He assembled one made from blockboard and softwood and fitted it with folding legs so it could be conveniently put away at the end of the working day.

Armed with workbench and toolkit and his own invincible self-assurance, Barry got stuck in. He cut through a wall and fitted new doors. He cut through another wall and fitted a serving-hatch made from chipboard, hardboard, hardwood and softwood. He lowered the staircase, holding it up with block-and-tackle. He put in a damp course and waged war on the dry rot and wet rot, then sprayed the joists in the kitchen ceiling with insecticide to send 'these little grubs with big appetites' packing. He installed a kitchen-sink unit with a laminated plastic top and drawers and sliding doors.

The deplorable state of the ceilings presented Barry with a tricky choice between taking them down and starting again – 'an arduous and messy job' – and strengthening them with battens and covering them in tiles of various kinds, many of them the newly popular polystyrene tiles. In the book that followed the TV series, Barry described how, when it was all over, the house was opened to the public for twenty days, allowing 40,000 people to inspect his handiwork. 'The ceiling tiles,' he said modestly, 'provided a major source of interest.'

As he progressed upwards, floor by floor – sanding floorboards, laying vinyl and parquet tiles, removing an old fireplace and replacing it with an electric unit, knocking up cabinets and shelves and tables and sliding doors, covering the odious door panels with hardboard, fitting new windows and replacing sash cords – the audience figures rose. With seven million viewers glued to their screens each week, Barry became a national celebrity. According to the *Daily Herald*, 79 The Grove, Ealing, had become the second-most famous residence in the country after Buckingham Palace. The newspaper's columnist, Dee Wells, wrote: 'No matter how increasingly ghastly the décor became, I could not possibly have switched Mr Bucknell off [. . .] he could have ripped out an Adam fireplace and replaced it with lino tiles and I would still have watched.' A staff of ten was recruited to handle the flood of correspondence addressed to the BBC, more than half a million letters in all.

No one could have accused Barry of being an innovator in matters of design. His taste in furniture and fittings came from the *Daily Mail* Ideal Home Exhibition and the pages of *Practical Householder* and *Do It Yourself*. Laminate, Formica, vinyl, polystyrene, hardboard, glass fibre, veneered boards, plastic sheeting – these were his favoured materials. Everything had to be smooth, shiny and sleek, able to be cleaned with one swish of a duster. Energetic flush panelling was the way to deal with dust-collecting door panels. Open fires looked nice, he conceded, but were 'extremely inefficient . . . modern appliances are much more efficient.'

To embrace the cult of 'the modern' to the full, he decided to convert the pigeon-infested attic – dark, dank, freezing in winter, roasting in summer – into 'the teenage room'. Major surgery was required: a new skylight, roof insulation, a concertina door at the top of the stairs, the addition of a layer of hardboard to the floor to reduce the noise of the 'continuous playing of pop records' expected of the occupant. To complete the picture, Barry installed a cabinet to contain the pop records and the machine on which to play them, and a desk at which the spotty sixteen-year-old might do his homework while the music played.

The last of the thirty-nine programmes of *Bucknell's House* was broadcast at 6.25pm on Wednesday, 27 February 1963. In it, Barry gave a tour of the house and his works, his now familiar voice as smooth and even as the many laminated surfaces he had left behind. A brass plate inscribed 'Bucknell's House' was fixed on the side of the new plywood porch. He had become a national treasure, his renown enhanced by the disclosure in the newspapers that – in the middle of an exhausting filming schedule – he had taken a little time out to deal with a request from his youngest son for him to design a basic sailing boat. The result was the eleven-foot Mirror Dinghy, a kit costing £63-11-0, that could be assembled by amateurs and transported on the roof of a car. Sponsored by the *Daily Mirror*, Barry's little boat was unveiled at the 1963 Boat Show and went on to sell in the tens of thousands.

Seen today, *Bucknell's House* seems as quaintly old-fashioned as the Victorian panelled door seemed to him. Barry's broadcasting style belongs to the Reithian era when the mission to inform and educate was paramount. His approach was entirely matter-of-fact and untouched by any hint of flamboyance. The programmes were almost austerely instructional; the jokiness, banter and raucous hilarity deemed essential to the later generation of makeover shows like *Changing Rooms* would have been as unthinkable to Barry as the suggestion that he wear a Stetson instead of a tie.

He was not really a TV construct. These days, he would probably have been recycled as a game-show or quiz host or the presenter of travelogues and haunted the schedules for years. But back then, his shelf life was short. He had arrived in television by chance, served his time happily and profitably, and moved on. He did present a series on independent TV called *The ABC of Do It Yourself*, but it had nothing of the impact of the two series he did for the BBC. For whatever reason, the BBC did not see a continuing role for Barry Bucknell, so he faded gracefully from the screen. He left London (where he had served as a Labour councillor on St Pancras council) for St Mawes in Cornwall, where his wife Betty came from. Barry died there in 2003 at the age of ninety-one, a figure from a long-departed black-and-white world, recalled by the obituarists as 'TV's Mr DIY'.

AT THE END OF the series, the BBC was left with an awkward loose end: what to do with Bucknell's House? Having spent £3,000 on buying it and roughly the same on materials to make it habitable, the public-spirited Corporation offered it to Ealing Council for £6,000. The council's officers, who wanted it as accommodation that could attract new staff, were keen, but the councillors were divided. Those on the finance committee agreed that it should be acquired, but the recommendation encountered a broadside of opposition when it was debated by the full council. Councillor Hether-ington said it would be necessary to charge £7-1-8 a week rent for the upper flat, and £3-16 for the lower one – which he said was exorbitant. He said that while 'Mr Bucknell has done a pretty good job', he understood it hadn't been finished. 'I hear tales of men with buckets of pitch up there,' he added, enigmatically. Councillor Gooderham claimed – without offering any evidence – that number 79 was 'a bodged-up job which is not worth the money'. Alderman Tann insisted it was worth nowhere near the £6,000 asking price, despite the District Valuer saying it was.

In the end, the opportunity to take Bucknell's House into public ownership was spurned, and it was sold at auction for £7,000 to a Mr Alfred Billig. A year later, it was being offered for sale again, for £9,750. Since then, the two flats have been through an unknown number of hands, and the fate of Barry Bucknell's handiwork is not recorded. It is in the nature of the materials he used so freely – particularly the composite wood panels – that time tends to be unkind to them. The boards warp, the chips degrade, the laminate peels off. Put baldly, they are more likely to end up in the skip than the solid, despised Victorian stuff they replaced. But what about the more durable features that Barry installed – the gas and electric fires, the bath, the banisters, and the polystyrene ceiling tiles and coping that aroused such admiration among the thousands allowed inside?

I went to Ealing one morning in July and walked down to The Grove from Ealing Broadway station. The shopping centre that came twenty years after Barry had folded away his workbench for the last time was evidently suffering from a Covid-induced identity crisis, like shopping centres everywhere, but there were plenty of upmarket bars and restaurants doing business along the High Street, and a Savills estate agents office, which is always a sign of an area on a socially upward path.

I turned left into The Grove. Number 79 is about half-way along on the north side. Outside, the leylandii tree that was hardly noticeable in the photographs taken when Barry went to work had grown into a monster so huge that, from a distance – despite it having had its upper part savagely ampu-tated – it obscured the front door and most of the frontage, and cast a pall of gloom over the front garden. I came closer so I could get a proper view.

The rendered front of the building, which Barry had got his assistants to paint cream, was now a tasteful dove grey, against which the white of his hardboard porch showed up nicely. The stairs up to the porch, which he had repaired with concrete, had, regrettably, been covered by a later and less skilful hand in ceramic brown tiles, several of which were cracked or leaning at angles, or missing altogether.

My heart quickened as my finger pressed the doorbell. This was, after all, primary source research. I could be on the verge of entering some hidden time warp. Would I find a treasure trove of Bucknelliana? Would the kitchen cabinet he made from plywood and prepared softwood, with a chrome strip with hooks and a catch that flicked open with a finger still be there? The wardrobes? The plastic-surfaced bath panels? The silicone shower curtains? Might there even be a spotty teenager playing pop music in the attic room?

Alas for my hopes! The door opened a little way, enough to reveal an elderly man with white hair. I stated my business and he began to close the door. 'I'm afraid I just can't talk about the house,' he said. 'I can't, that's all.' For the first time, it occurred to me that I might not be the first to have travelled the Bucknell historical path. I applied all the charm at my disposal to try to persuade him to let me in. I almost begged. The door opened a little wider and I thought he might be relenting. But he said again that he was sorry, but no – he really could not talk about it. Before he shut the door for good, I managed to twist my upper body to one side to see past him into the hall. I had a glimpse, just a glimpse, of the fabled polystyrene ceiling tiles.

I went around the side to the door leading to the downstairs flat. The tenant answered my knock and told me that the whole of it had been gutted long ago and refitted from a John Lewis furnishings catalogue. No feature from the Bucknell era had survived. I walked back to the station quite severely deflated, thinking about Barry and his legacy. His reputation had declined once he was no longer an active presence on the TV screen. He became an object of mockery as tastes changed. 'Doing a Bucknell' was adopted as a label for shoddy work and lousy taste. They even referred to him as 'Bodger Bucknell'. No wonder he went off to live out his days beside a distant sea.

It was utterly unfair. He was a man of his time, with an exceptional talent for communication and a limited skill in using tools and making things (revealingly, his wife Betty reported Barry as being a distinctly reluctant home DIYer). He was serious about his work and extremely conscientious. I do not believe that making a comfortable living from it was his chief motivation. He inspired countless thousands to try to follow his example and make their homes smarter, more comfortable, more pleasant to live in. Later arbiters of taste sneered at the results. But devotees of *Do It Yourself* and

*Bucknell's House* loved him for having liberated them from the darkness and dinginess of the rented homes in which so many of them had begun their adult lives. Even if their handiwork often fell short of the standard displayed by their instructor, he enabled them to fulfil a part of themselves.

## CHAPTER SEVEN

# Butcher's Hooks and Ideal Homes

I RATHER DOUBT if Barry Bucknell was much of a one for improvisation. He strikes me as a man who followed the manual, probably his own manual. Unlike Shro, whose mind flies when a challenge presents itself. As in the matter of the butcher's hooks.

One of the intractable problems with the shop is space and the acute lack of it. We are lucky to have the covered yard at the side and the uncovered yard at the back, where stock that is reasonably impervious to damp can be stored. But the shop itself is narrow, and there is never enough room for everything.

The hardware shopkeeper has to strike a balance. They have to be able to retrieve items that customers want without having to search for them – 'I know it's here somewhere, but I can't quite put my finger on it' is not a satisfactory sales technique. But, at the same time, the shop must both appear to have something that will meet every household eventuality, and yet still be full of surprises. It should be an Aladdin's cave – and that means it will be crammed to overflowing.

In our shop, every horizontal and vertical space is taken. Every cubic inch that could be occupied is occupied. There is a limit to how much can be kept on the floor, because customers have to be able to get around without setting off an avalanche. But the shelves are full and the space above head height is festooned with items hung from hooks or wire. Then there is the ceiling.

For some time, Shro had been looking at some unusual fittings at the far end of the shop, dating from its previous incarnation as a butcher's. Six metal bars, hooked at their bottom ends, descended from the ceiling and supported two further horizontal bars, which must once have had big S-bend hooks over them, from which the sanguineous carcasses of lambs and pigs would have been hung. These bars formed a wide rectangle – one that suggested possibilities.

Shro's first attempt involved fixing a metal mesh across the rectangle, but although it looked interesting, it sagged when she hung objects from it, so it was discarded. But the possibilities offered by the bars nagged at her, and she thought some more. Over many hours up a stepladder, drilling and bolting, she constructed an ingenious frame from the original rectangle, extended and embellished with additional metal struts and wooden cross-struts made from shortened broom handles. From the bars and handles, she hung multiple hooks, which now support a gleaming and glittering array of saucepans and frying pans, sieves and colanders, graters and washing-up racks and pastry-cutters.

Barry would have been impressed, I think.

IN 1949, A NEW quarterly magazine, *Pins and Needles*, was launched into the post-war world of aspirational home-making. Born from the 'Make Do and Mend' wartime campaign, its editor and publisher, Christine Veasey, initially confined its scope to advice on sewing, knitting, crochet, needlework and embroidery. But, over time, it extended its reach further around the home to include dress-making, cooking and other housewifely activities. It was successful enough to go monthly, and in 1955 introduced a new 'Home Making' section, with tips on how to make and repair furniture, devise colour schemes for rooms and carry out some limited DIY. Men were invited to join the readership and were shown the basics of plumbing and how to fit a TV aerial.

The two 'large and ferocious demons' besetting new homeowners, according to Christine Veasey in the *Pins and Needles Treasure Book of Home Making*, were called 'Housing Shortage' and 'Rising Prices'. 'That is why,' she declared, 'everywhere there is evidence of the tremendous do-it-yourself boom', which had helped turn her readers into 'a new generation of weekend decorators and carpenters'. The *Pins and Needles Treasure Book* endorsed the conventional gender demarcation. A young housewife is shown hanging wallpaper, but it is 'John' who makes the nest of tables, rewebs the chair and glues 'a colourful plastic fabric' to the handles of a cabinet. Women are steered towards the bright new curtains 'that can do wonders' for a tired room, and the 'charming effect' of a new window frill. Quilts, chair covers, bedspreads and basketry are for women; burst pipes and nail hammering are for men.

But, elsewhere, the dynamics were shifting. Paint manufacturers introduced exciting new colours with seductive names like viridian and zephyr. Archive footage of the time shown in a much later BBC TV series *All the Mod Cons* showed a young couple inspecting colour sheets in a showroom and discussing them as a partnership. In a promotional film advertising the virtues of Formica, a woman is shown applying the glue to the underside of the sheet; a man takes the glue pot from her, screws the top on, then saws off the edges.

A revised domestic paradigm was being promoted by the DIY supply industry, in which the woman made the decisions on how the home should look, and the husband was reduced to the role of instrument of her will. In an ICI Paints film, a young Valerie Singleton – later famous as a radio and TV presenter, particularly of the BBC's long-running children's programme *Blue Peter* – is shown lecturing her reluctant, fag-puffing husband on how they need to repaint their house to keep up with the couple next door, and then dragging him off to the paint shop. Evostick adhesive adopted a similar theme: husband with pipe in mouth, anxious to get away into the garden; wife wheedling away at him in honeyed tones to fit the acoustic tiles to the nursery ceiling, box in the bath and stick a laminated sheet on the kitchen table. 'Will you, sweetheart?' she coos. 'Do be a dear.'

One and a half million people flocked to the *Daily Mail* Ideal Home Exhibition at Olympia in 1957, and hundreds of thousands attended similar shows staged by *Practical Householder* and *Do It Yourself* magazines. The home-improvement publications continued to develop a more gender-inclusive approach – couples working in perfect harmony in spotlessly clean clothes – while focusing on practical DIY tasks. But other magazines – most notably *Homes and Gardens* – sought to position DIY within a wider and more upmarket branding bracket that, over time, became known as 'lifestyle'.

The May 1964 issue of *Homes and Gardens* featured interviews with Lady Douglas-Home and Mrs Mary Wilson – the wives of the prime minister and leader of the opposition respectively – conducted by the writer Elspeth Huxley. The detective story writer Marjery Allingham wrote about 'In My Garden'. There was a feature about the extremely stylish home of the actor Dirk Bogarde, and a wine column by the well-known journalist and *bon viveur* Denzil Batchelor. The travel section featured 'A Housewife in the Tropics' and an article entitled 'Driving Through Yugoslavia'.

But amid all the gloss, DIY still had its place. Towards the (admittedly less glamorous) end of the magazine was to be found W. A. G. Bradman, the author of *Wood Finishing, Wood Toymaking* and *Caravan Making*, giving detailed instructions on 'How to Tile a Sink Unit' ('it's not nearly as difficult as it might appear').

The DIY retail sector was also changing. Few of the traditional ironmongers or hardware shops had the space for a full range of the bigger products, such as panels of hardboard, plywood and Formica, that were now in demand. F. M. Woolworth, bouncing back after the war, did its best to fill the gap with a new generation of stores. Displays of tools, fixtures and DIY accessories were enlarged where possible. A photograph of the new Woolworths in Commercial Road, Portsmouth – which opened in 1953 in place of its predecessor, destroyed by German bombs in 1941 – shows boxes of cement and sand under the Odd Jobber's brand, alongside padlocks, curtain rails, hinges and a wide range of tools. In the past, the only paints Woolworths sold were the old-fashioned distemper and gloss in white or magnolia. But during the 1950s, many of the stores installed what were known as gondola islands, on which gloss and emulsion paints in a variety of sizes and with a wide choice of colours were displayed with brushes and other decorating requirements under the brand Household Paints.

But for DIYers unable to get to a big Woolworths, the alternative was the local builders' merchants. These were very much geared to the building trade and could be intimidating to the amateur who only wanted a couple of dozen nails and screws and a sheet of plywood to put in the boot of his car. The bigger hardware shops did their best to plug the gap, but the market was crying out for a revolution.

In the United States, the DIY flame was burning ever more brightly with each issue of *Better Homes and Gardens* and *The Family Handyman*, and demand was soaring. Retail space was much more freely available there, and stores could spread their wings. Chains of spacious hardware stores had been established and had spread long before the term DIY became current. One of the earliest – it claims to be *the* earliest – was Aubuchon Hardware, which was founded in 1908 in Fitchburg, Massachusetts, by a French-Canadian immigrant, William E. Aubuchon. Remarkably, it has remained a family firm, with more than twenty Aubuchons still helping run an empire of more than 130 stores in New England and upstate New York.

Ace Hardware – originally Ace Stores – was created in 1924, when the owners of four hardware stores in Chicago pooled their resources. It opened its first retail hardware warehouse in 1929, and by 1933 had thirty-eight outlets in Illinois, Indiana and Wisconsin. By 1949, this had grown to more than 130, with annual sales exceeding seven million dollars. Three years later, Ace opened their first self-service store in Merrillville, Illinois, and by the end of the decade, there were more than 350 Ace Hardware locations. In 1973, the company became a co-operative owned by its retailers; today, there are more than 4,000 Ace Hardware stores across the US, with outlets in sixty countries, and annual turnover is more than $20 billion USD.

Almost as familiar as Ace is Lowe's. Lucius Smith Lowe opened his first hardware store in Wilkesboro, North Carolina, in 1921. The second did not appear until 1949, but thereafter – fuelled by the DIY boom – the company expanded steadily. Today there are more than 2,100 Lowe's hardware and home-improvement stores in the US, putting it second as a public company only to The Home Depot, which came on the scene much later.

All over the US, lesser and greater chains of hardware stores flourished (and sometimes failed). Visitors from Britain used to tip-toeing around their local ironmonger or queuing self-consciously at the builders' merchants marvelled at the palatial scale of the American store, as well as the vast choice, and the friendliness and expertise of the staff. We had nothing to compare – until the seed of an idea was born and germinated in a suburb of Southampton.

It was planted by two brothers-in-law, Richard Block and David Quayle. Quayle was working for Marley Tiles at the time, and on a business trip to Belgium had been struck by the range of DIY stock available in a new hypermarket. He discussed the matter with brother-in-law Block, and they began looking for premises to pursue the idea. They took a lease on an empty showroom in Portswood, on the north-east side of Southampton. They fitted it out themselves, drafted in family members to work the tills, and did the deliveries in their own cars. Various names for the business were batted around until they settled on B&Q, and, on 5 March 1969, the first B&Q stored open its doors for customers – and a retail legend was created.

The word soon spread, and a second store was opened in Portsmouth the following year. Within ten years, there were twenty-six stores. By then, Richard Block had cashed in and decamped to Derbyshire to become a hypnotherapist. David Quayle stayed on to oversee further expansion, and he became a rich man when B&Q was taken over by Woolworths in 1980. He stuck around as a consultant for a while before migrating from emulsion and gloss to oils and canvas, enrolling on a fine art course in London and then founding the Beatrice Royal gallery of contemporary art in Eastleigh.

'You can do it if you B&Q it' was the company's immortal slogan, still current today. Other DIY chains followed Block and Quayle's pioneering path – Focus, Homebase and Wickes among them – but none ever managed to stamp such an indelible impression on the nation's consciousness.

It took some time for the B&Q brand of DIY magic to reach my corner of Berkshire, and I have no memory of being aware of its existence when my own patchy home-improvement journey began. In 1973, I became a homeowner for the first time by acquiring a small late-Victorian terraced cottage in Windsor. Interior design was not a strong point with me, so I painted all the walls and ceilings in all the rooms and the hall and the landing in brilliant white emulsion.

I then had the stairs and all the floors that required carpeting covered in the same olive-green nylon carpet. At £200 for the whole house, this struck me as a great bargain, an opinion I revised somewhat, as, within weeks, it began to stretch and bulge in annoying places.

Emboldened by my success with painting walls and ceilings, I decided to try something more ambitious. The kitchen ceiling, despite its coat of emulsion, was cracked and fissured and sad. I had been told that the way to address this was by sticking lining paper over it and then slapping on yet more emulsion. Had I been a subscriber to *Practical Householder*, or had I taken the trouble to consult one of the multitude of DIY books then available, I would have realised that this represented quite a challenge to a beginner, and actually required a degree of technical expertise.

Blithely I assumed you went about putting up lining paper in the same way as wallpaper, only horizontally instead of vertically. I cut the first strip to fit the length of the ceiling with a few inches extra, daubed on the paste, climbed the stepladder and pushed the end into the angle between ceiling and wall, using a big, soft brush to position and flatten it. I turned away from the wall and began to work the strip towards the centre but did not get far before feeling something clammy against the back of my head. I turned back to find that, under the weight of paste and in obedience to the laws of gravity, the strip had detached itself from where I had placed it and was resting against my head and back, lengthening as I progressed.

I reassessed. I began to suspect there might be something conceptually flawed in my method. I tried placing the stepladder in the middle of the kitchen and pushing the paper outwards, arms akimbo. But my arms were nowhere near long enough for the paper to establish a lasting attachment. Whichever way I tried to advance, it descended from the other. Gobbets of paste accumulated on my clothes and in my hair, and a familiar red mist of rage began to possess me. The notion of folding the paper concertina-style, as prescribed in the manuals, never occurred to me. In the end, I discovered from trial and error what length of paper was manageable with my method and covered the ceiling in short strips butted together. I hoped that if I applied enough emulsion, the many dividing lines would become invisible, but they did not.

In later life and with later houses, I generally restricted myself to basic painting. As children arrived, I never had enough money to pay a professional to do that kind of work. Anyway, there was a common feeling among young middle-class families starting along the massive mortgage/home-ownership road that you should do it yourself. Even my mother, who in her early married life would not have known one end of a paint brush from the other, took to doing her own painting and decorating, and, being a lot more capable than me, became accomplished at it.

In one house, much of the downstairs ceiling had, at some time in the past, been covered in a kind of textured plaster with added asbestos known as Artex. It became popular in the 1970s because it concealed imperfections in the original plaster and, with the use of a stipple brush or knife or even the fingers, could be worked into swirls and circles and random lines. These effects were considered very contemporary and stylish for a while, but quickly fell from favour. Ours, a heavy, spiky stipple, was particularly nasty, and my first wife and I decided that I should get rid of it (as Artex at that time was full of asbestos, the procedure I have described is not to be recommended).

It was the vilest job I have ever done. First, with a plastic bag over my hair and wearing a breathing mask, I tried brushing on some kind of sticky and acrid stripper, which was alleged to soften the rock-hard Artex sufficiently for it to be scraped off. The smell as the chemicals in the stripper encountered the asbestos was awful, and the efficacy was very limited, so I switched to using a wallpaper steamer. This involved climbing the stepladder and using one hand to apply a metal plate connected by a tube to a container on the floor full of boiling water, and the other to thrust a scraper into the softened Artex to prise it off. This worked better, but progress was agonisingly slow. If you left the metal plate against the Artex for too long, it tended to cause yet more cracks in the plaster underneath, or even bring it off altogether with a discouraging popping sound. If you withdrew the plate too soon, it left obstinate smears of the filthy stuff behind. It became obvious as I advanced why the previous owners had gone down the Artex route. The original plaster was a lunar landscape of cracks and holes, which continued to show through the several layers of emulsion we eventually put on top. We could not afford to replaster it, and I was disinclined to try the lining paper solution again, so we lived with it as one does and, in time, stopped fretting about it.

The habit that plaster has of deteriorating over time was a considerable issue when my second wife, Helen, and I moved into the house where we still live. Some of the walls had been papered and painted, concealing some unsavoury failings underneath. Most of the ceilings had been plastered long before, and in places the material was bowed under its own weight. We had the worst of it redone by a professional plasterer and forgot about the rest of it until one day, without warning, most of the ceiling in the room where our two infant daughters had been playing half an hour before collapsed. We called the plasterer back.

I did some painting during that characteristic initial burst of home-improvement energy. Then I thought I might install some shelving to take the several thousand books I had accumulated over the years. Had I been Barry Bucknell or Shro – or just a reasonably thoughtful DIYer – I would have considered the matter carefully and researched recommended procedures. As it was, I went down to Homebase in Reading and bought some brown metal twin slot uprights to fix to the wall, the brackets to fit in them and cheap MDF for the actual shelves. I reasoned that once the books were in place, it would not matter much how rough and ready the shelving was, because you would not really be able to see it. What I failed to take into account was the weight of the books and the consequent need to position the uprights fairly close together to support the load. I used two, quite far apart, and the shelves sagged in the middle. The next time, I put them closer together and the shelves sloped down at the ends.

They did not look good, and some years later I got the highly skilled carpenter who fitted our new kitchen to spend some time replacing my shelves. I am glad I did, because I can now look at the books and take one out without being distracted by feelings of past inadequacy.

As time went on, I generally restricted my DIY activities to slapping on emulsion paint where required and on outdoor projects. These included constructing bays for compost and leaf mould from old bits of wood and sheets of corrugated iron, making raised beds from gravel boards and posts, and improvising a fruit cage from wire netting and bigger posts. To combat a plague of muntjac deer, I even managed to erect a chain-link fence around the garden perimeter, a back-breaking endeavour that gave me considerable satisfaction and caused the muntjac to take their pesky chomping teeth elsewhere.

Anything that could be done with saw, wire, wire-cutters, pliers, nails, screws, metal staples, and brute strength and dogged persistence, I was game for. Anything that might be judged for finesse and skill was out.

## CHAPTER EIGHT

# A Man and His Toolbox

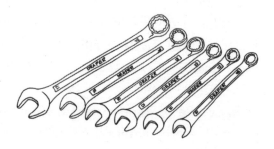

IT IS A FRIDAY MORNING in November. I began work on the writing of this book a few weeks ago, and it is time to confront the state of my toolbox. For as long as I can remember, I have tried to avoid looking at it when going into the shed, apart from on those occasions I needed something from it. It has always made me feel slightly ashamed of myself. What kind of a man, it seems to want to ask me, treats his tools like this?

But now I am making a study of tools and what they mean to us, because tools are a big part of what a hardware shop does. So I feel I need to deal with this personal issue before going on to consider the wider subject. This is my toolbox on this morning in November.

First, the box itself. It is made of plywood, which was once painted white, and it has a hinged lid. It is on one level only, which is divided into four compartments - a large one on the right, a smaller one on the left, and two much smaller ones in the middle. I do not know where the box came from; I think it may have been in the shed when we moved in. It stands on top of a very inferior plywood cabinet, which is used to store an assembly of bottles of chain oil, fuel cans, electric drills, a foot pump, a hazard triangle that should be in the car but isn't, some oily rags, various cycling accessories and some other stuff that might come in handy one day.

The spirit level, which is yellow and newish and in good working order, bar tooth marks at the end where the dog chewed it, rests diagonally across the other contents of the toolbox. It should not be there, because it is too long to fit into any of the compartments. It should be somewhere else, somewhere vertical rather than horizontal, but it has no fixed abode, so it is here.

The screwdrivers are supposed to be kept sharp-end down in the further of the two central compartments, so their handles are raised for easy removal. Thus arranged, they are both pleasing to look at, with their handles of various colours, and efficiently disposed. But they are not where they should be; at least, some are, but others are not. The others are all over the place. The biggest, which has a bottle-green handle and is vital for all kinds of prising, levering and chiselling functions unrelated to the turning of screws, is partially concealed under the spirit level. A smaller one, with a blue-and-grey handle, is at right angles to it, beside a chisel whose wooden handle has been flattened and somewhat splintered by some over-energetic bashing long ago.

Next to the chisel and at a slight angle to it is one of our two hammers, its head also underneath the spirit level. The other hammer is absent without leave. Resting on top of the hammer head and beneath the shank of the big screwdriver is one of my favourite tools, a pair of adjustable pliers, designed for gripping water pipes but adaptable to a wide variety of challenges requiring brute force to resolve.

Several more screwdrivers – flat-head and Phillips in various sizes and colours – can by glimpsed at different angles to the vertical and horizontal amid the confusion. There is a blue metal wedge that I cannot remember ever having used, but which I assume is for splitting recalcitrant bits of wood or opening manhole covers. There is a rusty adjustable spanner and a hacksaw with yet another screwdriver diagonally across its handle. There is a pair of wire-cutters, a wheel-nut wrench, a wire brush with most of its wire bristles missing, and a yellow object that I believe to be a metal pipe detector.

That is the right-hand compartment. The nearer of the two middle compartments is for spanners. It does have spanners in it, but they are partially obscured by a layer of dead brown leaves from the honeysuckle that grows with riotous abandon outside the window above the toolbox, sending its tendrils all around the inside of the shed to curl around broom handles and beams and lengths of two-by-four and the spokes of bicycle wheels, depositing leaves as they go. Moreover, not all the spanners are in there. Others are elsewhere in the box, or elsewhere in the shed, or elsewhere in the house or garden, or in the canvas bag that I use for transporting tools for use in other locations. A spanner that is not where you can put your hands on it is not much use.

Moving to the left-hand compartment, I see on top of the pile my Stanley planer file, in red. I bought this a long time ago, when I had ambitions to extend my woodworking capability, and I used it, although I cannot remember what for. But the blade is now rusted and clogged with ancient shavings and bits of dead honeysuckle leaf, and it is useless. But it is still here. Why? I have no answer.

To one side of it is a bone-handled dessert knife used for applying filler and putty, hardened accretions of which are smeared across the blade. Underneath the plane is a big spanner, with three screwdrivers and a chisel visible below. I see clamp, square, another wheel-nut spanner, a bradawl. At the bottom is the Stanley knife, one of the old-fashioned ones with a knobbly silver handle and a retractable blade that can be adjusted to different positions. The blade is rusty, and the spare blades that should be inside the handle are absent. It, too, is pretty much useless – unless I wish to give myself tetanus.

Over the years, I have periodically restored the toolbox to a state of order, discarding the dead leaves and putting everything back in the compartment where it belongs. But it never stays that way. There is a dark force that works against me. It does so by exercising an insidious temptation to take a tool away to do something and leave it there instead of bringing it back. I am sure I am guilty myself, but there are others in this household who make use of the toolbox – actually just one other, because our daughters would expire at the thought of personally undertaking DIY. I am not in the business of making accusations; all I will say is that I have found tools in some strange and unexpected places.

I concede that our tool discipline is reprehensibly slack. All over the civilised world are handicrafters and DIYers very unlike me: tidy practitioners with tidy minds, and tidy sheds and workshops, in which tools are tidily organised in toolboxes of an adequate capacity, with others in a cabinet or hung from hooks; people who know where everything is, who clean their tools, who replace useless tools with good tools, who know how to get the job done. I admire such people all the more for knowing that I can never be one of them.

Jim Tolpin is one. I came across his woodworking website and his celebration of his craft, *The Toolbox Book*, when searching online for exemplars of toolbox management. Tolpin was born and brought up in Springfield, Massachusetts, where he learned about wood from his grandfather, who ran a grocery store and made cabinets on the side. He became a geology lecturer at the University of New Hampshire, but was insistently pulled in a divergent direction towards working with wood. He built boats and cabinets, and moved to the coast of Washington, where he set up a woodworking school and wrote his first book, *Jim Tolpin's Guide to Becoming a Professional Cabinetmaker*. He wrote more books, taught, and made gypsy caravans, as well as more boats and cabinets, and eventually moved to Port Townsend, the historic port on the Quimper peninsula, where he co-founded the Port Townsend School of Woodworking.

*The Toolbox Book* was published in 1995. It is a richly researched and gorgeously illustrated homage to the American passion for skilled work with wood and its heritage. In the chapter on making your own traditional tool chest – which is featured on Tolpin's website – he lingers admiringly over the creations of several contemporary craftsmen. The chest made from maple, walnut and pine by Tim Kimack of Simi Valley, California, has three wells in the bottom for his various planes, a sliding till of seven drawers, and a till for saws against the inside cover. Judge Bill Tinney's mahogany box, designed specifically for boat-building tools, has saws fixed inside the top, a sliding three-drawer till and a tray with a fold-down handle. Tony Konovaloff, of Bellingham, Washington State, constructed his chest from black walnut, with the till drawers sliding sideways instead of back-to-front; fully loaded, it weighs around 400 pounds.

These are all amazing creations, but not quite as amazing, perhaps, as the one made by H. O. Studley – a name spoken with reverence among historians and connoisseurs of the American toolbox. Not a great deal is known about Henry Oscar Studley, beyond that he was born in 1838 and died in 1925, that he fought on the Union side in the Civil War, that he lived for most of his life in Quincy, just south of Boston, and that he was a dedicated Freemason and a craftsman of extraordinary talent. His profession was making organs and pianos; he worked for the Smith Organ Company in Quincy and subsequently for the Poole Piano Company of Boston. The only known photograph of him was in the December 1921 issue of the *Music Trade Review*; it shows him, aged over eighty, in his apron in the Poole workshop, 'still in active harness', according to the article. Hanging on the wall behind him is the reason for his legendary status.

Studley is believed to have fashioned this extraordinary artefact between 1890 and 1920. It is mainly mahogany, with ebony, ivory and mother-of-pearl fittings. It is thirty-nine inches long, nineteen-and-a-half wide and nine-and-a-half deep and is designed to contain nearly 300 tools – which included some particular to piano construction and a full range for woodworking. They are stored up to three layers deep. Each has its allotted place and fixtures to keep it there. The gaps are as small as one eighth of an inch, but no tool touches another. Ebony catches hold some groups in place, and other tiny catches stop the drawers sliding out. Whole sections swing out to reveal those underneath.

You really have to see a picture to appreciate this miracle of ingenuity and fine workmanship (or, to get the full story, read *Virtuoso: The Tool Cabinet and Workbench of Henry O. Studley*, the book written by the former chief conservator of furniture at the Smithsonian Institution, Donald Williams). The Studley toolbox is also, of course, more than mildly obsessive: almost literally a lifetime's work to create something that is more a sacred monument than a useful piece of equipment. Its creator had no one close to bequeath it to, so he left it to a lawyer in Quincy. One of his descendants inherited it and loaned it to the Smithsonian, where it was restored and repaired and displayed for a while. It was later sold to a collector but is sometimes made available for exhibitions.

IT WOULD BE HIGHLY INSULTING to the memory of H. O. Studley, or to living masters like Jim Tolpin and the woodworkers he honours, to associate them in any way with DIY. They belong to the highest echelon of craftsmen and craftswomen, standing in relation to the average DIYer as an elite Olympic athlete to the jogger in the park. But the principles laid down on the organisation and maintenance of the toolbox are universal – or should be. And having spent time with these exceptional individuals, I have vowed to change my ways.

I went out to the shed armed with dustpan and brush and vacuum cleaner. I removed the heap of tools from each compartment of my toolbox, swept up the honeysuckle leaves and vacuumed out the dust of twenty years. The screwdrivers, twenty of them, went bit-down, handle-up, into their places. The spanners, sixteen of them, went next door. On the left-hand side, I arranged chisels, knives, square, wire brush and wheel-nut wrenches parallel to each other. On the right, I put the blue wedge and the rusty but still salvageable Stanley knife along the near end, with the cutting, squeezing, gripping tools – pliers, wire-cutters, wrench, pincers – lengthways. The two claw hammers and the club hammer were laid on top.

I hung the spirit level, which should never have been in there in the first place, from a nail behind the lid of the toolbox, where it is easily accessible and does not get in the way. I took the Stanley planer file with its rusted blade to the shop in search of a replacement. Shro didn't have the right size but is trying to source one for me. I threw out a few items that were broken beyond repair, or to which I was unable to ascribe any known use. I wondered briefly if the little device for detecting metal pipes in walls should go as well. Its battery was dead, it didn't work, I had never used it and never would; but it did not take up much room, and somehow it seemed disrespectful to whoever had obtained it in the first place just to bin it, so I found a corner for it.

The toolbox stays where it always was but is – to use the jargon – 'in a better place'. I can look at it without a shudder of shame. And I have issued instructions to myself and others that items from it ARE TO BE RETURNED TO WHERE THEY CAME FROM. I fear it would not impress Jim Tolpin or H. O. Studley or any of those other unswerving perfectionists. But it impresses me for the moment. It is ready for action when the call comes.

## CHAPTER NINE

# 'Without Tools, He is Nothing'

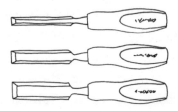

THERE HAVE BEEN TOOLS for as long as there have been hands to grasp them. At least two million years before *Homo sapiens* came on the scene, hominins were using hammer-stones to break off flakes from other stones to chop and cut with. What palaeontologists call the Oldowan Industry – named after a gorge in Tanzania where large quantities of the tools were found – was spread around Africa by *Homo habilis*, inherited by *Homo erectus* and taken north and east by travelling bands, reaching China by about 1.6 million years ago.

From the Oldowan developed the Acheulean stone-tool industry (named after Saint-Acheul near Amiens in south-west France), which produced axes, picks and cleavers. Blades appeared 50,000 years ago in the Upper Palaeolithic period, enabling the fashioning of spear points and arrowheads from flint or churt. The Neolithic era, the last of the Stone Age, saw the birth of agriculture and the development of more tools, including the adze, with its cutting edge at right angles to the handle rather than parallel, as with the axe. In varying sizes, the adze could be used for multiple functions, including carving wood and hoeing the soil. Neolithic people also used chisels, gouges, hammers, nails, clamps and the bow drill, with which a hole could be made by a sharp-ended spindle rotated with a cord held taut by a bow.

The coming of the saw represented a mighty technological breakthrough. In the eloquent words of the American collector and historian of early tools, Henry Chapman Mercer, it has been 'the master tool [. . .] outranging the edged tools because potent in cutting metal and stone as well as wood [. . .] it has outrivalled the axe and outclassed the wedge from the beginning of time'. Cutting tools with serrated edges, usually of flint, were evidently in use in pre-history, but the earliest-known manufactured saws, made 7,000 years ago from obsidian and with very short handles, were discovered in the excavation of the Sumerian capital, Ur of the Chaldees, between the Euphrates and Tigris rivers. Saws made of hardened copper and, later, bronze were also in use in Ancient Egypt, where – under later dynasties – they became much bigger to meet the need to cut blocks of limestone for the epic monuments required by the pharaohs. The British Museum has an Egyptian saw dating from 1450 BCE, with a five-inch handle and a ten-inch blade with unraked V-shaped teeth.

In medieval England, ironmonger's shops were common in cities and towns, and the 1356 inventory of the contents of John Leche's shop in Cornhill, London, suggests that they would have stocked a range of familiar tools. In around 1500, an English scribe named Rate or Rathe wrote down a lengthy poem in English entitled 'The Debate of the Carpenter's Tools'. One can only guess why; perhaps he was instructed to do so, or perhaps he composed it himself. If so, he evidently knew his subject, as a considerable range of implements are allowed their say about the faults and frailties – mainly alcohol-related – of their master. Some of the nomenclature is obscure – a wymbyll, for instance, may or may not be a kind of gimlet, and a skantyllon could be a measuring rule or something else entirely. Others are familiar and speak out plainly. The saw mocks the notion of their master ever making any serious money – 'He wones to nyghe the alewyffe' (he lives too near the tavern-keeper). The adze agrees – 'for he wyll drynke more on a dey/ Than thou cane lyghtly arne in twey', he tells his colleagues. It may not be great verse, but it undoubtedly has a rough Middle English vitality to it, and the absent carpenter seems an endearingly fallible and recognisable figure.

Skilled carpenters and joiners were highly prized. No ship would set sail without a master carpenter. When the wreck of Henry VIII's flagship, the *Mary Rose*, was salvaged, the carpenter's remains were found among coils of rope on the lower deck, with his sawhorse, chopping block and stool, and his tools – among them two adzes, a chisel and a hammer – nearby. Elsewhere were mallets, planes, a twenty-four-inch rule, a mortice gauge and the block from a block-and-tackle.

But the carpenter and joiner were only as good as their tools. The 1659 inventory of the possessions left by John Penney, a joiner from Eye in Suffolk, lists a vast range, including two lathes, two benches, hatchets, saws, forty-five chisels and a similar number of planes, glue pots, a spokeshave and a host of other items – valued in total at fourteen pounds and fifteen shillings.

Tools themselves were evidently widely available; what was missing was the manual of instruction as to how to use them. It took a remarkable man to address this deficiency; in doing so, Joseph Moxon conferred a status on working with hand tools that it had never enjoyed before. He called this massive work *Mechanick Exercises on the Doctrine of Handy Works*, and in the preamble he made a startling claim: 'Tho the Mechanicks be, by some, accounted ignoble and scandalous, yet it is very well known that many Gentlemen in this Nation, of good rank and high quality, are conversant in handy works.' In other words, according to Moxon – and why would he make it up? – there were educated men with a respectable position in society skilled enough with tools to fashion objects for the pleasure of it. DIY was alive in Carolingian England, but they called it 'handy works'.

Moxon was born in Wakefield in Yorkshire in 1627, and at the age of ten went with his family to live in Holland, where his father established a printing press in Rotterdam producing bibles in English to be smuggled back to England. After the execution of Charles I and the establishment of the Commonwealth, the family returned, and father and son set up a printing business 'at the upper end of Houndsditch'. But after a few years they went their separate ways, Joseph to pursue his aptitude for mathematics and the making of mathematical instruments (and to reposition himself politically and socially). He spent some time in Holland learning how to make globes and maps, then came back to London and published books on astronomy and mathematics, including one of his own about the motions of the planets.

With the restoration of Charles II, Moxon's cunningly contrived social manoeuvring paid off. In 1662, he was appointed Royal Hydrographer, his petition for the job supported in writing by a cluster of members of the immensely prestigious Royal Society. He had a close association with one of the towering geniuses of that dazzling age of scientific discovery, Robert Hooke; in his diary, Hooke mentions arranging for Moxon to come to his house 'to see comet but missed it, drank two bottles of claret'. Hooke advised him during the production of the *Mechanick Exercises*, which was published in fourteen issues between 1678 and 1680, each costing sixpence. Moxon presented the first six to the President of the Royal Society, Sir Joseph Williamson, and in November 1678 was elected a fellow.

Moxon's ascent from inky printer to royal office-holder and acknowledged man of science was complete. But he remained a businessman, with a shop in Cornhill (later Ludgate Hill), where he sold 'all manner of mathematical books or instruments and maps whatsoever'. And it was business that led to a rift with the Royal Society when he failed to secure the contract to be its official printer. Moxon signalled his displeasure by failing to pay his subscription, and in 1682 he was expelled.

The second part of the complete *Mechanick Exercises* was devoted to his first speciality: printing. The first part is, in effect, a comprehensive manual of instruction on working with tools. It begins with a lengthy section about the blacksmith and the operation of the well-equipped smithy, and subsequently covers everything from making a bowl to building a house. Much of it is clearly aimed at the professional rather than the rare gentleman handy worker – for example, the very detailed guidance on making locks and keys to fit them. And it is fair to say that Moxon's prose style is more functional than elegant.

Here he is on how to use the plow, a kind of plane:

The office of the plow is to plow a narrow square groove on the edge of a board [. . .] the board is set on edge with one end in the bench screw and its other edge upon a pin or pins put into a hole or holes in the leg or legs of the bench, such a hole or holes as will, for height, fit the breadth of the board; then the fence of the plow is set to that distance off the iron-plate of the plow that you intend the groove shall be off the edge of the board [. . .]

One feels there must be a simpler way of putting it.

But sometimes he speaks clearly across the centuries. Barry Bucknell himself would have approved of Moxon's words stressing the need for a solid workbench 'to keep the work fast while you either saw, tennant, mortess or plain upon it [. . .] if your board shakes or trembles under the plain your joint will hardly be truly straight'. In the section about 'glew' and 'the glew pot', Moxon writes: 'Your glew must be very warm [. . .] you must smear the glew well upon the joint of each piece [. . .] you must jostle them together that the glew may very well touch and take hold of the wood.'

The illustrations speak even more clearly. One plate in the joinery section shows the workbench, six different planes, six chisels, six saws of various kinds, a clamp, two squares, bevel, gimlet and hatchet ('its use is to hew the irregularities off such pieces of stuff which may sooner be hewn than sawn'). All these tools are instantly familiar, as are the axe, adze, hammer, mallet, plumb line, chisel and other implements displayed elsewhere. Most of them could be bought at our shop today, although Shro might struggle with some of the terminology – the Commander, for instance (a big mallet), and the Crow (crowbar).

Joseph Moxon's ABC of handywork is convincing evidence that the home-improvement enthusiast in Carolingian England would have been able to get hold of a range of tools identical in their principles of design to those available from any self-respecting hardware shop of today. Most of them had been in use for centuries before Moxon's time. The huge difference, of course, was the complete absence of standardisation in his day. The shape, weight and attributes of each hammer depended on which smith had fashioned it. The length, diameter and groove angle of your screws depended on which screw-maker you patronised. The same with nails. It required the coming of the machine age to bring a semblance of order to this infinitely varied tool landscape.

THE STORY OF WOODSCREWS is emblematic. The discovery that nails were good but screws were better belongs in the mists of ancient time. The principle of the helical screw was deployed to raise water at the Hanging Gardens of Nineveh in Iraq in 700 BCE, 400 years before Archimedes and his screw. In the first century CE, the Greek engineer and inventor Hero (or Heron) of Alexandria devised the direct screw press, and there is some evidence that he also used much smaller filed screws to make an early version of the theodolite. Roman engineers used screws, and in the Middle Ages their usefulness was generally acknowledged; the problem was that they were very laborious to make, as each one had to be held in a vice and the thread cut manually with a screw plate or file. They were, therefore, much more expensive than nails, and used only in exceptional circumstances, such as the making of armour, where the need for strength was paramount.

In 1760, two brothers from Tattenhill in Staffordshire, Job and William Wyatt, took out a patent for 'a method of cutting screws, commonly called wood screws, in a better manner than had been heretofore practised'. The Wyatt process was automatic – the screws were cut on a spindle turned by some kind of lathe, and the machine could produce ten screws a minute, which was considered almost hectic.

Sadly for them, the brothers were better at innovation than business. They acquired a watermill in Tattenhill and converted it into a water-powered screw factory, but it went bust and was taken over by another company, Shorthose, Wood and Co. This company thrived and output expanded, so that by 1792 there were sixty workers on thirty-six machines, turning out 16,000 screws a week.

This was certainly progress. But it remained the case that the manufactured screws were individual to each workshop. The ends were blunt; the lathes of that time could not cut a tapering thread. The uniqueness of each batch of screws – and of the bolts and nuts made on the same machines – was the source of much inconvenience. As the nineteenth-century industrial historian and self-help evangelist Samuel Smiles put it neatly, every bolt and nut was 'a speciality which neither owed nor admitted of any community with its neighbours'. Each had to be marked to distinguish it from any other.

The transformation of this anarchy into a state of proper Victorian order took half a century and was largely achieved by a quartet of outstanding mechanical problem-solvers: Joseph Bramah, Henry Maudslay, Joseph Clement and Joseph

Whitworth. Bramah was a farmer's son from near Barnsley in Yorkshire, whose exceptional manual skill and inventive tendency were evidenced as a teenage boy when he made a violin from a single block of wood, which became an object of wonder in the locality. An accident at the age of sixteen disqualified him from farming work, and he was apprenticed to the local carpenter. As a young man, he walked from Yorkshire to London and obtained work as a cabinet-maker. In 1778, Bramah patented a superior type of flushing water-closet. He became celebrated as a lock-maker, and subsequently for inventing a machine for printing the numbers and dates on banknotes.

Bramah was a brilliant innovator, and he also had an eye for unusual talent. One day, a young man, Henry Maudslay, came into his workshop in St Giles to ask for a job. Maudslay was a Londoner, and as a boy had worked as a 'powder monkey', making and filling cartridges at Woolwich Arsenal. Bramah recognised his exceptional ability at once, and within a year Maudslay had been made head foreman. Together, he and his boss developed the slide rest, an attachment on a lathe enabling precise cutting of metal. It was the self-tightening collar devised by Maudslay that made it possible for Bramah's hydraulic press to work in practice. They formed a creative partnership that achieved remarkable advances in a new generation of machine tools – until Maudslay had the cheek to ask for a significant pay rise, was rebuffed, and went off to set up in business on his own.

That was in 1797. In 1800, Maudslay succeeded in making a screw-cutting lathe far superior to anything seen before, and his work on refining and developing the technology continued until his death in 1830. By then, his business in

Lambeth employed several hundred men and produced a vast range of machines, machine tools and steam engines. John Jacob Holtzapffel, of the London tool-making dynasty and historian of the first machine age, wrote of Maudslay: 'It may be fairly advanced that during the period 1800 to 1810 he effected nearly the entire change from the old, imperfect, accidental practice of screw-making to the modern exact systematic mode.'

Some years after Maudslay had stomped out of Joseph Bramah's workshop, another amazingly ingenious young man seeking to make his way in the world turned up there seeking a position. Joseph Clement was born in Great Ashby in Westmorland in 1779, the son of a weaver. Like Bramah and Maudslay, he received very little in the way of formal schooling; like them, he was required at an early age to sink or swim in the world of work. At various times, Clement was a weaver, a roof thatcher and slater, and a maker of tools. He found employment locally at first, and then in Carlisle, Glasgow and Aberdeen, before yielding to the magnetic lure of London. He knew no one there and few could understand his strong Lakeland accent, but Bramah knew gold when he saw it and gave him the job. Clement excelled, but the following year, 1814, the old man died and the sons who succeeded him viewed the somewhat uncouth Clement with disfavour. He went to work for Maudslay for a time, mainly on marine steam engines, and subsequently set up his own workshop in Newington.

As with the other machine tool pioneers, Clement dealt with a range of products. But, for many years, he concentrated on improvements to the lathe, so that by 1828, using a revolving cutter, he was able to turn out screws of uniform length with standard threads at a regular pitch. He also found time to devise what became known as the 'Great Planer', which was able to finish large sheets of metal to a higher standard than anyone else could manage and was in such demand that it was often running day and night, making a major contribution to the profitability of the business. Clement's reputation was such that he was sought out by the wealthy mathematician, astronomer and theologian Charles Babbage to do the precision engineering of Babbage's celebrated Difference Machine, which was designed to calculate mathematical and astronomical tables of immense complexity, and is regarded as a milestone in early computing.

The last of these master toolmakers, Joseph Whitworth, followed the same path as the others. He was born in Stockport and – even though his father was a schoolmaster – was sent to work at his uncle's cotton-spinning business when he was fourteen. The lad showed no interest in the business side, but paid close attention to the machinery, finding much of it very imperfectly made. He learned his trade thoroughly before going to London, where, at the age of twenty-two, he secured a job with Maudslay. Under Maudslay's supervision, Whitworth worked extensively on methods to produce flat planes by removing all minute imperfections. From Maudslay's workshop, he moved to Holtzapffel's and then to Joseph Clement's. Aged thirty he returned to Manchester to set up his own business under the sign 'Joseph Whitworth Toolmaker from London'.

It thrived. Whitworth established a reputation for making machine tools to an exceptional standard, charged accordingly and became extremely rich. One of his most celebrated creations was known as the measuring machine, in which

– using a screw with twenty threads to an inch – he was able accurately to adjust the distance between parallel plates by a thousandth of an inch. Much later, he turned his fertile mind to weaponry. His rifle made the standard Enfield seem primitive in its accuracy, and he achieved great advances in making field guns safer (to their users) and more accurate and their shells more penetrative. He became a great name across Europe, was knighted, gave lavishly to good causes (the Whitworth Gallery in Manchester being one example), and lived in style on an estate in Derbyshire, where his park, gardens, trotting horses, pure-bred shorthorn cattle and perfectly flat iron billiards table were all regarded as models of their kind. Jane Carlyle met him and wrote to her husband Thomas: 'Whitworth, the inventor of the besom-cart [a horse-drawn street-sweeper] and many other wonderful machines, has a face not unlike that of a baboon; speaks the broadest Lancashire; could not invent an epigram to save his life; but when one talks to him, one feels to be talking with a real live man.'

In 1841, Whitworth read a paper to the Institution of Civil Engineers proposing the standardising of screw threads. He had made an intensive study of the many and varied possibilities and concluded that the angle of the thread should be fifty-five degrees, with the depth and pitch of constant proportion, and the number of threads per inch specified for various diameters. The force of his argument was irresistible and Whitworth championed it tirelessly, so that within twenty years, the British Standard Whitworth had been adopted throughout the country.

With the complacency characteristic of his time, Whitworth assumed that the booming manufacturing industry in the US should follow where Britain led. In 1853, he and George Wallis, who was in charge of the government's School of Design in Birmingham, made an extended visit to spread the word. Whitworth inspected factories and workshops in fifteen manufacturing centres, including Washington, Baltimore, Pittsburgh, New York and Buffalo. Overall, he was impressed by 'the eagerness with which they call in the aid of machinery in almost every department of industry [. . .] whenever it can be introduced as a substitute for manual labour is it universally and willingly resorted to'.

With hindsight, it is possible to see that, by the middle of the nineteenth century the creative balance in innovation was shifting westwards across the Atlantic. The great age of British invention was drawing to a close, while in America it was just getting into gear. American engineers were addressing the challenges presented by the industrial transformation in their own way; and in the matter of screws, they were not prepared to be told what was good for them by the British.

In 1842, a Rhode Island mechanic, Clarence Whipple, developed an automatic screw-making machine and formed the New England Screw Company (later amalgamated with the Eagle Screw Co. into the American Screw Co.). Seven years later, Thomas J. Sloan – collaborating with Clarence Whipple's company – patented a machine that tapered a screw to a pointed end, enabling it to be fixed without the tedious requirement first to drill a hole for it. It was a game-changer, the potential of which was recognised by British manufacturers after the machine was shown at the Great Exhibition in 1851. The rights to develop the technology on an industrial scale were acquired for £10,000 by Joseph Henry Nettlefold. In partnership with his brother-in-law, Joseph

Chamberlain, Nettlefold established a purpose-built factory at Smethwick, on the outskirts of Birmingham. By the early 1870s, Nettlefold & Chamberlain controlled seventy per cent of Birmingham's screw production and employed 2,500 men.

Meanwhile, the matter of the British Standard Whitworth screw thread had been receiving due consideration from American manufacturers. In 1864, William Sellers, the boss of a big Philadelphia machine factory, proposed a new system to replace the Whitworth standard. The main difference was to make the angle sixty degrees instead of fifty-five, which was easier to cut. Within a few years, the Sellers thread had been approved for all US government work, and, thirty years later, it was adopted at an international conference in Zurich. Britain clung on to its Whitworth, but the rest of the world voted Sellers.

THE TRANSATLANTIC MIGRATION of new thinking about the humble wood screw is just one example of the traffic in innovation between the two countries that transformed the industrial landscape in both over the course of the nineteenth century. Their common language may not have united them politically, but it made it very easy for a breakthrough patented in one to be closely studied in the other. Britain had led the way in devising new technologies in the making of machines and tools, but the dynamism and potential for growth in the much bigger country inevitably generated opportunities for ingenious minds to solve problems and address challenges on a scale that the old country could not match.

In 1859, the first issue of a new journal for the ironmongery trade in Britain appeared. It grew from a price list issued by a hardware shop in London that had been acquired by six industrious and enterprising brothers from Abergavenny in south Wales – William, Septimus, Thomas, Walter, Octavius and Edward Morgan. They began including items of trade news with their price list and expanded it into a publication, which they initially called *Morgan's Monthly Circular and Metal Trades Advertiser*, and later renamed *The Ironmonger and Metal Trades Advertiser*. It sold well and then very well; advertising poured in, and the Morgan brothers became publishers instead of ironmongers.

In time, it became a weekly and the brothers added a companion annual called *The Ironmonger Diary and Hardware Buyers Guide*. An early edition, published in 1877, provides a revealing snapshot of the impact of the mass production of tools and accessories. The story is really told in the advertisements rather than the editorial text, much of which consists of interminable tables in small print showing weights of various substances, specific heats of different bodies, the weight of copper balls per inch diameter and suchlike. The seventy pages of ads convey a vivid impression of what the factories and workshops in the new industrial power-houses were producing to satisfy the needs of the Victorian consumer.

Thomas Bradford and Co., with registered addresses in Manchester, London and Dublin, offered the Premier Box Mangle – 'the most perfect box mangle ever made' at £16-10-0 for the seven-foot version. From Sheffield, Frederick Brittan, toolmaker, declared the supremacy of his Improved Registered Spanner – 'For simplicity of construction, symmetry of shape and strength combined with lightness, this spanner has no equal'. Sutton & Ash, iron and steel merchants of Snow Hill, Birmingham, proclaimed the incomparable qualities of the Thackray washer – 'Locks the nuts perfectly, impossible to shake loose, cannot be broken by screwing up'. Julius Sax of Great Russell Street in London specialised in 'electric mercurial thermometers', electric bells, fire alarms and 'thief detectors' – 'Many of the largest hotels, club houses, mansions and private houses have been fitted up [. . .] continues to give great satisfaction'.

The American infiltration of the British market is clearly evidenced. Frederick Orme of Bishopsgate, London, labelled themselves 'importers of American labour-saving devices', including the Portable Liquid Manure Pump, the Improved Pillar Drilling Machine and the Patent Noiseless Fan and Exhauster ('A more powerful blast [. . .] at much less expenditure than that for any other Fan, Blower or Exhauster hitherto in use'). The great Philadelphia saw-making firm, Henry Disston and Sons, took out a full-page advertisement for their Patent Gauge Saw, Patent Skewback Saw and a range of lesser handsaws, ripsaws, and panel saws, to cover each and every carpentry requirement.

The reach of *The Ironmonger* was constantly expanding. The July 1882 issue carried an invitation to readers to subscribe to the journal's US counterpart, *The Iron Age: A Review of the American Hardware Iron and Metal Trades*, published in New York and with offices in Pittsburgh, Philadelphia and London. There were reports on trading conditions in Japan, France, Italy, Germany and Portugal, as well in the US, where 'the manufacture of locomotives is now in an extremely flourishing condition'. And not just locomotives – Gorse and Sons of Icknield Square, Birmingham, advertised the availability of the American Bicycle, 'a splendid machine for touring or racing'.

Within eight decades, the making of tools and the accessories that went with them had grown into a massive industry on both sides of the Atlantic. The Industrial Age had been forged through human ingenuity enabled by tools. 'Man is a tool-using animal,' Thomas Carlyle wrote in *Sartor Resartus*, 'weak in himself [. . .] nevertheless he can use tools, can devise tools: with these the granite mountains melt into light dust before him; seas are his smooth highway, winds and fire his unvarying steeds. Nowhere do you find him without tools; without tools he is nothing, with tools he is all.'

## CHAPTER TEN

# A Man and his Workshop

To have a workshop for your tools as opposed to a shed or garage where your tools share the space with a lot of other things is to belong to a higher level in the order of those who work with their hands. Behind our shop is Greg's workshop, where he heals the village's mowers, fixes the village's strimmers and hedge-cutters, sharpens the village's chainsaws and occasionally repairs a bicycle (Greg does not really like doing bicycles).

Greg has a rare talent for bringing apparently defunct motors back to life. It is not the kind of talent that brings renown and riches. But Greg is treasured by the part of the village that needs its machines in working order, even though the village doesn't show it. Very few settlements of our size have a repair shop where you can just drop off your clapped-out grass-cutter and hope to get it back before too long, ready to spring into life at the pull of a cord.

I say 'before too long' conscious of the elasticity of the term. There is a time of the year, the spring, when the grass is growing and the would-be mower discovers to their displeasure that the machine, which they fully intended to deliver to Greg last autumn for cleaning and servicing, was actually dumped back in the shed after the last cut, with mud and grass and shredded leaves plastered all over the roller and cutters; and that, however vigorously the starter cord is pulled, it will not start. At that time of year, the mowers multiply outside Greg's workshop. Customers are understandably keen to get them back in working order, and they sometimes express their impatience, and Greg can get snappy. He is a man who likes to have the time for a chat and a cup of tea, and he does not like to be hurried or badgered.

Having worked for a good many years as a groundsman, he knows mowers inside out. I do not, but I have had extensive dealings with them in the course of half a century of helping out with the maintenance work at my cricket club, not to mention keeping my own grass in order. Greg has worked wonders in keeping our club roller and pitch mower alive and kicking – each was acquired forty years or so ago, having already done twenty years' service elsewhere. Greg likes old machines that still run – or can be made to run – because they belong to that golden era when British machines were exported across the world and admired across the world, and the great British engineering companies were still properly British and their names were spoken with respect.

Of these names, none stands higher in Greg's view than Triumph, because in his heart he is not a mower repairman at all, but a motorcycle man; and he belongs, not in his workshop behind our shop, fixing carburettors and fitting replacement pull-cords, but flying around the Isle of Man TT course or along deserted roads built for speed, crouched over his beloved Triumph 650cc Thruxton Bonneville (number one of just fifty-two that were made). It, and the other models that came out of the Triumph factory at Meriden in Warwickshire before competition from Japan knocked the company off its perch – the Tiger, the Speed Twin, the Thunderbird, the Daytona, the Trident – are sacred to Greg. He has spent countless hours restoring the Bonneville, and his proudest day was when it was featured in glorious colour across several pages of the magazine *Vintage Bike*.

Greg loves to engage in talk about spring rear hubs and overhead cams and other arcane motorbike accessories. When someone who shares even a small part of his passion comes along, he downs whatever tool he is using, wipes his hands reflectively on an oily rag, and he is off, in the steady, unstoppable way of the obsessive, and nothing will stop him until – for whatever reason – his audience is no longer available. He and I do not talk about motorcycles, because I do not have anything to contribute on the subject. We do talk about mowers and chainsaws and family matters, and occasionally about fishing, because Greg was something of an angler in his youth. He talks about how much he dislikes the suburb of Reading where he and Emma live, and how he dreams of going to live in the West Country, because that is where he came from, but not too near the sea, because the salt is bad for motorbike engines. And we enquire about each other's wellbeing and discuss the characteristics of the well-known village irritants that he and I encounter along our very different paths.

His is a separate business, and he just pays a modest rent to Shro for the workshop and some space around it for his mowers. She has no interest in them or the fascinating subject of lawn care. But Greg and the workshop make a good fit for our shop. His customers are not numerous, but they are often talkative and take their time over their visits, and they bring life and occasional laughter to the yard. And some of them will combine buying hardware with their consultation with the mower man, which is good for business.

The workshop arrived in its present location when Heath & Watkins migrated from across the road in the 1950s. It shows its age, the green paint faded and flaked, the wooden boards cracked and some of them lopsided. It is dilapidated, even ramshackle, but it does retain a certain period charm. It does not present a dynamic, forward-looking, cutting-edge image – but neither does Greg. They belong together.

The inside of the workshop is in harmony with the outside. Underneath the filthy, cobwebbed window that looks out onto the yard is one of the original worktables: four sturdy legs supporting a thick top blackened with the grime and oil deposited over decades. The original vice is still in place, its handle worn and silvered by the tightening and loosening hand. There is a beaten-up Qualcast rotary mower next to the vice, awaiting attention, with two pairs of pliers just visible underneath it. There is a single shelf, on which are a miscellany of storage boxes and toolboxes crammed with dies and taps, pliers and screwdrivers, bolt grippers and sockets and gaskets and drill bits. Between the shelf and the floor are two big containers of WD-40 and two more toolboxes. Everything is extremely dirty and looks utterly disordered, although Greg claims that he can lay his hands on what he needs when he needs it.

The main workbench runs the length of the far side of the workshop. The ruinous asbestos cladding behind it supports an arbitrary arrangement of shelves crammed with what, to my eye, appears to be a total confusion of bits of old metal, rubber and plastic – but, again, Greg assures me there is order in the chaos. There are tools I recognise – chisels, screwdrivers, mole-grips, a hammer, a hacksaw – and plenty I do not. There are tubs of this lubricant and cans of that and canisters of another. There are goggles and ear-protectors and a Castrol mug hung from a hook, and a couple of plates bearing the Triumph logo, a bench grinder, drums of cord to make pull-cords for mowers. Cables, rubber tubes and lengths of wire twist in and out and vanish into the recesses. Almost everything is covered in a thickish layer of dust.

At the far end are more shelves, more boxes, more objects in corners, spray cans of paint and compounds for persuading damp engines to start, more drawers of nuts and bolts. Greg points out his welding machine, which is on the floor next to a compressor. There is a decrepit plywood cupboard where jump leads and inner tubes for cycle tires hang. Through the back is a dark storeroom, the floor space of which is mostly occupied by mowers. Greg claims that some are in his pending tray. But they all have an abandoned air about them. Cobwebs hang from the handles and are laid in delicate webs over the engines. Once they roared with life and travelled over cherished turf. Now they are silent and useless, forgotten by their owners, who have been forgotten in turn by Greg. Periodically, when lack of space becomes a problem, he offers them on eBay and some lawnmower-lover who has the same affection for names like Atco and Qualcast that Greg has for Triumph comes and takes them away to a better place.

Greg is a healer of machines and tools. But, as with all healers, the healing is not always effective (or, for whatever reason, is sometimes never attempted). The space not occupied by mowers is occupied by other casualties of garden warfare: strimmers that will never strim again, chainsaws damaged beyond repair, edging shears that came apart and will never be made whole. It is a mortuary, the workshop, as well as place of renewal and recovery.

GREG'S IS ONE species of workshop. There is another, which is the antithesis of his, where everything is meticulously ordered, where there is no layer of dust, where cobwebs do not fill the corners and loop between the shelves, where the tools are cleaned and put in their allotted place at the end of the day's work. This is the workshop of the dedicated specialist. They can be professional or amateur. They may make fishing tackle in it, or model aircraft; they may make boats of balsa wood and slip them into bottles; they may fashion bowls. Whatever the activity is, it is done with quiet and intense concentration and invokes Csikszentmihalyi's concept of flow. More often than not, it involves working with wood, the first and supreme material for manufacture.

I have made things with wood in my time, all of them badly. The first I can remember was an H-shaped bookshelf, which, as a ten-year-old, I glued together in school carpentry classes. I was so dismayed at the thought of showing it to my mother that I concealed it under some mail sacks on the platform at Northampton railway station on the way back for the school holidays and claimed, improbably, that it had been stolen. I have certainly never experienced the spiritual dimension of woodworking, but I acknowledge it as a powerful force. The playwright, Arthur Miller, was a lifelong woodworker. 'There is something unusual in that bed,' he remarked to his biographer, Christopher Bigsby, showing him the bed in which Miller and his wife slept, which Miller had made in his workshop. He later showed Bigsby a seat he had made from pale sassafras, commenting: 'I improvised the design . . . a bit like improvising a play.'

'A piece of wood is a challenge,' he said. 'It's like a blank piece of paper you could make into something boring or significant.'

Henry Thoreau built his wooden cabin in the woods by Walden Pond, and then the furniture – bed, table, three chairs ('one for solitude, two for friendship, three for society'), looking-glass – then kitchen items, including jugs and plates. He said: 'Thank God I can sit and stand without the aid of a furniture warehouse.'

Thoreau articulated the attraction of doing it yourself in matter-of-fact prose. Woodworkers tend to talk in simple, practical terms, because they work in simple, practical ways. But that spiritual dimension is always there beneath the surface. It comes from the sight and smell and feel of wood, its grain, its roughness and smoothness. All the adjectives associated with wood have positive moral connotations. Wood is strong, reliable, faithful, durable, tough, versatile, natural. It transmits – or can be interpreted as transmitting – qualities we would like to identify in ourselves: wisdom, authority, creative potential, warmth, strength, decency. Wood speaks to us of the world as we found it, of the simple life, of our early selves and challenges met and overcome. Of ancient tools and ancient skills and traditions long in the making. Of the real world, the physical world. There is a whole system of existence in a single tree. Trees were given to us for us to make use of. There is a world of possibility in the wood of a tree.

Many writers and artists have celebrated those possibilities and the traditional ways of working with wood. One who combined both disciplines with a peculiar degree of passion was born Everard Hinrichs in New York in 1905, but adopted the name Eric Sloane. As Hinrichs, he wrote this poem celebrating the handles of tools, the shavings from a blade, the smell of newly cut wood and the sound of kindling and logs burning, which ends:

> Abundant to all the needs of men,
> how poor the world would be
> Without wood.

Sloane was as gifted an artist and calligrapher as his alter ego Hinrichs was mediocre a versifier. As a young man, he travelled west, sketching and drawing and painting as he went. He moved from town to town, paying his way by painting signs and executing the lettering on bars and taverns and stores. He painted for the Amish and became fascinated by their barns and how they constructed them, and their extraordinary skill with traditional tools. He drew and painted anything that belonged to American's forgotten, agrarian, pioneering past, and developed an exquisite skill in old lettering fonts.

He also collected tools and, in a very beautiful, slim volume called *A Museum of Early American Tools*, he paid a devoted homage to them in words and drawings. Interspersed with the text of description, anecdote, history and comment, are pages illustrating axes, hatchets, hammers and mallets, adzes, wedges, froes, chisels, planes: the whole gamut of implements that the 'good woodsman' – Eric Sloane's ideal male – would have known and treasured. He depicts a nail-maker at work at his forge and all the different types of nail that would have been needed to build the home, the barn and other outbuildings, and the other essentials of the pioneer life. He dedicated the book to those early Americans 'who fashioned their own tools [...] these ancient implements are symbols of a sincerity, an integrity, an excellency that the craftsman of today might do well to emulate'.

In general, Sloane had a low opinion of the modern world. The intensity of his nostalgia for the vanished past was matched by an equivalent distaste for the modern. 'How poor and dishonest and ugly and temporary are the results of so many modern workers,' he lamented. He loathed modern art as much as he detested plastic handles. By the time of his death in 1985, Eric Sloane had created almost single-handedly a taxonomy for the world of the early settlers, and helped shape the mythology of that simpler, nobler way of life.

I RATHER ASSUME that most serious woodworkers have seriously tidy workshops, although I have no evidence to support this generalisation. By tidy, I really mean ordered, even if the order is in the mind of the woodworker and not immediately apparent to the casual observer. One of the best-known woodworkers in Britain is Paul Sellers, and he has a well-ordered but not obsessively tidy workshop.

Sellers learned his trade in north-west England, starting as an apprentice in Stockport at the age of fifteen. As a young man, he emigrated to the United States and lived and worked in Texas, making and designing furniture, teaching and appearing on TV. In 2009, he moved back to Britain, shortly after installing two cabinets of mesquite made by him and his team on either side of the doors leading from the Oval Office to the Cabinet Room at the White House.

He was fifty-nine and thinking of retirement. But, instead, he embarked on a new life as a teacher, film-maker, writer and standard-bearer for the traditional skills he'd learned as a lad. The YouTube channel, the books, the articles, the classes and talks have been borne along on a current of words composed for a blog that has been running for more than ten years. Like Thoreau's, Paul Sellers' prose is plain and straightforward, but eloquent and thoughtful with it. The blogs merge into a single narrative of a man's working life and his mission to explain and communicate as it unfolds. Workshops play their part.

Sellers favours a garage for a workshop, five metres or so by three, nothing fancy. He uses hand tools almost exclusively, and there they are: files, chisels, planes, rasps, gouges, spokeshaves, saws, braces, squares, rules, screwdrivers, spirit levels – the whole rich woodworking armoury, all within reach of the workbench on racks and shelves, in drawers, hung from hooks or magnetised strips. It is orderly, but there is an element of jumble as well. There are drifts of sawdust across the workbench, mixed with offcuts. Tools have been laid down for a moment because there is work going on here. And the tools are there to do a job, not because they are antique and have heritage value. Sellers treasures traditional tools for their usefulness, honouring the craftsmen who designed and made them with a single, noble purpose: to be used.

He has no problem with going modern and functional. In several blogs, he has lauded a set of four bevel-edged chisels branded Workzone and sold by Aldi for £7.95. 'They are not pretty,' he says in that plain, easy way, 'but I like the balance and I use them alongside my own.'

In terms of reputation, Joshua Farnsworth occupies a position in US woodworking comparable to that of Paul Sellers in Britain, but there are significant differences. The blog on Farnsworth's website, WoodAndShop.com, is much more geared to the business angle, and far less reflective and personal. Several hands contribute to it and its purpose is to support the marketing of the classes that Farnsworth runs at his home farm near Charlottesville in Virginia, and the sale of hand and power tools, workbenches, T-shirts, hats and other merchandise. This is the woodworking experience monetised to the full.

In one of the many videos accessible through the website, Farnsworth offers a whirlwind tour of 'ten jaw-dropping workshops'. To this non-woodworking viewer, this illustrates a tendency – how widespread in the American woodworking world I cannot say – to fetishise the workshop. These are not functional spaces for the working of wood (apart from one, a basement in Forest, Virginia, in which William Brown, a doctor, turns out furniture and gilded ornaments of baroque ornateness). They are statements about the woodworkers and their status in that arena. One is a gigantic converted barn, four storeys in height; another a converted water tower. They are conspicuously rooted in the past, made from clapboard or old bricks, and reached down rough tracks or leafy lanes to clearings in the woods, where they nestle far from the noisy world of machines. They breathe heritage and are stuffed with heritage – rows and shelves and racks of antique planes and chisels and saws with dark, burnished handles smoothed by the grip of generations of master craftsmen.

All these woodworkers make furniture in 'traditional' styles – generally variations on Colonial, Federal and Shaker – in traditional ways, except one, who makes old-fashioned guitars. They owe allegiance to the implements and techniques of the past; when they use machine tools, they are old machine tools. They are teachers, nurturing new generations of traditionalists. It goes without saying that they are skilled to a degree light years beyond anything the average DIYer could dream of. At least half of them have straggly beards, a significant proportion tie their sparse hair back with a band, and they are all male.

Woodworking has enjoyed a surge in popularity in recent years, and some of those taking it up are girls and women. Some of those attending the courses run by the owners of Joshua Farnsworth's jaw-dropping workshops are female. But the ethos of woodworking remains overwhelmingly and obstinately masculine.

A few years ago, Laura Mays, an Irish-born woman woodworker who runs the Fine Woodworking course for the College of the Redwoods in California, took one issue of the leading magazine in the field, *Fine Woodworking*, and dissected its contents from a gender perspective. There were no articles written by women. There was one female face featured in editorial and advertising material, compared with fifty-eight male faces. There was one person of colour. There were two pieces of work by women. According to Paul Sellers, fewer than two per cent of students attending his classes in the US were female; the proportion in Britain was around twenty-five per cent. He wrote that in 2011, and maybe there has been progress since then, although a skim through some recent issues of *Fine Woodworking* still shows almost exclusively men on the covers, men writing the articles, men in the pictures.

THE MOST CELEBRATED woodworker in America is very much a man, from the top of his luxuriant head of hair to the soles of his hand-tooled leather boots. His fans sometimes ask him – as if addressing his alter ego – if he has cut down any trees recently, or devoured any improbably huge platefuls of red meat, or emptied any bottles of Lagavulin single malt; and he answers: 'I am an actor and my name is Nick Offerman, and I am a separate and distinct person from Ron Swanson.' But because he inhabited the part for so long, and, in doing so, fashioned it in part in his own image, those fans can be hard to convince.

Unlike Swanson, who never watches TV and despises those who do, I have watched a lot in my time, and no long-running saga – not even the incomparable *Friday Night Lights* – has given me more pure, heart-warming pleasure than *Parks and Recreation*. Helen and I and our two daughters watched the first four seasons here in Britain, and then – in the course of a month-long trip down the west coast of America, mainly by train – we ended most days revisiting two or three episodes in our hotel or Airbnb and then finished off the whole seven-season epic when we got home.

The central premise of *Parks and Rec* – that everyday life in a small town in Indiana, focused on the activities of one department of the local council, could sustain a drama of infinite possibility – was a simple stroke of comedic genius.

The ensemble cast were perfect in every way, and at the heart of it was the utterly authentic relationship between the head of the department, Ron Swanson, and his deputy, Leslie Knope (played by Amy Poehler) – between the government man who has nothing but contempt for government, and the government woman who glories in it.

Swanson, of course, disdains to live in the town of Pawnee because of his unbounded distaste for urban life. He lives in the woods, in a wood cabin he has made himself. He hunts, he fishes, he traps; he communes with nature and is at one with the wilderness. He reverences wood and achieves fulfilment by working with wood.

Woodworking references and scenes are sewn seamlessly into several *Parks and Rec* episodes. When Leslie Knope takes charge of some important committee of the council and shows Swanson the chair that she will sit in, he admires it not for the status it embodies, but for the Corinthian leather and solid mahogany frame, and 'what I believe are hand-cut mortise-and-tenon joints'. He relates with pride how he has made a chair: 'A good chair, good enough to submit to the Indiana Fine Woodworking Association, who considered that it merited consideration for an award.' He pauses, shakes his head slightly, and adds: 'It's been a real whirlwind.' After a health scare lands him in hospital, he is asked by Nurse Anne if he exercises and replies gruffly, 'Lovemaking and woodworking.' Rebuked by Leslie for contributing no more than three lines to a job candidate evaluation, Swanson replies that he is describing a person, 'not something complicated like a wooden sailing ship or a proper dovetail technique'.

When *Parks and Recreation* finished in 2015, Nick Offerman presented each member of the cast and crew with a canoe paddle that he had shaped and finished using wood from the sets. As a lad, he had helped pay his way through theatre school by constructing the sets for productions and general building work. Long before the series that would make him a household name had been dreamed up, he had opened the Offerman Woodshop in east Los Angeles, a collective of woodworkers and furniture makers that is partnered with a social programme enabling homeless people to turn up and make items that they can sell or use to get credits. Its credo, expressed on the woodshop website, is: 'We proudly believe in the cultivation of elbow grease, grit, and love through an honest day's work.'

Offerman's woodshop avoids the temptation of fetishising the skills it promotes. It is big but plain – more of an outsized garage than a temple. They make big pieces there in volume, which necessarily means using machine tools. Offerman, conducting a tour of the premises, speaks up proudly for his machine tools, although he does like them old and heavy and machined by fine old American engineering firms. But it is with chisel or plane or saw in hand that his natural, soft-spoken eloquence flows forth. He picks up a square piece of big-leaf maple from Oregon. Start with this, he says, and with a little sanding and planing and cleaning and oiling, you have a chopping board. Then you make four of them and put them together with dowels, and you make a box. Then a set of drawers. Then you build a piano.

As he speaks, he demonstrates what the tool does, like an artist applying the first brushstrokes to a canvas. If you take nails and some planks and shape them into a doghouse, you are a woodworker, Offerman says. Then maybe you make a better doghouse, or you move on up to a horse house or a cow house and eventually a person house; then you find a mate and you have children and you teach them how to sand wood.

You are part of the circle of life.

## CHAPTER ELEVEN

# The Death of DIY?

MY TOUR OF NICK OFFERMAN'S woodshop was courtesy of YouTube, by invitation from the grandaddy of American DIY shows, *This Old House*. Since 1979, *This Old House's* team of genial experts – the great majority of them blokes, most of them in check shirts and blue denims – have been showing America how to lay flooring, paint and paper walls, sort out plumbing, install shelving and generally transform the shabby and neglected into a home that any decent American family would want to live in. With a smile on its wholesome face and a wry, self-deprecating chuckle, *This Old House* has consistently followed its calling to educate American hands to perform useful tasks.

On the way, it has swelled into a considerable media stable, with spin-off TV shows, a magazine, podcasts, newsletters, apps, an online shop – a whole stable of products, all marshalled by the website. Many home-improvement shows have trodden in the footsteps of *This Old House* without toppling it from its pedestal or emulating its longevity. Traditionally, American taste has tended to favour a homely, comfortable style of presentation. This could mean a husband-and-wife combination, as with *Fixer Upper* (Chip and Joanna Gaines), *Home Town* (Ben and Erin Napier), and *Flip or Flop* (Tarek El Moussa and Christina Horack); or siblings, as in *Property Brothers* (Drew and Jonathan Scott); or mother-and-daughter, as in *Good Bones* (Karen Lane and Mina Starsiak Hawk).

A favoured alternative to keeping it in the family has been to have proceedings anchored by a calm and reassuring father figure, such as Dean Johnson, who steered *Hometime* through twenty-nine seasons between 1986 and 2016, or the plaid-shirted master carpenter Norm Abram, who presented 284 episodes of *The New Yankee Workshop* between 1989 and 2009. A complementary role, of the apple-pie-making housewife/mother figure, meanwhile, was created by Joan Steffend, who laughed and hugged her way through thirty-one seasons, and more than 400 episodes, of *Decorating Cents*.

Thanks in no small part to *This Old House*, the old-fashioned educational strand in American DIY TV has been kept alive and kicking. But in doing so, it has bucked the trend, which has been to move away from true DIY to reality formats, as illustrated by a look at the menu available on Discovery's DIY Network. Shows like *Bath Crashers*, *Kitchen Crashers*, *Yard Crashers*, *Sledgehammer*, *Man Caves*, *Rehab Addict* and *Cool Tools* were not devised to lure the viewer into the workshop or inspire them to pick up their tools and embark on a project. The purpose is to keep the viewer slumped on the sofa, looking into a world that looks very much like their world, where people very much like them open the doors to admit a team of expert super-mortals. In the ensuing melo-drama, extreme challenges lead to triumphs snatched from the jaws of certain disaster, orchestrated by easy-mannered, folksy presenters who – as puppet masters – manipulate their casts of experts and 'ordinary people'.

The format – call it makeover or reality – was invented in Britain in the 1990s. Oddly enough, the huge success of the urbane Barry Bucknell in the early 1960s did not suggest to the bright commissioning minds at the BBC that there might be an appetite among viewers for more in the same vein. DIY segments regularly popped up in magazine programmes, but, unlike gardening or cooking, DIY was not seen as being able to sustain whole programmes or series on its own. In the 1970s, one of the regional networks, Yorkshire TV, ran two very low-key series, *Toolbox* and *Jobs Around the House*, which were shown on weekend mornings at a time when very few people watched daytime TV and had negligible impact.

*Home Front*, introduced by the BBC in 1992 as a half-hour programme presented by a design journalist, Tessa Shaw, was a hesitant first step towards embracing contemporary attitudes to home improvement. It had elements of the conventional how-to-do approach and elements of makeover, but did not linger in close-up on the emotional responses of those chosen to have their homes beautified. At that time, with the deregulation of television and the proliferation of new channels, the BBC was under pressure – or felt itself to be under pressure – to move away from the Reithian 'inform, educate and entertain' mantra, and towards a more 'democratic' and populist model. Increasingly, the making of programmes was being contracted out to independent production companies, which, by their nature, were not constrained in the way much in-house BBC work was.

In 1996, the magician of reality TV, Peter Bazalgette, introduced a new makeover creation that he called *Changing Rooms*.

The format, in which two couples swapped homes and each decorated a room in the other's, had nothing whatever in common with what had made Barry Bucknell a household name. Bucknell was an avatar, an embodiment of everyone's favourite design technology teacher (although at a time when design technology was still known as carpentry). His job was to teach viewers who aspired to make and build things how to fulfil that aspiration. *Changing Rooms* was spectacle, a riotous drama generated by the artfully manipulated collision between 'real people' and the gallery of presenters. The DIY was no more than an enabling mechanism. What kept a huge audience pinned to their chairs and sofas was partly the 'chemistry' between irrepressibly perky Carol Smillie, languid toff Laurence Llewelyn-Bowen, cheeky Cockney chippie 'Handy Andy' Kane and the rest – the banter, the laughs, the mishaps, the chat. But equally crucial were the emotional outpourings of the couples themselves. The format and direction were engineered to promote unrestrained emoting, so that the camera could linger almost lovingly on their faces as they registered their amazement, delight and disbelief – and, occasionally, disgust and outrage.

*Changing Rooms* hit a magic button with audiences. After two series on BBC Two, it was moved to the prime 8–9pm slot on BBC One, where it ran for six more years and seventeen series in all. Its format was globally adaptable and was sold across the world. It inspired many imitators in several fields of endeavour, among them another Bazalgette brainchild, *Ground Force*, which took makeover outside into the garden, and *DIY SOS* (later reconfigured as *DIY SOS: The Big Build*), which first aired on BBC One in 1999 and has sustained thirty-two series and almost 250 episodes. Even with *DIY SOS*, the actual doing-it-yourself was incidental. It was not an invitation to viewers to get their toolboxes out, but to witness and relish the humiliation of whichever duffer had botched up his loft conversion or new kitchen as the professionals went to work sorting out the mess, bantering away as they did so. The climax was soap opera in its predictability: the duffer reduced to amazed gratitude and deep emotion by the sight of the bodge-up miraculously rescued and transformed.

In makeover land, the home was no longer a setting in which practical challenges were discussed and addressed, but a theatre where impossible dreams could come true. A revamped *Home Front* was entrusted to Llewellyn-Bowen with curly-haired Irish joker Diarmuid Gavin as sidekick; together, they went forth and wrought miracles in homes and gardens, laughing as they went and spreading happiness among their punters. Other, lesser imitators tweaked the recipe, with varying results. *Sixty Minute Makeover*, for instance – which was made for ITV and has clocked up more than 600 episodes since 2004 – postulates a 'reality' in which a homeowner is persuaded to go somewhere else while the team of supermen and -women invade the property and turn it into a palace; the homeowner returns and is overwhelmed by wonder, happiness, gratitude, etc.

At the opposite end of the spectrum in terms of speed of execution is the supreme stayer in this field, *Grand Designs* (although *DIY SOS: The Big Build* is still going strong). Presented since its inception in 1999 by Kevin McCloud (one of the know-alls in the original *Home Front*), *Grand Designs* has achieved extraordinary success by turning the instant make-over concept on its head. Its premise is simple and unvaried: a couple (usually a couple) are seized by an insatiable and obsessive urge to build the house of their dreams or convert something into the house of their dreams. The process is protracted over months and even years and becomes an often harrowing and even agonising journey of self-discovery and self-laceration.

Home envy is part of the allure, because the houses are invariably astonishing. But the real key is the drama that comes from following the arc from burning hope through frustration, despair and gnawing anxiety to fulfilment and triumph (or, occasionally, disaster, bankruptcy and failed relationship). The cool, elegant and silver-tongued McCloud, who devised the programme, acts as a benign Svengali. He leads his subjects on, encouraging them, praising their exquisite taste and amazing resilience, sometimes raising a quizzical eyebrow at an individual item of expenditure or design choice. But beneath his friendly smile and sympathy is a steely ruthlessness and indifference to whatever self-inflicted crisis they are going through. He never intervenes to say what the viewer is internally shouting: 'You're mad, you don't need this, you're going to have a nervous breakdown, you're going to go bust.'

*Grand Designs* and its pallid imitators have nothing to do with practical DIY. But that is not to say that practical DIY is no longer catered for on TV, because there is a host of DIY shows available elsewhere in the televisual landscape. Much of it is accessible through what began as UK Style, became Home, and is now known as HGTV. In its schedules can be found mounds of old episodes of *Changing Rooms* and *DIY SOS*, alongside contemporary low-budget steady per-formers, such as *Builders – DIY Made Easy*, *Carter Can*, *Challenge Tommy Walsh*, *Disaster DIY* and *Completely Hammered*.

The responsibility for educating the great army of home-improvers on how to paint, wallpaper, plaster, lay floors, install sinks, check the wiring, put up shelves, and all the other basics is shared by another army – smaller, but still numerous – made up of the creators of YouTube videos. Why sit through half an hour of Barry Bucknell waiting to get round to Rawlplugs when you can stick your laptop on a table next to the wall that needs drilling and click on a five-minute film telling you exactly what to do? It is not art, it is not entertainment, but, by golly, it's handy. And now many of the big retailers, such as Ikea and Home Depot, have identified this as a prime way to reach customers, and have set up their own YouTube DIY channels.

PERIODICALLY, A CULTURAL commentator or journalist – drawing on selective statistics compiled in the course of a research project – proclaims that DIY in the age of the throwaway society is dying. A fairly typical piece in the *Guardian* a few years ago, headlined 'The Death of DIY – Why Can't I Do It Myself?', asserted that the 'tiny independent hardware shops that were once common on our high streets are long gone, swallowed up by chains of behemoths'. The reality is that, after a period of decline, the number of hardware shops in the UK increased from 2012 onwards, and, in 2019, according to the data provider Statista, there were nearly 6,000 of them.

Another trend seized upon by the commentators has been the decline in the number of twenty-three- to twenty-eight-year-olds doing DIY. That shows they're not interested, does it not? That they're too busy on their phones or playing video games? Wrong – the answer is that this age group are coming to home-ownership later than their parents did. They are living in rented accommodation or at home. Their reluctance to reach for a toolbox when something needs fixing has got nothing to do with age-related uselessness, and everything to do with being prepared to leave it to landlord or parent. When they get their first home, they learn fast enough.

All the market analysis in the United States and in the UK demonstrates that sales figures in the DIY sector were stable and pretty buoyant for several years up to 2020. In lockdown, they surged to unprecedented levels. By now they will have dropped back, but they remain steady. DIY is the way a great many people respond to the deep-rooted longing to have a home and make it a better place. While that need persists, DIY will never die.

# CHAPTER TWELVE

# Rivets, Trivets . . .

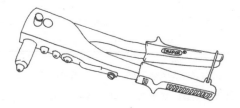

THE RIVETS RESIDE in a glass jam jar on a shelf behind and above the counter. There is a host of varieties of rivet, but our shop stocks only one. This is the blind rivet – otherwise known as the pop rivet – and it has a very particular use. It is about two-and-a-half inches long, slim and rather delicate in appearance, given the work it has to do; in profile, it looks rather like a miniature sword, but with hilt and blade rounded. I keep one on my key ring because I find the look and feel of it pleasing, but I think it is most unlikely I will ever put rivets to work in a practical sense. To do so requires the deployment of a rivet gun – available in our shop in the wall of tools at the far end. I have a rough theoretical grasp of how the rivet gun enables the blind rivet to do its business, but this is definitely something for those on a higher rung of the DIY ladder than mine.

The blind rivet is a twentieth-century advance on a very ancient method of fixing things together. Egyptian workmen under the pharaohs knew them; they were essential to Roman construction projects, and the Vikings riveted the

planks of their longboats. The word was in use in English by
the fifteenth century (probably derived from the Old French
'river', meaning to fix or fasten). On the eve of Agincourt,
according to Shakespeare in *Henry V, Part II*:

> . . . from the tents
> The armourers, accomplishing the knights,
> With busy hammers closing rivets up . . .

In *Mechanick Exercises*, Joseph Moxon described the technique thus: 'Rivetting is to batter the edges of a shank over
a plate or other iron the shank is let into so as the plate
or other iron may be clinched close and fixed between the
battering at the end of the shank and the shoulder.' There
is more, but the detail may be found . . . I was going to say,
'less than riveting', but wearisome covers it. Suffice to say
that the basic round-head rivet was a staple for all manner
of construction work; they were churned out in quantities
from smithies all over the land. They were strong, easy to fit,
reliable and cheap, and for centuries held things together.

That was the cold rivet. The hot rivet was even better.
Making the big machines and boilers demanded in the
Industrial Age, building the bridges, assembling the ships
and constructing the locomotives all required riveting on an
enormous scale. It was discovered that, if the little metal bolts
were heated until they glowed cherry red or even white, they
softened and could be fixed much more quickly and easily.

In 1836, Antoine Durenne, who ran a foundry in Paris
making ornamental ironwork, patented a machine to make
rivets, which had hitherto been forged by hand. A year later,
a Scottish-born engineer, William (later Sir William) Fairbairn, achieved a great automotive forward stride. A strike by

boilermakers at his factory in Manchester spurred him into swift action: 'I determined to do without them, and effect by machinery what we had heretofore been in the habit of executing by manual labour.' He and his assistant engineer, Robert Smith, devised a machine to punch rivets to fix boiler plates together. It was patented in the name of Smith and put into production and adopted by the ship-building industry.

Fairbairn's machine reduced the time taken to punch a rivet to eight seconds. But it was no longer a one-man job. It took a gang. One man drilled or punched the holes through the plates that were to be joined. The stoker heated the rivets in a furnace to a temperature between 950 and 1,100 °C. They were thrown, one by one, by the passer to the catcher, who picked up each one in tongs and placed it in the hole. The holder-on held it in place, while the driver secured it from the other side with a couple of meaty hammer blows.

Hot riveting became standard practice. Riveted loco-motives and carriages roared along the ever-expanding rail network. Riveted iron ships sailed the oceans. Riveted bridges soared high over rivers and gorges. Great public building projects employed swarms of riveters – the Eiffel Tower, com-pleted in 1889, is held together by 2.5 million rivets. Steel began to be used in the manufacture of rivets as well as iron, and the steam hammer superseded the hand-held hammer. What did not change was the noise level, which was prodigious.

Imagine the scene in the Harland & Wolff shipyard at Queen's Island, Belfast, in the months preceding the launch in May 1911 of the Royal Mail ship *Titanic*. Fifteen thousand men worked in the yard, a fifth of them on the *Titanic*, hundreds of them in riveting gangs. Three million iron rivets were driven home into her plates by pounding steam hammers. The din from them and the other construction work must have been stupendous (premature deafness was a common condition among riveters). It was standard practice after fitting each rivet to give it a tap with a hammer. If it gave a 'clean' sound in reply, it was sound. If the response was a dull thud, it was removed and done again.

One of the theories about the rivets on the *Titanic* is that the riveters were not able to carry out the normal sound checks properly because of the ambient racket. Another is that the quality of iron used to make the rivets was variable, with some batches weakened by excessive slag retained during smelting. What is certain is that, when the ship struck an iceberg off the west coast of Greenland in the early hours of 15 April 1912, some of the steel plates on the starboard side of the hull came apart, flooding six of her sixteen compartments and causing her to sink. Following the discovery of the wreck in 1985, forty-five rivets were recovered and subjected to metallurgical analysis. The results suggested that some made from inferior iron had popped from their holes after the interior heads broke off. It would have required the loss of comparatively few for those left – even if of approved standard – to be pushed beyond their failure threshold, causing both plates to pull apart.

Despite the occasional disaster, however, riveting remained indispensable to the construction of the twentieth-century world. Everything – trains, bridges, buildings, monuments, machines, ships, motor cars – depended on rivets. But there was one significant restraining factor – the riveters had to be able to access both sides of the plates being riveted. Overcoming that problem would open up a new dimension for the little connector.

The solution occurred to an otherwise obscure Scottish engineer called Hamilton Neil Wylye, who in 1916 patented a variant rivet with a mandrel through the centre. A hole was drilled through the two sheets of metal to be connected, the rivet inserted, and the mandrel tapped through and then pulled back so that the tube expanded, locking the sheets together. When the fitting was secure, the mandrel was snapped off. At the time, nobody paid Wylye or his invention much attention. But in the 1920s, he went to work for the aeronautical firm Armstrong Whitworth, who made the Siskin biplane fighter aircraft for the RAF. A rivet that could be fitted from one side only had evident potential for aircraft construction, and Armstrong Whitworth looked for a partner to develop it. A Birmingham firm, the George Tucker Eyelet Co., specialised in making eyelets for leather boots, and had independently developed a blind rivet that required a separate mandrel and was fiddly to deploy. Together, the two companies perfected the one-piece blind rivet and it went into production. At some point it became known as a pop rivet, probably because of the noise made when the mandrel was snapped off, and this was registered as a brand name by George Tucker.

It was a little thing, but it had a mighty impact. Billions of blind rivets were used to build the planes that fought the Second World War in the sky. Subsequently, the blind rivet proved to be indispensable in any process using overlapping metal sheets, and its use soon spread across the world. Armstrong Whitworth and Hamilton Neil Wylye faded from the scene, but the George Tucker Eyelet Co. prospered on the back of its pop rivet, setting up manufacturing plants in Germany, Spain, Denmark, Japan, Australia and the US. The company renamed itself Tucker Fasteners and was eventually taken over by the American toolmakers Stanley (which subsequently merged with Black & Decker).

Blind rivets and the tools required to fit them are still used all over the world. The aerospace industry, for example, continues to rely upon them because the alternative method of joining metal sheets together, which is welding, cannot be safely used with the aluminium preferred for aircraft bodies. But the place in the construction industry occupied for so long by the humble round-head rivet has largely disappeared. Welding gives greater strength, and the rivet's other functions have been generally usurped by high-strength friction grip (HSFG) bolts and tension control (TC) bolts, which do the same job but are easier to install. The riveters of old have become a threatened species, occasionally called out for heritage work, such as replacing the rivets in an historic structure.

But there is one situation in which the rivet still reigns supreme. You see it everywhere: on the tube and train, in the coffee shop and the pub and the park, on every street and street corner. Anywhere where anyone is wearing a pair of blue jeans.

TO THE OFFICIALS OF the US Circuit Court, California District, it must have seemed like just another patent infringement case, of which there were plenty. Levi Strauss *et al.* versus A. B. Elfelt and partners of San Francisco, January 1874. It concerned:

> the art of making pantaloons, to wit: of an improvement in fastening pocket openings [. . .] that the same

was a new and useful invention, and consisted of the employment of a metal rivet or eyelet at each edge of the pocket opening to prevent the ripping of the seams at those points, the said rivets or eyelets being so fastened in the seams as to bind the two parts of cloth which each seam united, so as to prevent the strain or pressure from coming upon the thread with which the seam was sewed.

The papers remained undisturbed in the San Bruno branch of the National Archives for more than a century, until Ann Morgan Campbell, who was the archivist, dug them out in order to write an article for the Nevada Historical Society, in which she answered the question: who put the copper rivet in Levi's jeans?

Included in the papers was the deposition of Jacob W. Davis, a tailor in the railroad town of Reno, just across the border in Nevada. He was born Jacob Youphas in 1831 in Riga, now the capital of Latvia but then in Germany. At the age of twenty-three, he joined the westward flow of emigrants intent on taking their chance in the land of hope and opportunity. He experienced ups and downs in several parts of the US and in Canada, where he lived for nine years, before arriving in Reno. He was now Jacob Davis and he had a wife and children. He reverted to his first trade and opened his tailor's shop in Virginia Street. That was in 1869, the year after Reno was officially recognised as a town. He made a go of it, cutting and stitching clothes. He also had a line in tents and wagon covers, which he sewed together from duck cloth supplied by Levi Strauss of San Francisco.

According to Davis's court deposition:

I could not tell the name of the man. He was a large man
– sick with dropsy – could not get a pair of pants in the
stores to fit him. He lived across the railroad track from
my place. He was a poor laboring man. She, his wife, said
she wanted to send him up to chop some wood but he
had no pants to put on. I never spoke to the man – the
wife brought his measure to me – the man being sick at
the time. I saw him afterwards wearing these pants.

Davis made the trousers from Levi Strauss white duck. When
they were done, his eye happened to alight on a little pile of
copper rivets that he had been using to make straps. 'The
thought struck me to fasten the pockets with rivets,' he
related. 'I had never thought of it before.'

Word spread that the tailor on Virginia Street could
provide real hard-wearing work clothes for hard-working
men. Over the next eighteen months, Davis made 200 pairs
of trousers and overalls, some from cotton duck and some
from the equally sturdy cotton denim also supplied from
San Francisco by Levi Strauss. He sold them at three dollars,
which was a top price, but demand kept growing. Eventually, Davis asked Levi Strauss to help him prepare a patent
application: 'The secret of them Pents,' he wrote, 'is the
Rivits I put in those Pockots [. . .] I cannot make them fast
enough [. . .] my nabors are getting yealouse of these success.'

A full patent was granted in May 1870, by which time
Strauss had persuaded Davis to move to San Francisco and
run a factory built to manufacture the riveted pants and
overalls in volume. By then, Davis had added a second distinguishing mark, the double arc in orange thread stitched onto
the back pockets. Having seen off the underhand attempt by

Mr Elfelt and his associates to pirate the rivet innovation – the case was settled out of court, with Elfelt paying \$2,000 in damages – Jacob Davis and Levi Strauss prospered considerably from the ingenuity of the one and the investment of the other. Davis ran the factory for the rest of his life and died a rich man in 1908, aged seventy-seven.

For a long time, the blue denim trousers made by Levi Strauss – and by other manufacturers once the patent had expired – were worn as work wear by working men and women. They were often bought in larger sizes and worn over ordinary trousers and were known as overalls (they were held up by shoulder straps, but did not have the upper bib until later). For miners, cowboys, farmers and other outdoor workers, they simply met the need for something hard-wearing to cover the lower half. It was not until the 1950s that denim – also known as jeans – made the cultural leap to becoming leisure wear for all and sundry. Cultural historians attribute the step change to the influence of Hollywood – Marlon Brando in denim in *The Wild One*, James Dean in his Lee jeans in *Rebel Without a Cause* – and the cult of the western on television and in the cinema. One way or another denim conquered the world, seducing people of all ages, classes and genders. Incidentals of design vary, with Levi's retaining their position as global leader, but the fundamentals are constant. Among them, without which jeans are simply not jeans but something else, is the little rivet – a direct descendant of the little rivets that Jacob Davis's eyes fell upon in his tailor's shop in Reno.

'I HATE IT WHEN someone asks for something and I haven't got it.' That is why Shro has two jam jars containing pop rivets. She sells no more than a handful each year, and has sold just one rivet gun in three years. But they don't take up much room, nor do they have a sell-by date. And for the hardware shopkeeper, not wanting to disappoint the customer is a primary impulse.

It applies equally to the trivet, which is even less in demand than the rivet or rivet gun. A trivet can be round, oblong, hexagonal, pentagonal, irregular, square, rectangular – any shape. It can be ornate or plain. It can display heraldic or occult or even erotic designs. It can be almost infinitely varied. But it must have legs, or at least feet (three is the standard number, hence the word trivet, but four, five or even six are acceptable). That is my view.

What a trivet is not, in my view, is a circular heat diffuser made of silicone; but the term has been larcenously appropriated and is widely applied to these utterly uninteresting kitchen objects sold by retailers such as John Lewis. Indeed, when I asked Shro – who does not share my interest in the subject – if I could see the trivets she had just received from her suppliers, she showed me a little stack of these grey discs. I told her forcibly that a trivet without legs or feet was not a trivet at all. I think she found my warmth on the issue mystifying, but she is happy to humour me, and now you can buy – or just admire – a proper cast-iron heart-shaped trivet with four legs and some fancy scrollwork at the shop.

A trivet is a metal stand, originally designed to support a pot or kettle on a hot stove, or to keep a hot vessel above a surface or inside a pan (for example, when making a steam pudding). The word has been familiar in English since the fifteenth century, and large numbers of trivets were made and sold in Victorian times. Many were purely functional, but

George Mence Smith's hardware shop in Bexleyheath, south-east London – which he called an 'Italian warehouse' – one of a chain of around seventy outlets bearing his name.

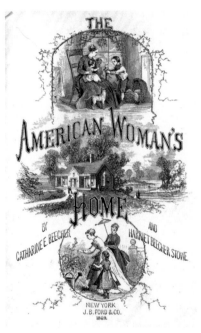

*The American Woman's Home* by Catharine Beecher and her sister Harriet Beecher Stowe. Published in 1869, it advanced the novel suggestion that women might use a hammer and nails.

The introduction of Black & Decker power tools post-1945 helped DIY to come of age.

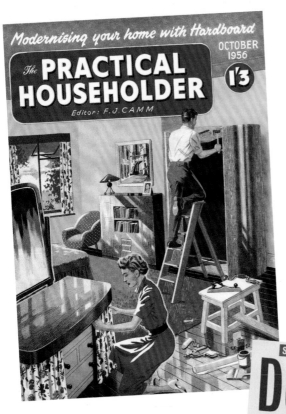

*Practical Householder* – the first of the specialised DIY magazines launched in the UK in 1955.

*Do It Yourself* – launched in 1957, it embraced home design as well as practical jobs.

*Homemaker* – came on the scene two years after *Do It Yourself* and attempted to bring glamour into DIY.

Barry Bucknell – TV's Mr DIY, he introduced millions to the joys of home improvement in the 1960s.

My toolbox – not something to be proud of but in a better state than it was.

The first B&Q, in a showroom in Southampton – opened in 1969 it was the first UK DIY superstore.

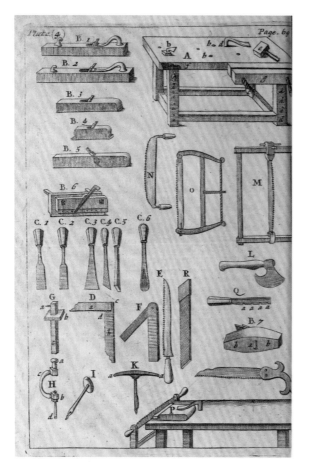

Tools illustrated in Joseph Moxon's *Mechanick Exercises on the Doctrine of Handy Works*, first published between 1678 and 1680. It was the first comprehensive DIY manual.

Illustrations from Eric Sloane's *A Museum of Early American Tools*, looking back to the pioneer days when wood was the essential building material and tools evolved to work it.

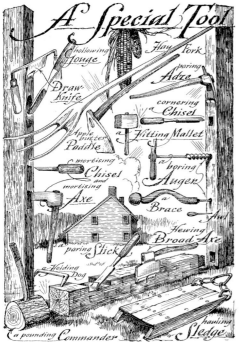

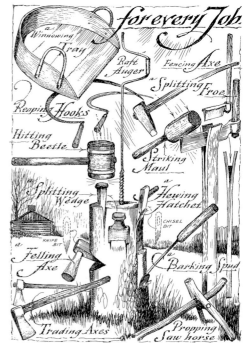

RMS *Titanic* under construction in Belfast; three millions rivets were used. Launched in 1911, the ship sank the following year after hitting an iceberg.

When the US joined the Allies in the Second World War, women took over men's work in the factories – including riveting.

A trivet made in Baltimore in the 1840s, the work of W. B. Rimby.

Nissen huts photographed during the 1914-18 war – made of corrugated galvanised metal, they provided warm and comparatively dry accommodation for millions of soldiers.

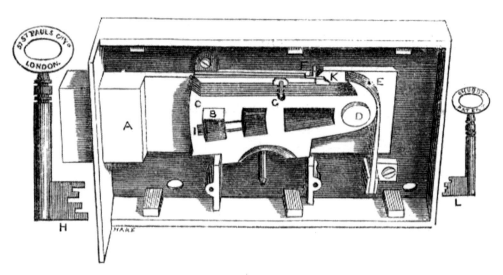

An old Chubb lock. The company advertised them as unpickable, but Alfred C. Hobbs, the champion lockpicker, proved them wrong.

A Kilner Jar. British-made, but the method of sealing the top came from the US.

The Phillips cross-head screw was adopted by the US car industry in the 1930s and subsequently conquered the world.

Spirit levels ancient and modern.

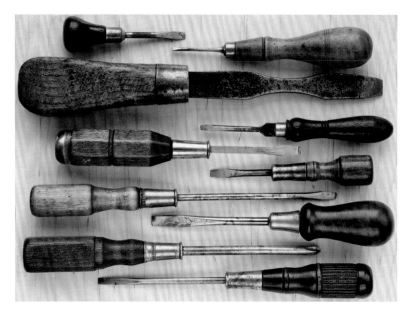

A collection
of old
screwdrivers.

An early advertising poster for The North British Rubber Co., which supplied
millions of pairs of black rubber boots for the troops in both world wars
and introduced the green welly in the 1950s.

others were endowed with all kinds of decorative flourish. Most were made of cast iron or brass, but there was a fondness for ceramic trivets (or stands, as they were often termed in Britain). A particularly impressive example is the Jubilee Tea Pot Stand, made by Deykin and Sons of Birmingham, which has a glazed ceramic surface inset into an electroplated silver frame and three small, rounded feet. It shows Queen Victoria in crown, headdress and diamond necklace, as photographed for her 1887 jubilee, with 'Long May She Reign' underneath.

I assume there are people who collect trivets in Britain, but they seem to keep themselves to themselves. The Antique Metalware Society, which seeks, in its own words, to 'promote the appreciation of base metal objects' (i.e. non-precious metals), gets very exercised about warming pans, door knockers, bells, cooking pots, candlesticks and the like, but pays little or no attention to the trivet. But, in the United States, the trivet is taken seriously. It has status in the collecting world and a sizeable community of admirers. It also has a champion, a supreme triveteer, in the form of Lynn Rosack, who lives in Florida in a house full of trivets, and maintains an amazing blog called Trivetology.

Since 2008, she has posted reports, on average, once or twice a month about the rich history of the trivet. Taken with her two books - *The A–Z Guide to Collecting Trivets* and *The Expanded A–Z Guide to Collecting Trivets* - these dispatches form an immense body of scholarship and research, one as formidable as any definitive work in any conventional branch of academic research. As Lynn Rosack says in the introduction to her blog, it has been the birth and maturing of the internet that have made possible this extraordinary labour of love, allowing her to collect trivets offered for sale on eBay and by websites and auctions, ferret out the histories of individual trivets and their manufacturers from records carefully made long ago and then forgotten, and bring together the community of trivet-lovers from all over the US and from foreign outposts. It is fair to say, with reference to trivets, that if Lynn Rosack doesn't know it, it either isn't true or it isn't worth knowing.

The basic trivet was really an item of kitchenware. But in the second half of the nineteenth century, it was adapted to an additional use: to support the weighty sad irons ('sad' is a linguistic corruption of 'solid'), which were heated and used to press clothes. These trivets were necessarily triangular, to match the shape of the iron.

Distinctiveness in the look of a trivet was easily contrived. It could be any shape and any size, within reason, and the wrought iron or brass could be forged into whatever motif the maker fancied. Cherubs, angels, owls, eagles, fish, cats, fruit and flowers, horseshoes, hearts, vines, sheaves of corn, and real and mythic creatures abounded. Unlike with a chair, for instance, there was no structural constraint on the number of legs or feet it could have, or their length. Some foundries incorporated their trademarks and initials into the metalwork. Others preferred anonymous ornate scrollwork and other assorted decorative flourishes. Because the trivet occupied such a lowly position in the hierarchy of kitchen fixtures and fittings, there were no accepted canons of taste, and it was almost unheard of for an individual designer to be identified. Apart from Rimby.

'Mention the name William Rimby among trivet collectors,' Lynn Rosack wrote in her *Expanded A–Z Guide*, 'and the group will become animated with comments from those who have added at least one Rimby to their collection and those who are still hoping to.' Nothing is known about this craftsman beyond that he worked in a foundry in Baltimore in the 1840s, and that he was permitted to identify himself – or perhaps insisted on identifying himself – as the designer of his trivets. Some bear the initials WBR, others the name Rimby. Of exceptional rarity is the one stamped 'W. B. Rimby Baltimore', the acquisition of which Lynn Rosack announced with undisguised elation in 2011. It is a beautiful thing, dark and graceful, with a five-inch handle supporting an eight-inch-diameter circle enclosing twelve contiguous hearts around the circumference and a four-leaf motif in the centre.

In Britain, the proposition that usefulness and beauty could and should be combined was an article of faith embraced wholeheartedly by the aesthetic movement of the late-nineteenth century. In the sphere of the home, the Glasgow-born designer Christopher Dresser exercised great influence, both as theorist and practitioner. As a young man, Dresser was a botanist, and he remained highly conscious of the form, beauty and complexity of flowers when he branched out into designing wallpapers, carpets, textiles, ceramics and metalware. He wrote a number of books, including *The Art of Decorative Design*, which was intended to open the minds of a general readership to the possibilities of creating beauty in their homes. Dresser lectured in America, and travelled and studied in Japan, whose traditions influenced him deeply.

He worked at a fierce tempo, at least partly driven by the need to support his wife and their thirteen children. He died in 1904, on his own in a hotel in the city of Mulhouse in eastern France (then Mulhausen in German Alsace-Lorraine), where he had gone to show designs to the bosses of local textile-printing firms. Because he was so prolific in so many fields of design, and because so little of his work bore his name, Dresser's reputation faded rapidly after his death. It was not revived until the late 1930s, when the architectural historian Nikolaus Pevsner stumbled across two examples of Dresser's work, electroplated nickel silver and glass cruets manufactured by Hukin & Heath of Birmingham in around 1878. In an article for the *Architectural Review*, illustrated by photographs of the cruets, Pevsner hailed Dresser as a designer of exceptional talent. Since then, he has been accorded his rightful position as one of the leaders of the design revolution labelled 'Arts and Crafts'.

But unlike William Morris, the best-known figure in the movement, Dresser did not view the Industrial Revolution with horror. Instead he embraced the possibilities offered by mass production. He saw, as Morris did not, how homes and thus lives could be improved by allying his aesthetic sensibilities with the sound and fury of the foundry and the textiles mill. He worked closely with a number of manufacturers in Sheffield and Birmingham, including Hukin & Heath, several of whose lines were stamped 'Designed by Dr. Dresser'. These included the cruets that later delighted Pevsner, as well as ink stands, tureens and a silver-plated teapot with a plain three-legged trivet. Dresser was also retained by Archibald Kenrick and Sons, a renowned metalware firm based on the Birmingham Canal in West Bromwich (and still in business today), for whom he designed a series of exuberantly decorated cast-iron and brass trivets. Definitive attribution is problematic, as they were sold as a numbered series without any name apart from the manufacturer's, and the documentation has largely disappeared. But the stylistic evidence of Dresser's hand, with lovingly executed motifs drawn from the plants he had studied so closely, is persuasive.

There is no evidence of any other British designer taking any interest in the lowly trivet. But in the US, the trivet continued to stimulate innovative thinking. In 1952, Virginia Metalcrafters of Waynesboro, Virginia, came up with a new line in cast-iron trivets, which they called The Ranch Brand. Priced at a dollar each, they were designed to evoke the mythology of the American West – coming, as the sales brochure stated, 'out of our nation's heritage'. There were twelve motifs, including Crown Bar, Dog Iron, 3 Lazy Y and Double H – each realised by the company's long-serving trivet designer, Horace Burns, and each artfully conjuring the vision of wide-open grass country under endless skies, and the sharp smell of hot metal stamping cattle hide.

Between 1944 and 1958, the boss of the Union Manufacturing Co. in Boyertown, Pennsylvania, John Zimmerman Harner, had made what were known as the JZH Alphabet series of trivets. The designs were varied – hearts, leaves, wreaths, tulips, stars, even the Swedish soprano Jenny Lind – each with its assigned letter stamped on the back with Harner's initials. They were initially intended as presents for his friends, but word spread and they became a popular selling line – as well as being extensively pirated by other foundries.

Harner was proud of his German antecedents and the survival in his home state of fine old German traditions, as well as a version of the language known vulgarly as Pennsylvania Dutch ('Dutch' being a corruption of 'Deutsch'). In 1956, his company produced 900 large trivets inscribed: '*Grundsow*

*Lodge Nummer Ains on Da Lechaw'* – meaning: 'Groundhog Lodge Number One on the Lehigh River' – with a groundhog in the middle and three hearts on either side. They were cast to mark an annual shindig for the Pennsylvania Dutch, at which the meteorological portents provided by the little animal (immortalised as Punxsutawney Phil in the film *Groundhog Day*) were analysed and discussed amid the consumption of much beer and many German-style sausages.

The attraction (but also perhaps the drawback) of the trivet from the collecting perspective is its durability. Short of beating one with a sledgehammer or melting it down, they are near indestructible. As they were manufactured in large numbers, the inevitable corollary is that a large proportion of the metal trivets ever made have survived, which means that they can be fairly easily obtained and – compared with, say, nineteenth-century fine furniture or ceramics – they are cheap.

But that has the advantage of making trivetology, to use Lynn Rosack's word, appealingly democratic and welcoming. Regrettably, some collectors and dealers in other fields – antique fishing tackle would be one example – tend to be secretive, devious, slippery, evasive and given to gross exaggeration, subterfuge and even downright dishonesty when trying to acquire or dispose of particularly rare and desirable items. The triveteers, I am confident, are an open and friendly bunch. Each year (apart from 2020, Covid year) the Pressing Irons and Trivet Collectors of America, PITCA, hold a convention somewhere in the Midwest, where they gather for outings, talks, bring-and-sell sessions, a banquet, and to spend a few days, as the organisers put it, 'immersed in irons and trivets'. It is obvious from the galleries of pictures that the members of PITCA regard each other as friends and as belonging to a fellowship bound by admiration for a craft that receives little attention from the wider world.

The 2022 annual convention was once again held at the Marriott in Cranberry Township near Pittsburgh in July. Even more exciting was the staging in September of the seventeenth *Reunion Internacional de Colleccionistas de Planchas Antiguas* (translated as 'Reunion of Collectors of Old Flat Irons') in Torre del Mar on the southern coast of Spain. The organisers held out the promise that this would be an UNFORGETTABLE trip – 'we all have the same faith, the same madness', they proclaimed. 'We have many things to tell each other, to know each other, to make friendships'.

I was tempted for a moment to attend, if only to find out what the madness uniting an assembly of trivetologists was like. But I thought four days of trivetology might be excessive, and anyway my own collection – one four-footed steel square enclosing three fish and a classic iron-shaped design in heavy brass with three feet and some twirly scrollwork – might be considered somewhat underwhelming, although I am sure I would have been given a warm welcome by these friendly people.

## CHAPTER THIRTEEN

# . . . and Galvanised Buckets

UNLIKE RIVETS AND TRIVETS, the galvanised bucket is a steady seller in the shop, as are its bigger cousins, the galvanised mop pail, the galvanised dustbin and the galvanised incinerator. But why do we like our buckets and mop pails and dustbins and incinerators to be galvanised? What is the appeal? Plastic would do just as well, except in the case of the incinerator. In our house, we used to have a green plastic bucket in which we put the compostable kitchen waste. It was perfectly adequate for the job, but one day it was replaced – I had no part in the decision – by a gleaming silver galvanised bucket. This performs the same function as its predecessor, in that it contains vegetable peel, apple cores, coffee grinds and the rest of it, until it is full and it is time to empty it on the compost heap.

You might say that it's the look of it: that bright brilliance that no plastic can match. But we know that the brilliance will not last. Within a few weeks of taking over compost duty, the interior of our bucket began to darken and no amount of scrubbing would restore it. The startling silver of the new dustbin's exterior soon fades, and the incinerator blackens after a few blazes within.

But we still prefer our galvanised bucket, even in its tarnished state. There is a solidity to it that reassures. The clang of the handle against the top is comforting. Plastic utensils are anonymous, characterless, devoid of any cultural or historic hinterland. The galvanised bucket has a place in our folk memory, speaking to us of a past populated by familiar receptacles and devices, like breadbins and mangles and washing tubs, that aroused our curiosity when we were children. That past preceded the era of throwaway, in which convenience replaced value. We created that era and continue to inhabit it, but we have become increasingly uneasy about its impact on our world and the implications of the way we casually discard its products when they no longer suit us. The galvanised bucket reminds us of a time when things lasted and we looked after them.

Maybe that's why we got rid of the plastic bucket.

GALVANISATION IS the process of coating metals in zinc to protect them from rust. The origin of the term is one of those linguistic quirks that delight etymologists and seem perverse to the rest of us. Luigi Galvani was an eighteenth-century dabbler in the sciences, who flitted from one discipline to another – surgery, anatomy, the auditory organs of birds, animals and humans – without achieving anything of lasting value in any of them. His breakthrough came as a result of experiments he carried out on the corpses or legs of frogs, which, when hung on metal hooks, were observed to twitch when touched with a scalpel (another version has the frogs' legs dangling from hooks suspended from a metal railing on his balcony, which quivered convulsively when the wind brought them in contact with the railing).

Keen to justify the stipend he received as a fellow of the Academy of Sciences in his native Bologna, Galvani seized upon the quivering limbs of his defunct amphibians as the means to make his name. He coined the term 'animal electricity' to explain the involuntary movements and asserted in several weighty papers that this energy source was stored in the creature's pelvic muscle.

He was hopelessly wrong, of course, although he never admitted it. The twitching was in fact caused by a current of electricity between two metals, as was demonstrated by Galvani's rival from the University of Padua, Alessandro Volta. In 1800 – two years after Galvani had died in obscurity – Volta demonstrated the prototype of his electric battery, in which copper and zinc discs were alternately stacked, separated by pieces of cloth or cardboard soaked in brine. When a wire was attached to the top and bottom, an electric current flowed through the stack. This was a genuine breakthrough, which became known as the Voltaic Pile, and opened the way to further advances in the infant science of electricity. Although Volta had demolished Galvani's theory, he was generous enough to acknowledge its part in stimulating his thinking and used the term 'galvanism' for a current produced by chemical action.

But the process that immortalised Galvani's name – the coating of metals in zinc to protect them – had nothing to do with him or Alessandro Volta. It had actually been devised by a French medical doctor and chemist, Pierre Jacques Malouin, thirty years before it occurred to Luigi Galvani that poking around with frogs' legs might get him somewhere. Malouin described his work in a paper presented to the Royal Academy in Paris in 1742. Although no one at the time paid much attention to it or him, passing references to coating metal containers and vessels in zinc suggest that news of Malouin's discovery did spread. For instance, Bishop Richard Watson of Llandaff, an eminent late-eighteenth-century theologian, observed on a visit to Rouen that iron pots were scrubbed bright with salamonniac and then 'dipped in an iron pot full of melted zinc'.

It was the great Cornish-born chemist, Sir Humphry Davy, who first showed that when two dissimilar metals were connected electrically and immersed in water, the corrosion of one was accelerated while the other received a degree of protection. And it was another great English chemist, Michael Faraday, who first analysed and made sense of zinc's protective power. In a series of experiments in 1829, Faraday found that when iron nails were placed on a sheet of zinc and partially covered in salt water, the zinc corroded and the nails did not. This was the so-called 'sacrificial action' of zinc at work, and while Faraday himself soon moved on to more exciting discoveries concerning electricity, the metal industry was beginning to sit up and take notice.

Eight years after Faraday had recorded his observations in his diary, a French inventor, Stanislas Sorel, took out a patent for dipping iron previously cleaned by immersion in hydrochloric acid in a bath of molten zinc. He called the process 'galvanisation'; it is not known why, although in the text for his patent application he paid tribute to the work of Galvani and Volta in discovering that 'electricity is generated by the contact of dissimilar metals'.

Eyes and ears must have been on the alert across the Channel, as within a few months of Sorel submitting his patent application, an otherwise obscure English naval officer, Commander Henry Craufurd, had applied for a patent for a process identical in its essentials to Sorel's. By then, Henry Palmer, chief engineer of the London Dock Company, had developed and patented his technique for making what he called 'indented or corrugated' iron, and, by the middle of the nineteenth century, a considerable business had developed in galvanised corrugated iron. The sheets were comparatively light and strong, and their resistance to corrosion made them doubly useful. Corrugated iron became the roofing material of choice in far-flung parts of the US, South America and Australasia, where ease of construction counted for more than permanence or aesthetic considerations. Galvanised wire for keeping cattle and sheep in their place and galvanised telegraph wiring soon followed.

On 24 May 1883, one of the great symbols of American engineering prowess, the Brooklyn Suspension Bridge, was opened. Its construction, which had taken thirteen years, took a considerable toll. Between twenty and thirty men lost their lives working on it, most of them from falls. But the first fatality occurred a year before work even began, when the designer of the bridge, John Augustus Roebling, died of tetanus after having his toes crushed by a passing boat while he was on a ferry pier making measurements. The baton was passed to his son, Washington Roebling, who himself suffered a complete health collapse and became an invalid as a result of decompression sickness ('the bends'), brought on by working in one of the pneumatic caissons used to clear silt from the riverbed.

Roebling developed a severe aversion to light and noise, as a result of which he was unable to leave his home to visit the site or speak to contractors. His remarkable wife, Emily, became his eyes and ears, and it was she who ensured that his instructions were followed and saw the project through to completion. And at the opening ceremony, it was Emily Roebling who first crossed the bridge ahead of the assorted city worthies and the investors who had put their money into it.

The chief wonders of the Brooklyn Bridge were the four great steel cables that looped between the two arched towers of limestone, granite and cement, and then on to the suspension anchorages on either bank of the river. Each cable was composed of more than 5,000 wires in nineteen strands, and from them hung a web of steel ropes, cross-beams and stays reaching to the deck. Altogether, more than 14,000 miles of galvanised steel wire was used. And a century later, when a major refurbishment was carried out, most of them were in good condition, even though the cables were replaced.

Seventeen years after the cables on the Brooklyn Bridge were first put to the test, the process of hot-dipping in molten zinc was extended to another significant – if mundane – use. George C. Witt, founder and boss of the Witt Cornice Co. in Cincinnati, Ohio, obtained a patent for a corrugated galvanised steel can for rubbish and ash. At a stroke, he offered a solution to what had grown into a major social problem for city council officials and health inspectors as the cities grew – what to do with the piles of garbage and waste left in the streets for dogs, cats and vermin to enjoy and distribute. As a 1906 ad for Witt's lucrative innovation proclaimed: 'You wouldn't take chances with sewer gas – why risk disease from the offensive odours of decaying garbage? The only way to make garbage odourless and harmless is to keep it in a Witt's Corrugated Can – then no matter which way the wind is blowing, nobody gets a whiff.'

The outbreak of war in Europe in 1914 presented a host of challenges for the armaments and supply industries, one of which was how to provide accommodation for the troops at speed. Once again, galvanised corrugated iron provided the answer in a semi-circular form that soon became – and remains – a familiar sight. The beauty of the Nissen hut was that its constituent parts could be easily transported by lorry and assembled within a few hours to make a dry, warm and reasonably spacious living quarters. They sprang up at barracks and airfields and on training grounds and battle grounds all over Europe. They were a key facility in both World Wars, and the model was so adaptable that it was replicated from the wilds of Canada to the frozen wastes of Antarctica.

It was the brainchild of an American-born engineer, Peter Nissen, who found himself on the Western Front in 1916, pondering the problem of how to provide some comfort for his fellow soldiers. As a lad, he'd studied in North Carolina before his parents, originally immigrants from Norway, moved the family to Nova Scotia. He worked with his father and on his own in various parts of Canada, got married, and emigrated to South Africa to take up a position in the gold mining industry centred on Witwatersrand in the Transvaal. In 1913, Nissen and his family moved to England, where he set up a construction company. He was forty-three when war broke out but was evidently intent on doing his bit for King and Country, despite still being a US citizen.

His engineering skills made him a valuable asset, and in 1915 he joined the Royal Engineers and was made captain. He worked steadily on his ideas for a novel form of accommodation for the troops and discussed them with fellow and senior officers. Initially, he envisaged a wooden roof, but switched to galvanised corrugated iron as being more convenient in every way. The first version, named the Nissen Bow Hut, was twenty-seven feet long and eight feet high. But the model could be made to any size – the field hospital version was sixty feet long, forty feet wide and ten feet high.

The Nissen hut had wooden floors and wooden end walls with windows. The steel floor frame had steel bows, onto which the sheets of corrugated iron were bolted. The only tool required was a spanner, and the average time for a six-man team to put up the standard version was four hours. As long as the ground was reasonably flat, it could be installed anywhere. The first ones appeared in France in September 1916, and by the end of the war, an estimated 100,000 were in use. The press took an interest. A *Daily Mirror* reporter described how, overnight, a piece of empty ground would be occupied by 'an immense creature of the tortoise species', and within a week, the whole valley could be covered in them. 'These are the new homes,' he wrote, 'for which many a soldier on the Somme is thanking his lucky stars in this bitter weather [. . .] In short, among the creatures to which the war has given birth, it has already earned a high character as a useful, kindly, tractable domestic beast.'

It is estimated that more than two million soldiers slept, ate and relaxed in the dry warmth of a Nissen hut in the last two years of the First World War. More than 200,000 beds were provided for the wounded in 10,000 Nissen field hospitals. Peter Nissen's contribution to the eventual Allied victory was immense – had they known who he was, the men would certainly have held him in higher esteem than they did any of their generals. His work was recognised by the authorities: he was made lieutenant-colonel and was awarded the Distinguished Service Order. Of more practical use was the £13,400 he got from the War Office for waiving his patent rights while the war was in progress. With this, he was able to establish his company, Nissen Buildings Ltd, at Hoddesdon in Hertfordshire. He bought the unused stock of huts from the government and set about adapting his classic design to civilian use, designing and building aircraft hangars, small factories and even churches.

For a time, the principle of the Nissen hut was embraced as a possible answer to the country's housing shortage. In Yeovil, the district council built a terrace of three pairs of homes based on the design, with concrete walls at either end and the galvanised corrugated sheets bolted to a concrete floor. Others appeared elsewhere in the same area, notably at South Petherton and West Camel. However, they turned out not to be as cheap as the makers promised, and in the end no more than fifty were built.

The inventor of the Nissen hut died at his home in Kent in 1930 at the age of fifty-eight. His company carried on without him, and the outbreak of war in 1939 triggered a major resurgence in production of the basic hut. Post-1945, the company continued trading for a time but was eventually wound up in 1971.

Nissen himself was soon forgotten, but his huts have proved remarkably durable. They survive in many parts of the world, their rounded profile making them instantly recognisable. Some are still in use at army camps; others have been converted for a wide variety of uses. There is even one around the corner from our house, which was at one time used in a family coffin-making business, before becoming a splendid shed.

A double-length Nissen hut was installed on the Orkney island of Lamb Holm to accommodate Italian prisoners-of-war, and was converted by them into a chapel. One of the prisoners, Domenico Chiocchetti, painted much of the ornate interior decoration, including a Madonna and Child on the wall behind the altar. He stayed on after the hostilities ceased in order to finish decorating the font, which is believed to have been constructed from a car exhaust covered in concrete. Chiocchetti returned to Orkney in 1960 to restore the chapel and wrote an open letter to the people: 'The chapel is yours for you to love and preserve. I take with me to Italy the remembrance of your kindness and wonderful hospitality [. . .] my children will learn from me to love you.'

Another application of galvanisation – less noticeable than the Nissen hut, but even more ubiquitous – was the wash tub. The coming of the semi-automatic and then the fully automatic washing machine from the 1950s onwards has gone a long way to freeing working-class women from one of the most insistent of the several forms of drudgery that once filled their lives. It is therefore difficult for us to imagine what the start of the week was like in millions of households, as the women of the house surveyed the piles of dirty laundry to be done and organised themselves for their day's toil.

Over the previous days, the dirty clothes were generally dumped in and around the wash tub, which was kept in the pantry, and then, on Monday morning, the whole lot was transferred to the scullery. There, the clothes were sorted into separate heaps – whites, coloureds, exceptionally filthy, and so on – and ordered for sequential washing. In the meantime, the fire would have been lit under the copper to heat the water. When steaming hot, the water was tipped into the wash tub, which was also known in Britain as the dolly tub (the instrument used for agitating the clothes during washing was a pole with a crossways handle at the top and up to six legs radiating from the bottom, and was widely known as the dolly). Then the hard work began, as the dolly was grasped and lifted and plunged and turned one way and then the other.

Whites were done first, then the other heaps. After washing, each item was rinsed, put through the mangle, rinsed again, mangled again, and then – depending on the weather, hung up on the washing line outside or on a drying rack indoors. Exceptionally filthy clothes were stretched over the washing board and scrubbed before being consigned to the tub. Until the development of hot-dip galvanising, the tub was generally made of wood; the galvanised tub was eagerly adopted because it was both lighter and easier to clean. Increasingly, washing boards were also made of galvanised metal.

On both sides of the Atlantic, Monday was conventionally washing day – the weather forecast on Monday morning was expected to include a prediction as to whether or not it would be 'a good drying day'. 'Anyone who did not wash on a Monday was not considered a good housekeeper,' Frances Brands of Belle Plains, Minnesota, related in her memories of growing up pre-1914, when starching aprons, collars, cuffs and dresses was still part of the rigmarole. George Thom, writing in the Canadian edition of *Reader's Digest* about his boyhood in Winnipeg in the early 1930s, recalled that the first task on Monday morning was to get the water from the community pump down the road, as there was no running water in the house. For his mother, Monday wash day was followed by Tuesday ironing day, for which she had to heat the heavy sad-iron on the kitchen stove, doubtless placing it on a trivet as she turned and folded the clothes.

The man of the house played no part in the proceedings, although children were expected to help out when they were big enough, particularly with the mangling. In many British towns and cities, communal laundries were set up – forerunners of the laundrette – where the payment of a small fee entitled the housewife to use the hot water, wash tubs and implements. That represented a small step forward, as it took away some of the most laborious and tedious aspects of the operation, and also provided an opportunity for chat and gossip. But it was still drudgery; it was no wonder that the Ascot electric water heater (which came on the market in the 1930s) and the twin-tub washing machine (introduced in the 1950s) were hailed as liberators.

Like old drinking troughs, terracotta olive oil jars and cast-iron mangles, the galvanised wash tub has evolved from indispensable farm or household object to garden ornament. Any self-respecting retailer of garden antiquities and bric-a-brac will have one or two for sale at a price comfortably in excess of the annual incomes of those for whom they were once a symbol of endless drudgery. Shro sells a reduced-size version custom-made for the market; they are expensive, but popular as planters.

*

IN AN ISSUE OF the *American Zinc Lead and Oil Journal* in 1921, the editor, tongue in cheek, produced a list of the Ten Commandments for zinc producers. The last two read: 'If you must have iron or steel in your building exposed to the elements, zincize (galvanise) it', and 'Eliminate the word galvanize from your dictionary and substitute for it the word zincize'. The inaccurate terminology was clearly a matter of concern in the US, because a few years later the *Bulletin* of the American Zinc Institute published a letter from W. D. Fleming, author of an authoritative book entitled *Galvanizing and Tinning*, calling for the process to be renamed 'zincing'. 'We have the art of tinning,' Mr Fleming argued, 'why not zincing?'

The reformers were fighting a losing battle, and 'galvanising' it remained. What really mattered was fighting the common enemy. 'Rust,' the editor of the *Bulletin* affirmed in 1923, 'is nature's way of taking back the metals that man has wrested from the bosom of Mother Earth [. . .] to build in the metals that are subject to rust is to invite desecration of objects that should stand as lasting testaments to the idealism that conceived them, the genius that executed them and the frugality that founded them.'

Across the world, hot-dip galvanising has remained the principal defence against corrosion. The buckets and dustbins and incinerators that we sell at the shop have been armoured as far as is possible against the creeping decay of oxidisation. The story that began in eighteenth-century Italy with Luigi Galvani and his frogs' legs and Alessandro Volta and his electric pile has not finished, because no one has yet devised a better way to keep this insidious foe at bay.

CHAPTER FOURTEEN

# Lockpickers, Nail-makers and Fruit-bottlers

SHRO IS BENT OVER the key-cutting machine, which is fixed at one end of the counter by the window. She is a study in concentration as she turns the knobs that adjust the jaws holding the blank mortice key. A few inches away, the original key has already been locked into position. The tiniest error produces that most useless of objects – the key that cannot open the lock – so she takes extreme care to ensure that everything is exactly as it should be.

She pulls down the goggles over her eyes, switches on the cutting disc and engages it with the blank. The shop, normally quiet but for low-level conversational exchanges, is filled with the sharp, dissonant rasp of metal being cut. Tiny particles are thrown from the machine, silvering the counter.

'There you go, my dear,' Shro says, lifting her goggles and handing over the cut key and the original. 'Remember, bring it back if it doesn't work.' Sometimes they don't, and have to be cut again, which is a bore. But cutting keys is a solid earner, because keys get lost in the same way that light bulbs cease to light, and the nearest alternative key-cutter is in the town several miles away. The people in the village depend on being able to get their keys done close to home.

THE GREAT EXHIBITION, which opened at the Crystal Palace in London in May 1851, was trumpeted as the supreme showcase of British dominance in global technological innovation. Its full title was the Great Exhibition of the Industry of All Nations; inviting competitors from foreign lands would, the organisers complacently believed, demonstrate the superiority of British inventors, engineers and craftsmen. But the very presence of the foreigners inevitably carried the risk of undermining the image of ascendancy central to the whole show. The confidence and boastfulness that characterised the promotion and the press coverage was partly a mask. Beneath it, anxiety lurked.

A couple of weeks before the exhibition was opened by Queen Victoria, the American steamship *Washington I* docked at Southampton after an uneventful passage from New York. Among the passengers disembarking was a thickset Bostonian in a dark suit, with a mane of hair and a fine beard. He paid very close attention to the transfer of his luggage, in which was a small chest of drawers containing an interesting collection of slender tools, which E. W. Hornung's immortal amateur cracksman Raffles would have recognised immediately as having been designed for the picking of locks. But the American, Alfred C. Hobbs, was no common or uncommon criminal – indeed, he carried with him a letter from the

Chief of Police in New York, testifying to his character as a 'gentleman and a citizen'.

Hobbs had come to England to represent his employers, the respected New York locksmiths Day & Newell, at the Great Exhibition. He also had it in mind to show the home country a thing or two about security and its limitations. At that time, the acknowledged kingpins in the growing British security business were Chubb of Wolverhampton. In 1818 one of the founding brothers, Jeremiah Chubb, had devised what he called the 'detector lock', in which any attempt to pick it or open it with the wrong key triggered a mechanism that jammed it. It was a significant advance on earlier security locks, and the reputation of the company grew steadily, so that, by the time of the Great Exhibition, they had a factory in London making safes and strongroom doors as well as the lock works in Wolverhampton.

One of the big draws at the Exhibition was the 105-carat Koh-i-Noor diamond, which had been surrendered to Queen Victoria as a spoil of war after the annexation of Punjab in 1849. During the day, this was exhibited on a cushion inside a gilded cage, and at night it was locked away in a specially commissioned Chubb safe. Chubb also displayed a full range of their locks, along with promotional material bragging about their impregnability.

The American salesman Alfred C. Hobbs spent the first few days at Crystal Palace setting up the stand exhibiting the locks made in New York by Day & Newell. He then announced publicly that he would open one of the celebrated Chubb Detector locks, which – in front of onlookers and journalists – he did inside fifteen minutes. An indignant John

Chubb – who had taken over the running of the company from his father and uncle – promptly challenged the upstart Yankee to try his dexterous hand on a locked strongroom door fitted by Chubb at offices in Westminster. In front of a considerable audience, Hobbs produced his tools from his waistcoat pocket and bent over the lock. After twenty-five minutes, a sharp click was heard and the door swung open.

The English lock-makers were astonished and outraged. But worse was to follow. For half a century, the window of Joseph Bramah's shop at 124 Piccadilly had displayed a very different species of lock made by the great engineer and his redoubtable assistant, Henry Maudslay. It was circular and was opened by a small, circular key with a series of longitudinal slots at the end, which, when inserted, depressed a configuration of eighteen sliders, resulting in the release of the bolt. In 1801, Bramah had placed this padlock in his shop window with this challenge beside it: 'The Artist who can make an Instrument that will pick or open this Lock shall receive 200 guineas the moment it is produced.'

Various nimble-fingered lock pickers had tried to open the Bramah lock and had failed, and it had become an accepted truth that it was invincible – until Alfred C. Hobbs arrived on the scene. Hobbs, who effortlessly combined the roles of salesman for his company and natural showman, informed Bramah and Co. of his intention to pick the lock. A committee was formed to supervise the challenge. The lock was removed to an upstairs room and sealed in a box with only the keyhole accessible. Hobbs had thirty days to win or lose. After fifty hours of poking and fiddling, spread over sixteen days, he announced that he had succeeded. The committee met, ruled in his favour, and the 200 guineas were handed over.

The whole event aroused tremendous media interest. The dominant motif of the coverage was 'John Bull' versus 'The Yankee', and the fact that the Yankee had triumphed stuck in John Bull's throat. To redress the balance, a London lock-smith, a Mr Garbutt, ill-advisedly informed the press that he would pick one of the so-called Parautoptic locks that Alfred Hobbs had brought from New York to form the centrepiece of the Day & Newell display. The Parautoptic was taken to a house in Knightsbridge and sealed in the same way that the Bramah had been. Mr Garbutt bent to his task, but in vain. After thirty days he was forced to admit ignominious defeat.

The Great Lock Controversy, as it was dubbed by the newspapers, provoked huge and sustained public interest, which persisted for a time after the Great Exhibition had ended. Public contests between lock-maker and lock-picker continued to be staged in front of noisy audiences. John Goater, chief foreman at Chubb's Locks and a jealous defender of the company's name, claimed he had managed to pick one of Hobbs' locks; Hobbs retorted that it was an inferior model. In 1854, Hobbs himself, obviously having an off-day, failed to open the Royal Climax Detector Lock made by Edwin Cotterill at Ashted in Birmingham within the allotted twenty-four hours. Later that year, Goater publicly boasted about picking a lock made by a London locksmith, Michael Parnell, who then sued for defamation and won.

Despite the theatrical and much-publicised revelations of the fallibility of individual locks, the trade of Chubb and other lock-makers – many of them operating in the Midlands town of Willenhall, which became synonymous with the industry – continued to flourish. Hobbs himself decided to stay in England and set up his own business in Cheapside, making and selling a range of locks, including a version of the Parautoptic. He must have done reasonably well, as he stayed for the best part of a decade before returning to the US to take up the position of superintendent at the Hawk Sewing Co. in Bridgeport, Connecticut, where he died in 1891 aged eighty-eight.

The fear of crime, and in particularly robbery and burglary, became more acute in well-to-do Victorian households as the quantity and value of possessions worth stealing increased. Sensational coverage of crime in the newspapers and periodicals stoked this sense of insecurity. The burgeoning security industry's promises to keep valuables safe, enabling homeowners and the proprietors of jewellery businesses to sleep soundly at night, were eagerly embraced. At one point in the Great Lock Controversy, *The Times* wondered if all the publicity was not having the unintended effect of stimulating 'the taste for lock-picking [. . .] among a class where perfection in the operation is not at all to be desired'.

In fact, the class of professional criminal generally had neither the time nor the aptitude to graduate in advanced lock-picking and preferred more direct methods. The most celebrated heist of the time was the South-Eastern Railway bullion robbery of May 1855, when three boxes of gold bars and coins were stolen from the guard's van on the service between London Bridge and Folkestone. The gang did indeed succeed in opening the Chubb safe in which the gold was secured – but they used copies of the original keys that had been 'borrowed' by a disaffected employee of the rail company. In another celebrated robbery, at a jeweller in Cornhill in 1865, the thieves had no time to waste on fiddling with the safe lock; they slammed wedges around the door with a sledgehammer until it could be prised off with a crowbar.

Attention shifted from the locks to the safes themselves. At the Paris Exhibition in 1867, a New York safe-maker, Silas Herring, displayed a notice on his Banker's Safe challenging anyone to try to break into it. Samuel Chatwood, whose lock and safe company was based in Bolton, Lancashire, rose like a feeding trout to the fly and announced that he would match his safe against Herring's. The Battle of the Safes, as it was inevitably dubbed by the newspapers (with the strapline 'British Invincible versus Yankee Ironclad') began with Herring's gang of hired safe-breakers going to work with ratchet drill, sledgehammers, twenty-inch steel wedges and crowbars. After 232 minutes, they levered the door off Chatwood's safe with the wedges and crowbar and smashed their way inside. Chatwood's men had the door off Herring's safe inside half an hour, but breaking into the inner chest was tougher; altogether, they took 254 minutes. The Americans claimed victory, but subsequent investigation revealed that Silas Herring had resorted to a number of sneaky subterfuges, including 'improper communication' with Monsieur Duliot, the chairman of the supervisors of the contest. The Battle was eventually declared null and void, and Herring was ordered to pay costs to his opponent.

The great age when British and American lock-makers led the world in keeping intruders out of places where they were not wanted has long gone. Willenhall, once home to more than 300 manufacturers, now has its lock museum to recall departed glories but no more than a handful of businesses actively involved in the trade. The name of Chubb was sold to a Swedish conglomerate.

But the desire to lock and bolt and chain, which is as old as ownership itself, is still amply catered for in the shop, as evidenced by the peg boards behind the counter, on which are displayed the blank keys, hundreds of them – cylinder keys to the right, mortice keys to the left. Over the door leading out into the yard are the brass and chrome door handles, each with its keyhole, and next to them are door bolts. On the corner is a column of padlocks – cheap ones that would not hold up a thief for more than a minute or two, above more formidable, heavy-duty and expensive ones that would definitely take some picking, although Alfred Hobbs would doubtless fathom their complexities in a trice.

> For want of a naile the shoe is lost
> for want of a shoe the horse is lost
> for want of a horse the rider is lost.

This saying, included by the seventeenth-century poet George Herbert in his collection of *Outlandish Proverbs*, published in 1640, is ancient, and versions of it appear in many languages to illustrate the proposition of causality. It also illustrates the indispensability of the nail – life without nails, and a hammer to bang them in, is difficult to imagine.

The first nail in human history was probably a sharp fragment of animal bone or flint driven in by a hand-sized stone for a hammer. Nails were used in construction and boat building in Ancient Egypt. Wrought-iron nails were forged in volume at smithies in Roman times. Each had to be hammered into shape by hand, and it was not until the early nineteenth century that machines were developed to cut nails from flat sheets of metal and turn and shape them.

The Tudor chronicler John Leland visited Birmingham in 1538 and noted 'the many smithies [. . .] and a great many nailers'. Traditionally, the West Midlands was the heartland of English nail-making. Dudley was known for horseshoe nails, Sedgeley for gate nails, Bromsgove for hobnails and tacks. Nail-making in the ages before the Machine Age was generally a family affair, in which children heated the rods and pumped the bellows while their elders fashioned the nails. By 1798, it was estimate that 35,000 men, women and children worked in the Black Country nail industry.

In 1814, Joseph Dyer, an American immigrant from Connecticut, converted a vacant brewery beside the Birmingham and Fazeley canal into a nail factory. He installed his own patented nail-cutting machines, powered by a Boulton & Watt steam engine, and quickly became a dominant figure in Black Country nail production. After the expiry of his patents in the late 1820s, Dyer's machine was widely copied. By 1860, there were seventeen nail-makers in Birmingham and seven in Wolverhampton. One of the most important producers was the Nail Mistress of the Black Country, Eliza Tinsley, who established an empire of half a dozen factories and warehouses employing 4,000 workers. Born in Wolverhampton in 1813, she had married a nail-maker, and upon his early death had taken over his business and rapidly expanded it. Eliza Tinsley sold up and retired in 1871, but the company was still in business under her name seventy years later.

The old family-based cottage industry producing wrought nails quickly disappeared, but the heyday of the cut nail was comparatively short-lived, abbreviated by the advent of wire nails – originally developed in Belgium – which were cut from steel wire, sharpened at one end, with a flat, round head at the other and straight sides, all done by machines. The holding power of the wire nails was inferior to that of tapered cut nails, but they were vastly cheaper to make, and by 1900 had captured ninety per cent of the global market. It is the wire nail, very often galvanised to resist corrosion, that continues to hold sway today.

After blazing a nail trail and making a small fortune in Birmingham, Joseph Dyer relocated to Manchester to apply his inventive ingenuity to the cotton industry. He patented and subsequently improved a roving machine for use in spinning cotton and made a lot more money. He built himself a fine mansion, Mauldeth Hall in Burnage, and, as time went on, devoted his energies increasingly to social issues and political reform. He helped found the *Manchester Guardian* newspaper, organised and personally delivered relief for those wounded in the 1830 revolution in Paris, and became a leading figure in the Manchester Literary and Philosophical Society, to which he read numerous papers about physics, mechanics and political science. Dyer was a fierce campaigner against slavery and wrote several pamphlets denouncing his fellow Americans for allowing it to persist.

It can therefore be assumed that he would have had strong, if possibly conflicted, views about his compatriot, Thomas Jefferson – the founding father and third president – who managed somewhat uneasily to combine presenting eloquent arguments against slavery with owning hundreds of slaves on his estates in Virginia and fathering several children with one of them. Whatever Joseph Dyer or anyone else thought of Jefferson's moral character, there is no doubt that he was a man of extraordinary talents and achievements; and that when he put his mind to an undertaking, he did so thoroughly. As with the making of nails.

Mulberry Row, named after the trees planted along it, was the principal street in Monticello, Jefferson's 5,000-acre estate in Virginia, and its commercial heart. Among the enterprises he set up was a blacksmith's shop, to which, in 1794, he added a workshop for making nails. In October of that year, Jefferson wrote to his friend Henry Remsen (who became his private secretary during his presidency) to say that he was so immersed in farming and nail-making 'that politics are entirely banished from my mind'. Jefferson's plan was to deploy the profits from making nails in improving the whole of the estate. 'My new trade of nail-making,' he wrote proudly to Remsen, 'is to me in this country what an additional title of nobility or the ensigns of a new order are in Europe.'

About a dozen male slaves aged between ten and sixteen worked at the forges in the nailery. Jefferson checked their productivity and the quality of their work on a daily basis. The nails sold well to local farmers and tradespeople, and to builders engaged in expanding the nearby town of Richmond into a major industrial centre. In 1795, Jefferson invested in a new machine to cut the nails. He reported that the nailery was turning out 8,000–10,000 nails a day and was providing 'completely for the maintenance of my family'.

The following year, he returned to frontline politics as vice-president to John Adams, and his close supervision of the nail operation necessarily lapsed. There were problems with the maintenance and operation of the cutting machine, and profits were further eroded by competition from rivals – in particular, a local slave owner, Kate Flood McCall, who set up nail factories in Richmond and Alexandria, and from the nail workshop established at the state penitentiary in Richmond. References to the Mulberry Row nailery in Jefferson's letters and notebooks became infrequent. At one point, a new stone workshop was built, but the war with England between 1812 and 1815 had a severe impact on trade, and at times production ceased entirely.

The last order for Jefferson's nails was recorded in 1823, three years before his death. His remarkable range of talents did not include prudent financial management, and by then he and his estate were enmeshed in debts that he had no hope of paying off. Sure enough, after he died, everything – Monticello, all his land, his paintings, his furniture and books, the remaining 130 slaves – were all sold, including the nail forge.

The range of nails beaten into shape at Jefferson's forge was necessarily extremely restricted, and he would have raised a quizzical eyebrow if he could have seen the vast diversity available today to the dedicated hammer-wielder. In our shop, the range occupies a sizeable stretch of shelf behind the counter, immediately above the array of liquid dispensers. There are clout nails, felt nails, round nails, oval nails, huge four-inch nails, nails of more manageable size and tiny tacks. They come in boxes in a rather fetching livery of mustard yellow and royal blue under the Challenge brand, which identifies them as having been made at the Frank Shaw nail factory in Gloucester. The boxes arrive in bigger boxes of the same colour scheme, which bear the company's reassuring – if unexciting – slogan: 'Quality Fastenings for the Handy Person'.

IT IS TOWARDS the end of November as I write these words, and the wind came into the north today after a few weeks of mild southerlies and south-westerlies. It was a reminder that winter should be here or hereabouts; another was the appearance in the shop window of the Christmas tree and its little bubbles of winking light. It is hung once more with wooden spoons and honey drizzlers, along with white-frosted pine cones and white bells with black top hats. For tinsel, Shro has cut strips of hessian and concertinaed them. There are eco-crackers of brown paper tied with twine and glistening red berries. The inverted retro Fairy Liquid bottle, as festive as any conventional Christmas fairy, is once again in the position of honour at the top.

Shro has announced her intention to implement a significant change to the display behind the counters. She has turned against the row of jam jars containing the pop rivets, grips, bath plugs, grommets, teapot spout protectors, suction hooks, pipe clips, croc clips, brass nipples, door stops and other small and fiddly items. In her view, they convey a faintly amateurish impression at odds with her professionalism and efficiency. More to the point, they take up too much room, and every time something is needed from one, the entire contents have to be tipped out for it to be retrieved.

The jam jars are condemned. New, wider shelves are to be installed. She has been to Ikea and bought several units of little drawers, which she plans to knock the backs out of and fix together to make extra-deep drawers. These will be methodically labelled and filled with the relevant stock. They will, she says, look better and work better, and no one is inclined to disagree with her.

But the other shelves behind the counter will be left as they are, including the uppermost one, on which, in elevated glory, stand the Kilner jars. No self-respecting hardware store would be without a selection of Kilner jars. But what is so special about them? And why Kilner?

There are two basic versions that come in various sizes and shapes – the clip top and the screw top, both with separate seal lids. The name reaches reassuringly far back in time. The original firm of glass-makers was established by John Kilner in Wakefield, Yorkshire, in the 1840s. Assorted Kilner brothers and sons and other family members were involved over the succeeding decades as the fortunes of the company prospered. It expanded, opening bottle- and jar-making factories in Dewsbury and Conisbrough. In the 1890s, it employed more than 400 workers, but around that time there was some kind of parting of the ways between Kilners, and the enterprise was divided into two parts. The economic slump of the 1920s combined with competition from abroad did for both; the Dewsbury operation shut down in 1922, and the Conisbrough branch in 1936.

But what of the jar? It turns out there was never one particular and innovative version, and no patent was ever taken out. From around 1910 onwards (glass bottle historians are not precise about the date), Kilner Brothers started referring to their screw-top jars with separate glass lids as Kilner jars. The lids were embossed with 'Original Kilner Jar' and 'English Made'. Others were marketed as the 'Kilner Dual Purpose Jar'. The name was registered as a trademark, and at the sale following bankruptcy proceedings in 1937, this was acquired by United Glass and production continued. Today, the jars are made in China, but the good old Yorkshire name endures.

According to the Society for Industrial Archaeology in the US, Kilner Brothers were able to make wide-mouth bottles and jars only after they installed American-made machines in around 1900. These had been devised and patented by a prolific inventor, Charles Edwin Blue of Wheeling, West Virginia, and manufactured by the Hazel Glass Company (later Atlas Glass Co.) in Wellsburg. It further transpires – disappointingly, for anyone inclined to think of the Kilner jar as a British breakthrough – that all the significant advances in jar technology took place on the other side of the Atlantic (where, confusingly, the whole business is called 'canning').

The chief honours go to an obscure New Jersey tinsmith, John Laudis Mason, who, in 1858, patented a method of sealing a square-shouldered jar with a screw thread designed to press a separate metal disc down onto the rim. Mason sold the rights to a company in Clyde, New York State, which subsequently licensed glass-makers to produce what was known as the Mason jar. The expiry of the patent after thirteen years triggered a vitreous free-for-all, and a bewildering variety of jars that employed the Mason principle flooded out of bottling plants across the country.

As with the humble trivet, the history of the glass preserving jar has been exhaustively researched in the US and little touched upon in Britain. Two monumental works of scholarship stand as landmarks in the field: *Bottle Makers and their Marks* and *Fruit Jars: A Collector's Manual*, both the work of the one-time head of the War Production Board's glass containers division, Julian Harrison Toulouse. The latter, published in 1971, runs to more than 550 pages, of which more than half are devoted to a glossary of jars, distinguishing marks of jars, the companies that made the jars and the people who made the companies.

It is difficult for someone who is not a connoisseur of bottles and jars to imagine that there could be much more to say on the subject. But a trot through the Historic Glass Bottle website, created and maintained by Bill Lindsey of Klamath Falls, Oregon, and hosted by the Bureau of Land Management and the Society for Historical Archaeology, reveals this to be a misapprehension. There is no corner of the United States' bottle- and jar-making heritage that has not been researched, from milk bottles in El Paso and beer bottles in Tucson to medicine bottles, Pepsi bottles and the original Budweiser beer bottle in St Louis – and the whole colossal body of bottle and jar history can be accessed through this website.

As for John Laudis Mason, his great innovation did not bring him the comfort and prosperity he deserved. His business venture thrived for a time, but the expiry of his patent was followed by what Julian H. Toulouse described as 'the most flagrant, widespread and unabashed piracy of a man's name and reputation in the history of glass making'. Rival manufacturers did not only take his invention, they took his name as well. Within a few years, as many as fifty factories were advertising their versions of 'the Mason jar'. In the meantime, the circumstances of Mason himself declined; he died in 1902 at the age of seventy, an inmate of the House of Relief on Hudson Street, New York.

The Kilner jar is one of a small and select group of brand names to have acquired, through long-lasting familiarity, a status completely out of proportion to its usefulness. Generations of jam- and jelly- and chutney-makers, onion-picklers and fruit-bottlers have reached for the Kilner jar when all the boiling and stirring is done and the product is ready. As a dedicated maker of jams and marmalade, I should be a Kilner person myself. But, somewhat heretically, I confess that I find them a bit unwieldy; I prefer simple screw-top jars or the collection of instant coffee jars that I inherited from my mother when she announced that her marmalade-making days were over (along with her preserving pan, ancient funnel and wooden stirring spoon).

## CHAPTER FIFTEEN

# Let There Be Light (and Sandpaper, Masking Tape and Rawlplugs)

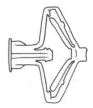

IT'S DIFFICULT TO GET too excited about light bulbs. The light bulb is pure functionality. Yes, they enable a great deal of the life we take for granted to happen, but people do not buy them thinking about that. They buy them because a previous one no longer works, and they do not want to be in darkness. There is no good conversation to be had about light bulbs. They do not come with associations attached or stimulate memories. To almost everyone apart from the small community of light-bulb enthusiasts, they are quite boring.

Shro and Helen, keepers of the shop, find them so. They talk about them sometimes because they have to. But the exchanges are severely practical – where they should be stored, whether or not to order more non-dimmables or dimmables or both, whether to opt for clear glass or frosted glass, and so forth. And they are a source of irritation, because customers complain about them. There are too many different kinds. They are confusing. They are too expensive. They don't last as long as they should. They're too bright, or not bright enough, or don't fit the socket. No one is ever pleased to buy a light bulb; it's just something you need, like lavatory paper.

But, like keys, they are essential hardware business. The trade in light bulbs is a significant contributor to turnover, and it's constant, year-round – in fact, unlike garden stuff and all the outdoors DIY stuff, it is better during the winter, presumably because there's more darkness around. The light-bulb section is to the left of the counter looking down the shop, and it consists of more than fifteen shelves. Much of the space in the storage cupboard inside the back door is taken up with reserves of the strongest selling lines. You have to carry a big stock, because it annoys customers if you do not have the one they need.

I referred earlier to the small community of light-bulb enthusiasts. That is the beauty of our fascination with the past – that every object, however overlooked, has a history – and the beauty of the internet is that it enables those who share an interest in that overlooked object to come together, to pool knowledge, to speak to each other and thereby immeasurably increase the pleasure they get from the shared enthusiasm. There is a website, lamptech.co.uk, which unlocks the doors into the extraordinarily rich world of the light bulb (referred to in the US as a lamp) and the light-bulb lover. Established and maintained by James D. Hooker – of whom I know nothing except that he seems to work for a Belgian lighting company – it incorporates the Museum of Electric Lamp Technology. At the click of a mouse, you can inspect the technological history, meet the pioneers, dead and alive, look at the literature, dip into the films, and – best of all – follow the links. In the lighting world, there are no national frontiers. Nearly 200 manufacturers from every part of the developed world are referenced. Seventy 'historic light collections' from all over Europe and America are listed. Nine forums are featured, each a portal into a room full of kindred spirits. For those curious about old street lamps, there is UKASTLE – the UK Association of Street Lighting Enthusiasts. For those wishing to know more about how they do things in Russia, there's Old Lighting Russia, although you really need to be able to read Russian to get the best out of it. Germany's lighting heritage is covered in Stefans Lichtparade – again, a command of German comes in handy.

One of the forums based in the US is Kilokat's antique light bulb site, flagged as 'an illustrated history of an art'. It is the brainchild of Tim Tromp, who has collected vintage lights for more than thirty years and said of himself in an interview: 'I do not consider myself an obsessive compulsive collector, it's only a pastime that I find interesting and stress-relieving [. . .] if I ever feel that my hobby becomes a challenge I will stop collecting.' The website is built around his own collection, which includes a bulb dating from 1882 in which the filament is held in place by minute nuts and bolts. It was designed by Hiram Maxim, famous as the inventor of the Maxim automatic machine gun and much else – including a steam-driven flying machine that almost flew, an inhaler to alleviate bronchitis and an automatic sprinkler (he settled in England and, in 1901, became Sir Hiram Maxim.)

Like Lamptech.com, Kilokat's umbrella of information spreads far and wide, covering the stories of individual bulbs and their makers, as well as patents, fuses, plugs and other accessories. There is guidance on how to find books and articles, and information on where you might hope to acquire the light bulb for the lamp that you seek. It is a great, warm, well-lit welcoming chamber where, Tim Tromp says, 'I invite visitors to browse.'

FIRE CAME FIRST in the story of light in darkness. The arc of time from the cave fire by whose flickering light early humans first used pigments to depict the animals they hunted to the light switch we unthinkingly press as we enter a darkened room is very long, but, over most of it, progress was minimal. The rushlight – reeds dipped in grease and ignited – was a step beyond a blazing piece of wood, and the earliest-known oil lamp – using a wick in a vessel containing vegetable or animal fat – was found in the prehistoric caves at Lascaux in France, which were in use 10,000–15,000 years ago. Tallow candles made from animal fat were used by the Romans, and possibly the Phoenicians before them. Wax candles gave off more light than tallow candles and did not smell so disgusting, but they were much more expensive. Economic circumstances tended to determine the quality of artificial lighting. Rushlights were still being used by the rural poor in Britain well into the nineteenth century. In her book *Old West Surrey: Some Notes and Memories,* the great garden designer Gertrude Jekyll recalls being told by a ninety-year-old woman how they were prepared: 'You peels away the rind from the peth, leaving only a little strip of rind. And when the rushes is dry you dips 'em through the grease, keeping 'em well under. And my mother she always laid hers to dry in a bit of hollow bark. Mutton fat's the best; it dries hardest.'

For the middle and upper classes, lighting meant candles. Sperm whale oil, which became available in the second half of the eighteenth century, made for brighter light, but they were still candles. The poet and clergyman George Crabbe provided this snapshot of how an evening might be spent in a middle-class home in Suffolk in the last decade of the eighteenth century: 'Mrs Forest sat at a small table on which in the evening stood one small candle in an iron candlestick, plying her needle by the feeble glimmer surrounded by her maids all busy in the same employment [. . .]'

Help was at hand, however, although probably too late for Mrs Forest. A Swiss chemist and experimenter, François-Pierre-Amédée Argand, had devised an oil lamp with a glass chimney fitted over a wick and enclosed within an inner and an outer metal cylinder. The arrangement ensured an improved air flow, which kept the flame burning brighter. Thomas Jefferson saw one in Paris in 1784 and reported that it gave a light 'equal to six or eight candles'. Although Argand did not personally benefit greatly from his invention – he died of malaria aged fifty-three – society at large did. Later versions of the Argand lamp, lighter and more manageable than the original, were installed in most of the better class of houses across Europe. When the Duke of Rutland and his family and retainers were in residence at Belvoir Castle – usually for no more than four months a year, for the winter hunting season – 400 lamps were kept blazing, burning their way through 600 gallons of oil.

The performance of the descendants of the Argand lamp was considerably improved by using kerosene (generally called paraffin in Britain), which was invented by a Canadian geologist, Abraham Gesner. Initially, it was distilled from coal, but the cost was high, and it became commercially viable only after Samuel Martin Kier showed how it could be refined from petroleum and established the first oil refinery at his works in Pittsburgh. Kerosene lamps were cheap to make and power and continued to burn brightly well into the twentieth century. Their only drawbacks were the smell of the fuel and the potentially disastrous consequences if they were knocked over. In 1871, much of Chicago was destroyed by a fire that began in a barn on DeKoven Street, owned by the O'Leary family. In a disgraceful example of gutter journalism, a Chicago newspaper alleged that a kerosene lamp had been kicked over by a cow while it was being milked. Mrs O'Leary and her cow were publicly blamed across the US for the catastrophe. It was more than twenty-five years later that the reporter who wrote the story admitted making it up, and another 100 years before the city council passed a motion formally exonerating the lady and the beast.

Over the first half of the nineteenth century, the technology of heating coal to make gas advanced sufficiently for the streets of many European and American cities to be illuminated to a degree by gas lamps. However, the light was pretty feeble, and the lamps deposited quantities of black muck, making them unsuitable for domestic use. The situation was crying out for a stroke – or multiple strokes – of genius. The rival and complementary work of two great inventors – one British, one American – met that need, and the result was electric lighting, which changed everything.

The British innovator, Joseph Swan, had begun working on a prototype light bulb as early as 1850, when he was a mere stripling of twenty-two. The problem he wrestled with was that the filament would only work effectively in a vacuum, and the means to engineer a proper vacuum did not exist. The invention of the vacuum pump by the German scientist Hermann Sprengel, and its use by William (later Sir William) Crookes to develop the Crookes Tube made it possible to achieve a near perfect vacuum within a glass bulb. Joseph Swan resumed his work, and in 1879 was able to demonstrate his incandescent lamp with its carbon filament in front of a large and appreciative audience in Newcastle.

In New York, the American, Thomas Edison, was moving in the same direction by a somewhat different path. Swan's lamp was suitable for the homes of rich people able to afford their own electricity supply. Edison's ambition was to create a system capable of lighting many homes at once. In 1878, he convinced investors, including J. P. Morgan and members of the Vanderbilt family, to put money into the Edison Electric Illuminating Company. The following year, he demonstrated his own incandescent light bulb – which was very similar to Joseph Swan's – with the prophecy: 'We will make electricity so cheap that only the rich will burn candles.'

He and Swan followed each other's work with close and jealous interest. Swan wrote to his rival in generous terms:

> I had the mortification one fine morning of finding you on my track and in several particulars ahead of me – but now I think I have shot ahead of you and yet I feel there is almost an infinity of detail to be wrought out in the large application now awaiting development and that your inventive genius as well as my own will find very ample room for exercise in carrying out this gigantic work that awaits execution.

And so it came to pass. Having battled each other over patents for a time, these two remarkable men came together to establish the Edison Swan Electric Light Company, known as Ediswan. In Britain, it sold light bulbs with a cellulose filament devised by Swan; in New York, Edison used his own filament made from bamboo. The first grand house in England to be fully lit by electric lamps was Cragside in Northumberland, owned by Swan's friend Sir William Armstrong, who declared that they presented 'a very beautiful and starlike appearance, not so bright as to pain the eye in passing and very efficient in lighting the way'. Other grand houses followed, including Tatton Park in Cheshire and Lanhydrock in Cornwall. In January 1883, *The Times* published a letter from the Conservative MP and brewing tycoon Octavius E. Coope, expressing his satisfaction at having gone over from gas to electricity. But he gave a clue as to why take-up was restricted – the annual cost of providing electricity from his generator to his 200 eighteen-candlepower lamps was £232, the equivalent of around £25,000 today.

In New York, the Edison Electric Light Co. established the world's first coal-fired power station in Pearl Street, and began laying cabling beneath the streets. By December 1882, the company had put down thirteen miles of cable and had 203 customers with 3,144 lamps. Ten years later, there were fewer than 10,000 users, and the company was steadily losing money. Installing the cabling was prohibitively expensive, and the new technology was eclipsed by the much improved gas lighting made possible by the invention of the gas mantle by the Austrian chemist Carl Auer von Welsbach in the 1880s. Although hot and dirty, gas mantle lamps burned as brightly as Edison and Swan's incandescent light bulbs and were very much cheaper.

In the end, electric lighting triumphed over gas, but – because of the cost of the infrastructure – the victory was a long time coming. In Britain, most streetlighting was by gas until the 1950s, although by then electricity was the norm for domestic lighting as a result of the establishment of the National Grid in 1936 and the subsequent spread of its network across the country. In America, twenty per cent of homes were electrified by 1920, but the spread away from the towns and cities was very slow – by 1935, ninety per cent of rural homes still used gas.

Now our world is lit day and night, and darkness is banished. The circadian rhythms that dictated the lives of our ancestors have been thrust into the shadows. The notion of rising with the sun and going to bed when it sinks below the horizon is no more applicable to our existence than a proposal to go and hunt a woolly mammoth. Even among those who question the idea of social progress, very few would willingly exchange the home illuminated by the flick of a switch with one dependent on the sickly, evil-smelling glow of a tallow candle.

In Old Order Amish communities in America, lighting is generally provided by kerosene lamps. Electricity is used, but connection to a central grid is forbidden. This rejection is one part of the Amish creed of separation. Donald Kraybill, the pre-eminent American authority on the Amish and other Anabaptist groups, reported an Amish elder telling him: 'Electric would lead to worldliness. What would come with electric? All the things we don't need . . . the Amish are human, you know.'

As for light-bulb technology, it has marched on in step with the relentless creep of cabling: tungsten filaments, frosted glass, neon, soft light, halogen, fluorescent tubes. Now halogen bulbs, standard for so long, have been elbowed out of the way by LEDs (light-emitting diodes), and the filaments devised by the fertile minds of Joseph Swan and

Thomas Edison are being relegated to luminescent history. Such is progress, reflected in the rich – some would say bewildering – choice available on the shelves of Heath & Watkins.

IN OUR SHOP, the close neighbours of the light bulbs are the sandpaper, the masking tape and the Rawlplugs. All three are hardware essentials and steady sellers. Anyone who does any DIY at any level will need them. They are unglamorous but indispensable. Sandpaper smooths the edges of wood; masking tape makes it possible to apply paint without it getting where it is not wanted; Rawlplugs give screws traction in places where they would otherwise be useless. They all contribute significantly in our efforts to improve our homes, but I think it's fair to say we tend to take them for granted, not thinking how difficult it would be without them. Each is the product of some very clever thinking on the part of an ingenious innovator to whom all DIYers owe a debt of gratitude.

Pieces of paper with sand or tiny fragments of glass glued to them to rub down wood were in use two centuries ago, and were recommended in John Nicholson's 1825 manual *The Operative Mechanic and British Machinist*. A patent was granted in Britain in 1833 to John Oakey, who had developed his own sandpaper while working as an apprentice piano-maker in London and went on to create a good business out of abrasives. A year later, an American version, called glass paper but actually made using pulverised quartz, was patented by Isaac Fisher of Springfield, Vermont. In his book *Turning and Mechanical Manipulation*, published in 1843, John Jacob Holtzapffel referred to sandpaper being made 'with common sand and of only one degree of coarseness but in other respects exactly like glass paper'. It was subsequently adapted for machine use – the Egan Co. of Cincinnati advertised a formidable engine called a 'drum sander' in their catalogue of 1886.

The snag with this sandpaper was that it had to be dry, and that it produced an unwholesome volume of dust particles that were inevitably inhaled by the operator. This failing was addressed by the strange and subtle mind of Francis Gurney Okie, a maker of printer's inks in Philadelphia. In 1920, Okie contacted William L. McKnight, vice-president of the Minnesota Mining and Manufacturing Co. (later 3M) to ask for samples of their abrasive grits. McKnight eventually hired Okie to work on his ideas for a water-resistant sandpaper. The result was Wet-or-Dry sandpaper, launched in 1921 and an almost immediate commercial hit. The beauty of Wet-or-Dry was that, with its garnet surface, it lasted well, smoothed well, and caught much of the dust, greatly reducing the risk to health.

It was eagerly embraced by the burgeoning automotive industry, and it made 3M a fortune. Okie himself retired from the company in the 1930s and spent much of the rest of his very long life (he died in 1975 aged ninety-five) at his home beside White Bear Lake, composing mystical poetry using the alphanumerical cypher known as Gematria. This allots a numerical value to each letter, and requires that each line must add up to an unvarying total chosen by the writer. The number chosen by Okie was 869, because that was the aggregate in the line 'He That Hath Understanding' in the Book of Revelation. The lines Okie composed that met the test were retained in piles of yellow foolscap; the order in which they were arranged to make finished poems seems to have been arbitrary.

One of Francis Okie's younger colleagues at 3M was Richard Gurney Drew. He began there as a lowly lab technician and then graduated to the sandpaper project. Part of his job was to take samples to car makers, and he became accustomed to hearing them complain bitterly about the problems they had in painting two-tone colour schemes. They used butcher's paper or newspaper stuck on with surgical cloth tape to mask one area while they sprayed the other, but removing the masking often left an unsightly mess of adhesive or bits of paper that then had to be scraped off.

Drew went to the lab and experimented with applying some of the adhesives Okie had been working with to paper tape. He found that a combination of wood glue with glycerine laid on kraft paper (the kind used for paper bags) would stick down well, but could be detached without leaving any adhesive behind. It could also be produced in handy rolls, which the company marketed as Scotch Brand masking tape (3M company legend has it that an early sample was rejected by a car body painter with the words 'take that back to your Scotch bosses and tell them to put more adhesive on it'.) It was the answer to a prayer in the automotive industry, and was found to have many other useful applications, such as taping up parcels and labelling.

Richard Drew was not finished. Cellophane, a thin transparent sheet derived from cellulose, had been invented and patented by a Swiss chemist, Jacques Brandenberger, just before the First World War. After the war, a research chemist with DuPont, William Hale Charch, developed a lacquer to make Cellophane waterproof. It became the food packaging material of choice and earned DuPont many millions of dollars. Drew began experimenting with applying different combinations of glue to strips of Cellophane to make a transparent adhesive tape. In 1930, it was ready for the market, with the label Scotch Brand Cellulose Tape, later renamed Scotch Transparent Tape.

Scotch tape was an instant runaway commercial success. Like masking tape, it could be used for parcels and packages, but its transparency made it ideal for sticking torn pages and even bank notes together. The two rolls of sticky tape and Francis Okie's Wet-or-Dry sandpaper helped propel 3M towards becoming the giant multinational it is today (still producing more than five million miles of Scotch tape a year).

William McKnight, the vice-president and later chairman of 3M, who had hired Francis Okie and overseen the work of Richard Drew, learned an important lesson from their breakthroughs. McKnight had originally urged Drew to concentrate on sandpaper instead of fiddling around in the lab with strips of tape. As profits from Drew's invention soared, he came up with what he called 'the fifteen per cent policy', which encouraged researchers to spend that proportion of their time on pet projects. 'If you put fences around people, you get sheep,' McKnight sagely observed. His principle has been embraced to useful effect by some of the biggest names in Silicon Valley, including Google and Hewlett Packard.

Drew remained with 3M for more than forty years, heading the Products Fabrication Laboratory, known as Pro-Fab Lab, which came up with a range of money-earners including surgical tape, foam tape, decorative ribbon, face masks and respirators. He once said: 'What I really want is a creative person. You can always hire a PhD to take care of the detail.'

*

RICHARD DREW would have loved James Joseph Rawlings, who certainly did not have a PhD, but who found the answer to an age-old problem, which is as good today as it was when he hit on it. This was the problem: how to fix something quite heavy – say, a picture or a shelf of books – into a plaster wall? Until Rawlings came on the scene, the answer was to chisel out a square hole in the plaster and fill it as snugly as possible with a wooden bung, then screw into that. But there were obvious drawbacks – it was difficult to get the bung solid and flush with the wall, and the operation often damaged the surrounding plaster.

Rawlings and his brother ran a small plumbing and repair company in South Kensington, London. In 1910, he was hired by the British Museum to install electric fittings in the walls. They needed to be screwed into position as unobtrusively as possible. Rawlings went away to ponder the matter. Was there a way to expand whatever was inserted into the hole so that it would fit really tightly? He made a small plug of jute held together by glue with an opening to take the point of the screw. He made a hole roughly the same size as the plug and tapped it in until it was flush with the wall. Turning the screw into it until it was fully home had the effect of causing the plug to expand and secure itself tightly.

It worked. Of course it worked. It was a stroke of genius.

Rawlings called it the Rawlplug, registered it as a trade-mark, and obtained a patent in 1913. That gave him protection from competitors for fourteen years; he secured an extension to 1931 to compensate for the war years. Rawlings Brothers became the Rawlplug Company, with offices in Cromwell Road and a factory nearby. The little plug was a boon to builders and trade blossomed. The company invested heavily in advertising: 'The simplest to fix, the cheapest to buy, the firmest when fixed, invisible when in position', was one inducement splashed across the trade papers; another, rather snappier, was: 'Rawlplugs Never Let You Down'.

The Rawlplug Co. has continued to prosper. It introduced variations on James Joseph's original brainwave, including the Rawlbolt for heavy anchorage in concrete and masonry; all useful, but none as celebrated as their diminutive ancestor. James Joseph died a rich man at his home in a select part of Wimbledon in 1942 at the age of eighty-two. Much later, the fibre model of the Rawlplug was joined by a plastic version available in a range of cheery colours. The Rawlplug Co. was eventually taken under the umbrella of BPB (British Plasterboard) but continues to operate from a factory in Glasgow.

For a British DIYer, life without Rawlplugs is unimaginable (in the US, the name is hardly known, and the same device is referred to as a wall anchor). There is not a hardware shop in the land that does not stock them. When contemplating a wall and the question of how to fix something to it, the first word that springs to mind is: Rawlplug. But it is important to remember that even the Rawlplug is not a miracle-worker, and that it is possible to ask too much from them. This recalls what I still regard as – from a number of contenders – the most painful disaster in my patchy DIY life. It was a long time ago, but it still hurts.

There were two alcoves in one of our downstairs rooms, and I made the ill-fated decision to fill one of them with shelves to hold the cream of my collection of 700 or so books about fish and angling. As usual, my approach to the task was dictated by cheapskate cheeseparing rather than any aspiration to craftsmanship. I bought the metal uprights that I had used elsewhere, and the most inferior melamine-faced chipboard, arguing to myself that in an alcove it didn't matter in the least what the shelving was made of, because no one would be able to see it.

Having cut the chipboard to fit the space and marked where the supporting screws would go in, I set to work with drill and Rawlplug. As I tapped the little plastic plugs into the holes, it did fleetingly occur to me that they seemed to go in very easily compared with the other walls I had tackled. I believe I may also have heard an occasional rattle from within the wall and may have briefly wondered what the cause might be.

I finished the shelving and it looked good. I spent a happy couple of hours dusting the fishing books, admiring the covers, occasionally dipping into the text for a few moments, and then putting each volume in its rightful place according to alphabetical order: Adams and Aflalo at the top, followed by Barder and Chalmers, then Zane Grey and F. M. Halford, and so on. I do not recall how far through the alphabet I had got, but I know that I had just finished filling the bottom shelf and had stepped back to admire the effect when there was a series of rattling sounds from behind the shelving and the whole lot came away from the wall and collapsed around me. I was up to my knees in tales of great salmon and pike and fat trout landed and lost, and advice on entomology and the technical way to approach roach fishing.

And somewhere in the wreckage were the Rawlplugs.

## CHAPTER SIXTEEN

# If I Had a Plunger (and a Hammer)

THE PLUNGERS RESIDE upside down in one of the galvanised buckets on the floor at the far end of the shop, looking like a clump of elongated fungi, but with their cups inverted. They work in this way. The wooden handle is grasped and the cup placed over the plughole or down the lavatory, and then vigorously depressed several times. If you are in luck, there is a convulsive gurgle and the obstruction – whatever it may be – goes on its way.

According to internet pundits, its operation is dictated by Boyle's law governing the relationship between the volume of a gas and its pressure, although I do not, for the life of me, understand its application in this case. Certainly Robert Boyle, seventh son and fifteenth child of the Earl of Cork, did not have a plunger in mind when he published his findings in the 1660s, and it would be another two centuries before this invaluable device was introduced to a grateful world.

Blockages are one of the many inconveniences that complicate domestic life. Out of sight, out of mind is generally the principle – or lack of principle – that informs how we view the disposal of our waste and filth. It disappears from the lavatory bowl and the basin and the sink and the shower into a Stygian underworld that we prefer not to think about, policed by shadowy operatives in huge boots and protective overalls whose task is to keep the heaving mass of detritus moving along pipes and tunnels and down chutes and channels until it reaches a destination where even they do not have to think about it. Occasionally, faced by pale and grotesquely shaped crags and crevasses of congealed fat mixed with discarded wet wipes, condoms, nappy pads, sanitary towels and God knows what other species of foulness, they are forced to resort to high-pressure water jets to dislodge the greasy fatbergs. Somehow they keep the sewers open, but we do not care to know too much about their heroics.

Sometimes, we are compelled to deal with our own minor problems of disposal. The lavatory bowl obstinately refuses to empty, leaving turds to twist and turn like distantly glimpsed humpback whales. Grey, greasy water thick with coffee grinds and grains of rice and blobs of egg white slops against the sides of the kitchen sink and declines to leave the scene via the plug. Clods of hair caught in the shower outflow float like seaweed as the rising water threatens to invade the bathroom floor.

A few years ago, we had a problem known to plumbers as backing up, which afflicted the shower and lavatory in our downstairs bathroom. Raising the hatch in my office over the exit drain revealed a very bad situation – I will not go into detail. I tried extended rods, I tried feeding the garden hose along the pipes, I poked and prodded and gagged as the awful stench assailed my nostrils. In the end, we had to seek help from the professionals, who began by feeding a camera into the pipes. This showed the clay walls to have been invaded by what looked like mangrove roots but were, in fact, ordinary tree roots. They then sent an amazing machine into action that travelled along the subterranean pipe system, severing the roots and laying plastic lining as it went. With a whoosh and a rush, the backup said farewell and vanished.

That was an extreme case. Usually, the clearing of a blockage is pretty straightforward. It is said that a combination of bicarbonate of soda, vinegar and very hot water is effective. Shro stocks a range of chemical unblockers that have sodium hydroxide as their main component. but speaking for myself, I much prefer the magnificently simple and effective plunger.

Only this morning, taking a break from the chore of writing, I retrieved our plunger from its resting place beneath the kitchen sink and went to tackle one of the basins upstairs, where some slimy black agglomeration of nastiness had been causing trouble. I filled the basin half-full, thrust the suction cup over the plug hole and vigorously pumped a few times. There was a gurgle down below, a hiccup, a few bubbles, then a dimple as the water hastened away. I waved the plunger in triumph and Helen congratulated me on being so useful, which does not happen often.

We owe the genesis of this indispensable appliance to a New Yorker, John Savage Hawley, who developed what he called the 'elastic force-cup' while working for a confectionery firm and patented it in 1874. It drew the attention of the journal *Scientific American*, which described it as being 'for clearing the discharge pipes of wash bowls, bath tubs etc when they become partially or entirely blocked [. . .] the handle is forced down three or four times with a quick motion, the water beneath the cup is forced into the discharge pipe with a sudden impulse dislodging the obstruction.'

An advertisement appeared in the *Metal Worker: A Weekly Journal of the Stove, Tin, Plumbing and House Furnishing Trades* stating that 'the elastic force-cup will usually clear the pipe without difficulty and will always be found convenient wherever there are waste pipes'. They were available from 'Mr John S. Hawley, No. 144 Chambers St., N.Y.', but it seems Mr Hawley must have sold the rights, as in 1876, D. Hodgman and Co. were advertised as the sole manufacturers. Hawley moved on to start a confectionery business of his own. He acquired a partner, Herman W. Hoops, and they flourished with their patented line of 'chocolate candy cigars, old-fashioned liquorice, Union cream bonbons, genuine marshmallows' and other tooth-rotting delights.

In the 1880s, Hawley & Hoops moved to premises that eventually occupied almost an entire block on Mulberry Street, Jersey Street and Marion Street, and employed 800 workers. Hawley became a big name in the city, and was, according to one admiring writer, 'inscribed high on the roll of New York's prominent representatives of business [. . .] in control of one of the mammoth industrial concerns of that city and yet who is not without a large share of that deep human sympathy and Christ-like spirit [. . .]' In other words, having left the drain-unblocking scene far behind, John S. Hawley made a great deal of money and became an upright citizen, a regular worshipper at the Church of the Eternal Hope, and a philanthropist who funded the establishment of the Charlton Industrial School at Ballstone Lake in Saratoga County (described as 'A Christian Family Home for Wayward and Hopeless Boys', it closed after being destroyed by fire in 1938, but subsequently reopened as a girls' school and is still going today). He wrote several religious books – including

*Fearless Bible Reading: Tradition v. Truth* and *Creeds and Religious Beliefs as They Appear to a Plain Business Man* – and eventually became a Christian Scientist, dying in San Diego in 1913. The company that made his fortune remained in New York, manufacturing sweet delights including chocolate buffaloes, lobsters, alligators, violins, cigars and pipes until 1952, when it was taken over and incorporated into M&M Mars ('M&Ms Melt in the Mouth Not in the Hand').

His great pipe-clearing invention continued to be known as 'the elastic force-cup' for a while. In the 1890s, a very similar device using the same principle appeared on the market described as 'the plumber's friend', a name that is still current. It is an etymological mystery why and how the word 'plunger' – originally applied to a very different type of pipe-cleaning tool – came to attach itself to the appliance we know and cherish today.

THE PLUNGERS are in one bucket. In another one, close by, are the hammers. The selection includes claw hammers, cross and straight pein hammers (also peen), club hammers (sometimes known as lump hammers) and mallets with hard rubber faces. The plunger is a pretty lowly utensil, whereas by rights the hammers belong in the main tool section, which is displayed on the wall right up to the ceiling. On the top shelf, in a position of eminence in keeping with their cost, are the Black & Decker power tools in their black-and-orange boxes. Below, suspended from hooks on the peg board, are ranks of screwdrivers, spanners, Stanley knives, pliers, scrapers, chisels and other familiar tools. Others are less familiar to me – the spokeshaver, for instance, the tapered reamer, the holesaw arbor, the torx key set.

But they all have their uses, presumably, and together they compose a formidable armoury. The hardware shop does not make much money from selling tools, for the obvious reason that – unlike light bulbs or compostable food bags, for example, or indeed electric kettles – they last a long time; or should do. But a hardware shop must, absolutely, carry a full range of standard tools; otherwise it cannot reasonably call itself a hardware shop.

The hammers are excluded from the main tool display because they are too heavy for the hooks and the peg board. But perhaps there is also a subtle acknowledgment of distinction here, because the hammer could be said to be somewhat lacking in creative potential. It is undoubtedly useful, even indispensable, but it is somewhat one-dimensional in application. With the hammer, it is all force and no nuance. And as well as being a problem-solver, it can be a problem-maker (witness the blackened thumbnail where you missed the metal nail, the shattered batten that you hit too hard, the bent nail that will not straighten).

The hammer did not require inventing. It is the same in its essentials as the one fashioned with a lump of stone, a stick and some twine by our Stone Age ancestors 30,000 years ago. It becomes interesting when we consider the hammer, not as an object but as a means to many ends, and how we think of it, and where it fits into our notion of ourselves as makers, repairers and fixers.

Karl Marx famously returned from a visit to investigate industrial conditions in Birmingham and noted that, in this one city, 'five hundred varieties of hammers are produced and not only is each adapted to one process, but several varieties often serve exclusively for the different operations in one and the same process'. Marx argued that this multiplicity of hammer types illustrated how 'the implements of labour' were adapted to specific functions. It is unlikely that Marx was much of a DIY man himself, otherwise he might have considered this figure of 500 more deeply. Had he inspected all the different hammers more closely, he would have realised that there was no standard system for naming them; and that the same hammer made for the same specific use might have half a dozen different names according to the whim of the maker. It might also have occurred to him that he had been on the receiving end of some Brummie hammer-maker's idea of a joke. But then, he was always more of a theorist than a nail-banger.

Professor Henry Petroski, a teacher of engineering as well as a practical engineer and a prolific writer on engineering history and design, considered this matter of Marx and the 500 hammers in his splendid and endlessly stimulating book *The Evolution of Useful Things*. The point Petroski makes is that if you have only one hammer, you are likely to use it for various jobs, for some of which – such as getting lids back on paint pots or fixing very small tacks – it is far from ideal. 'If I were to try and accomplish 500 different things with a single hammer,' he says, 'I might find at least 500 faults and invent more than 500 variations.'

This brings us to the place of the hammer in philosophy, and specifically to the Law of the Instrument. This is defined as a cognitive bias associated with over-reliance on a single tool and is commonly illustrated thus: 'If all you have is a hammer, you treat everything as if it were a nail.' The saying has been appropriated, adapted and attributed far and wide, often presented as a remarkable specimen of deep thinking.

Its provenance has been pleasingly untangled by a computer scientist, Gregory F. Sullivan, who – under the pseudonym Garson O'Toole – runs the website quoteinvestigator.com. Its first iteration, according to Sullivan, was in a Victorian periodical, *Once A Week*: 'Give a boy a hammer and chisel; show him how to use them; at once he begins to hack the doorpost, to take off the corners of a shutter and window frames until you teach him a better use for them [. . .]'

It seems improbable that this obscure reference was known to Abraham Kaplan, Professor of Philosophy at the University of California, Los Angeles, when he addressed a conference of the American Educational Research Association in February 1962. The professor was talking about how to choose the best methods for research and observed that just because a method is easily available, or because the researcher has been trained in it, it offers no assurance that it is appropriate in all situations. He cited what he called Kaplan's Law of the Instrument: 'Give a boy a hammer and everything he meets needs to be pounded.'

A year later, Silvan Tomkins, one of the editors of an influential book called *Computer Simulation of Personality: Frontiers of Psychological Theory*, wrote: 'If one has a hammer one tends to look for nails, and if one has a computer with storage capacity but no feelings, one is more likely to concern oneself with remembering and problem solving than with loving and hating.'

Abraham Kaplan may or may not have read Tomkins' comments, but he was evidently attached to his Law of the Instrument, as it appears again in his best-known work, *The Conduct of Inquiry: Methodology for Behavioral Science*, which was published in 1964. It may have been somewhat galling for him to have his dictum borrowed and adapted by the psychologist Abraham Mallow in his 1966 book *The Psychology of Science: A Reconnaissance* to read thus: 'It is tempting, if the only tool you have is a hammer, to treat everything as if it were a nail.' It is in this form that the saying has achieved its position as a modern proverb – indeed, it is often referred to as Mallow's Hammer.

Whoever gets the credit for it, abiding by the Law of the Instrument can have unfortunate consequences. A long time ago, my first wife reported that the control knob on the shower was sticking, probably because of a build-up of limescale. I went to investigate. She was right; it wouldn't turn and needed to be shifted. I went to my toolbox, surveyed its contents and concluded that force was the answer. I picked up the hammer and returned to the shower. I tapped the knob a few times. No movement. I tapped a little harder. Still no movement. Irritation gathered like a cloud. More force was obviously required.

The knob shattered. A plumber had to be called. The installation of a new turning mechanism cost over £100, money we could ill afford. I learned a lesson that day.

## Chapter Seventeen

# If I Had a Screwdriver
# (or a Spirit Level)

THERE ARE TWO BASIC types of screwdriver that are stocked in most hardware shops, including ours. One is the slotted screwdriver – also known as a flat-head because of the shape of the tip – which is used with slotted screws. Its drawback, familiar to anyone who has ever thrown down their screwdriver with a violent oath and clutched their wounded finger, is that the tip or head of the screwdriver tends to slip from the slot when force is increased to try to turn a recalcitrant screw. In addition, screws of that type are very difficult to get out once they have been in place for a few years, because the definition of the slot degenerates and the head of the screwdriver cannot obtain sufficient purchase to turn it.

The Phillips cross-head or cruciform screwdriver and screws came into existence to address these problems, which they do. Their flaw is that, under force, the cross-head recess tends to flatten, causing the head to slip. You then tighten your grip on the handle, grimace and press harder, which flattens it further. The law of diminishing returns kicks in. It may be that you achieve full penetration, but sometimes you don't, and then the head no longer grips enough to get the damn thing to go in or come out. This is maddening.

The story of the screwdriver has been told with considerable elegance in a book called *One Good Turn: A Natural History of the Screwdriver and the Screw* by Witold Rybczynski, the Professor of Urbanism at Pennsylvania University and a prolific writer about culture and architecture. Rybczynski is an amateur woodworker himself, and he clearly spent many happy hours combing through old books and ancient texts in search of early references to this most useful of tools. He believes the implement itself may have been a French invention – it first appears as a '*tourne-vis*' in the *Dictionnaire Général de la Langue Francaise* in 1723. But screws had evidently been around much earlier; there is a reference to them in the *Medieval Housebook (Das Mittelalterliche Hausbuch)* compiled at Wolfegg Castle in southern Germany in the late fifteenth century. They would have been in use for an unknown period before that – and where there was a screw, there must have been something to turn it.

Over the succeeding centuries, there were advances in screw-making technology, but the essential features of the slotted screwdriver could not really be improved upon and remained unaltered (as they do today). But its failings were clear, and in the evolution of technology, failings inevitably lead to solutions, or at least alternatives.

John Frearson was born in Leicestershire in 1811 and learned his trade as a mechanic in Manchester, where he was radicalised politically and became an ardent campaigner for the ideals of Chartism. He emigrated to America and made his living there for a while before returning to set up a workshop in Birmingham, where he and his father specialised in making hooks and eyes for women's dresses. In 1857, he was granted a patent for a cruciform screw-head that pre-dated the world-conquering Phillips by eighty years. Some years later, he developed an improved model with a deeper recess, which was then granted patent rights in the US and Canada. An American company, Reed & Prince of Worcester, Massachusetts, subsequently bought the exclusive rights to the Frearson screw-head, by which time its inventor was dead and forgotten. It became and remained popular with boat-builders because of the amount of torque that could be applied to it, but failed to get the attention it deserved in the wider world. The Frearson is still acknowledged by boat-builders in the US and Canada as the supreme screw, and a few niche makers can provide them.

At the start of the twentieth century, most woodworkers had no choice but the slotted screw and screwdriver. In his indispensable manual *The Handyman's Enquire Within*, Paul Hasluck featured a London screwdriver with a flattened handle, a Cabinet screwdriver with an oval handle and a gimlet-handled screwdriver, which he said should be more widely used because of the extra power that could be exercised with a horizontal handle. But the only screw was the slotted screw.

Across the Atlantic, in Ontario, Canada, a salesman for a Philadelphia tools company, Peter Lymburner Robertson, was pondering the drawbacks of the slotted screwdriver after cutting his hand with one during a demonstration to a potential customer. In 1909, he patented his design for a screw-head with a square-socket drive 'with chamfered edges, slightly tapering sides and a pyramidal bottom', as Witold Rybczynski described it. Its beauty was that, once inserted, the screwdriver head could not slip. It had nowhere to go, and the fit was so snug that it could be used one-handed or even held in the air. Its major advantage from the manufacturing point of view was that the heads could be cold-formed (i.e., stamped with a die at ambient temperature), which was quick, easy and cheap.

Robertson established a screw-making factory in Milton, Ontario, in 1908, and little by little, the unique attributes of his method were recognised in Canada. His eyes were raised to wider horizons and, in 1912, having obtained British patents, he came to England and set up Recess Screws Ltd in Gillingham, Kent. With the advertising slogan 'The Screw that Grips the Drive', the business was performing solidly when war broke out and the government took over the factory to make armaments, mainly mortars and grenade pins.

Disillusioned, Robertson cut his ties with the British company and returned home to look for new markets. Henry Ford was already using the Robertson screw and was the major customer for the output from the factory in Milton. In the 1920s, US car production was booming, and Robertson went to Detroit to talk to Ford about how to meet the soaring demand. He was evidently no pushover and would not accede to Ford's demand for control over how and where the screws should be produced. In the context of the history of the screwdriver, it was a fateful disagreement. Robertson went back to Milton and remained there running his factory until his death in 1951; meanwhile, over in Portland, Oregon, the answer to Henry Ford's pressing need was taking shape.

An otherwise obscure car mechanic, John P. Thompson, had devised a screw that observed the same principle as Frearson's, but with a less defined cruciform in the centre of the head, and a screwdriver to go with it. He attempted to arouse the interest of manufacturers, but they found there was a problem with punching the recess into the screw-head, and in the end he sold the rights to a fellow Portlander, Henry Frank Phillips, at that time the boss of a copper-mining company. Phillips obtained patents and funding to set up the Phillips Screw Co., and went back to the screw-makers who had told Thompson the cross-head could not be done to urge them to think again. One of them, Eugene Clark, President of the American Screw Co., based in Providence, Rhode Island, was persuaded. Modifications were made to the design to enable the head of the screw to be cold-punched and it went into production.

The first major customer was General Motors, which began using the Phillips screw to assemble its range of Cadillacs. Within a few years, the screw had been embraced by all other car makers, as well as the rail and aviation industries. Business boomed at the American Screw Co., while Henry Phillips himself was busy making a fortune by selling manufacturing licences – most significantly to the British firm Guest, Keen and Nettlefold, the biggest suppliers of screws, nuts, bolts and other fasteners in the world (later, the giant components multinational GKN).

'I go where I'm driven without fuss and with the minimum of effort', was the slogan dreamed up for the Phillips screw in Britain. The principle behind it – that the screw would self-centre and give secure grip – ensured that it became first choice wherever power tools were the norm. It remains universally dominant, even though subsequent refinements to the design – such as the Pozidriv and the Torq-set – have replaced it in some specialist fields. Every DIYer has Phillips screwdrivers and uses Phillips screws and curses them because sooner or later the cruciform recess flattens and the screwdriver tip no longer grips sufficiently to turn the screw. This intensely annoying outcome, called 'camming out' by those who know what they are talking about, explains why the Robertson screw retains its toehold in the screw-turning world.

It is commonly available in hardware shops in Canada and – along with the Frearson – is sought out by boat-builders and woodworkers all over North America. Witold Rybczynski prefers the Robertson to the Phillips when he is engaged at his workbench. He says it is faster and much less prone to cam-out – and 'no matter how old, or rusty or painted over, a Robertson screw can always be unturned'.

I HAVE ONE big screwdriver with a handsome bottle-green handle and a tip too massive for any screw I have ever used or am ever likely to use, but it excels in brute-force tasks involving chiselling, splintering, levering and prising. I would miss it if it went missing, but I have no particular feelings towards the rest of my screwdrivers.

My spirit level is another matter. You cannot really call a spirit level a tool, even though mine hangs behind my toolbox (no longer across the top of it), and in the shop the small ones are on the peg board beside the spanner sets and the ratchets, and the big ones in a bucket on the floor beside the hammers. The spirit level is defined as an instrument for measuring, in this case horizontality. You do not need one very often, but when you do, it is very satisfying in its function.

When I was constructing my raised beds for growing vegetables, I was not really interested in achieving extreme neatness, but I did want the gravel boards making up the sides to be level. The easiest way was to make sure the tops of the posts at the corners and in the middle of the longer sides were level, and then to nail or screw the gravel boards so that the tops of each were flush. I would bang in the posts until they looked reasonably level to my eye, then lay a plank on the tops of two of them, put the spirit level on the plank and tap the posts with the lump hammer to get the height exactly right. I liked the silence of the spirit level between the thuds as hammer struck post, and the way the bubble would edge sideways with each tap until it came to rest in the central vial, equidistant between the indicator lines. It sat there, motionless and at peace, testifying to my ability to get at least one part of the job done properly.

In the histories of tools and useful instruments, the invention of the spirit level is credited to a curiously named Frenchman, Melchisédech Thévenot, who was Louis XIV's royal librarian. Called *un niveau à bulle d'air*, it seems to have been some kind of vial containing water or alcohol with a viewing lens, mounted on a stone ruler, although it is not at all clear if Thévenot actually made one or merely conceptualised it. He certainly described it in correspondence in the early 1660s with three much more distinguished scientists of the age: Robert Hooke in England, Christian Huygens in Holland, and Vincenzo Viviani in Florence. Hooke and Huygens seem to have devised their own versions of it, but the spirit level did not come into general use until much later. In the meantime, seekers after horizontal exactitude had to be content with the old Roman method of placing a glass container partially filled with water on the surface and checking the level of the liquid.

Thévenot evidently had one of those restless minds so characteristic of that age of scientific discovery. In addition to looking after the king's books, he dabbled in astronomy and magnetism, learned numerous languages, including English, Turkish and Arabic, and – most notably – wrote the first book about how to swim, translated into English as *The Art of Swimming*. 'Lie down gently on your belly,' Thévenot wrote, 'keep your head and neck upright, your breast advancing forward, your back bending, withdraw your legs from the bottom and immediately stretch them out again, strike out your arms forward and spread them apart, draw them in again [. . .] you will find this way easy and pleasant.' As a description of basic breaststroke, it can hardly be improved upon, even if the reasons advanced by Thévenot for learning to swim – to save yourself when shipwrecked and to be able to escape across a river when being pursued by an enemy – may seem less applicable today.

In time, the superiority of the spirit level in establishing the horizontal came to be recognised. The early models were generally banana-shaped with a bubble in each upraised end. Paul Hasluck, in *The Handyman's Enquire Within*, illustrates three of this type, but also one that is very similar in its principles to the one I use, except that it has two vials filled with alcohol. The development of the single vial spirit level, with its single and beautiful bubble, was the inspiration of Henry Ziemann of Mukwonago, Wisconsin, who patented it in the 1920s and established the Empire Level Co. to make and sell it.

Was Henry Ziemann a lover of poetry? Or even, like Francis Okie of sandpaper fame, a composer of poetry? I have no idea, but there is clearly a poetic quality to his invention. Seamus Heaney called one of his collections of verse *The Spirit Level*, although – rather disappointingly – none of the poems has that name or references the implement. Another poet, the American David Barber, also published a collection called *The Spirit Level*, and the title poem is actually about his father's – I presume it is his father's – workshop, where 'you kept your tools sequestered out of sight'. The spirit level – 'so ingenious / in the essence of its unvarnished purpose' – becomes a toy shotgun for the boy, but:

> I found it even more ingratiating
> for what it was, how its stripped-down upshot
> was both transparent and inscrutable.
> Winking in their banded tubes of tinted glass,
> Those emerald bubbles never burst
> or vanished [. . .]

# CHAPTER EIGHTEEN

# The Indispensables

IT BELONGS TO another age, almost another world: that moment when the young woman destined to be Princess of Wales stepped in front of the cameras at Balmoral to show her shy smile and her idea of what a princess should wear on such an occasion. She wore a Fair Isle sweater over a pale polo-neck top, moleskin breeks and a pair of green Hunter wellington boots with red socks peeping over the top. Within a week, production of the boot at the Hunter factory near Dumfries – which had been jogging along at one day a week – was upped to five days, and still they couldn't meet the demand. The green welly brigade was born that day, and it is marching still.

In our village, anyone who does anything outside needs wellies, which means our shop must have them. Actually, at the time of writing, the brand (absolutely not Hunters) made in China that Shro has always stocked are in disgrace, and the few remaining pairs have been banished to the uppermost shelf, where they stand like children on detention. There have been complaints about the quality; customers have brought them back, saying they let the water in, and Shro has had to replace them. She hates that – not the replacing but letting her customers down. It quite spoils her day when it happens, and when there is a pattern, she becomes unforgiving towards the product. She is selling the ones she has left with a warning and is looking for a new supplier.

HERE IS A SPARKLING example of royal humour. A youngish Queen Victoria had given an audience to an elderly Duke of Wellington and had commented on the close-fitting calfskin boots he was wearing under his trousers. 'They call them Wellingtons, ma'am,' the duke said with proper humility.

'How absurd,' the Queen replied vivaciously. 'Where, I should like to know, would they find a PAIR of Wellingtons?'

It is pleasant to think of the grizzled face of the victor of Waterloo, the man who saved us from Boney, crinkling in amusement at this sally.

At the duke's funeral procession, on 18 November 1852, the forward carriage was followed by a riderless horse with a pair of the duke's boots in the stirrups. It must have made stirring theatre, but those Wellingtons had nothing except the name in common with the black or green rubber (or, for the cheap option, PVC) boots in which we stride across wet fields or slosh down muddy lanes today. They were calf- or ankle-length, leather, snug-fitting, suitable for riding and for informal indoor occasions. They became very popular among well-bred gentlemen and those who wished to be thought of as gentlemen; they were comfortable, practical and self-advertisingly British.

In another arena altogether, technology was on the move. In 1823, a Scottish chemist, Charles Macintosh, obtained a patent for his process of treating fabric with a solution of rubber and ammonia, using coal tar as a solvent, in order to make it waterproof. At about the same time, but quite separately, Thomas Hancock – born in Wiltshire, resident in London – devised a machine to slice rubber into shreds, which, when heated, could then be pressed into blocks or sheets. Hancock called it the pickle, but it was more generally known as the masticator. He and Macintosh were aware of each other's innovations and could see advantages in cooperation. Eventually, they pooled their wits and resources and became partners in the great company Charles Macintosh & Co., making the coats and capes that immortalised the name.

Wearing one of their products when it was raining was much preferable to not, but it had its limitations. When it was hot, the coat or cape became sticky, and when it was very cold, it stiffened. Correcting this defect in rubber had become a consuming preoccupation of an American inventor, Charles Goodyear, who was toiling night and day in various makeshift laboratories, trying all manner of chemical treatments for it. By the time Hancock and Macintosh had joined forces, Goodyear had already spent several years on his experiments. He was an ill-starred individual, attracting misfortune on a grand scale, and his loyal wife and children languished in poverty as he went from business failure to business failure in his quest to devise a treatment that would make the rubber stable in varying temperatures.

Exposure to nitric acid and lead oxide fumes had undermined his already delicate health, but Goodyear was nothing if not persistent. In 1839 he discovered, almost by accident, that heating rubber with sulphur caused its composition to change significantly. It became more rigid and durable, and – crucially – this transformation was irreversible. He called the process vulcanisation and obtained a US patent.

He also obtained a partner, Horace Cutler, and, within a few years, they were turning out hundreds of pairs of rubber boots a day from their factory in Springfield, Massachusetts, as well as vulcanised clothing, life-preservers and other rubber goods. At last, Goodyear seemed to have turned the corner from poverty to prosperity. But he was a driven man, and for his great innovation to achieve its full potential, it had to conquer the British market as well. Cutler proved to be a wholly unsatisfactory partner; they fell out, and, in 1842, Goodyear dispatched an Englishman of his acquaintance, Stephen Moulton, to England with samples of the vulcanised rubber and instructions to show them to Thomas Hancock. Goodyear told Moulton to demand £50,000 for the rights.

At this point, the clear line of the rubber narrative becomes blurred in a fog of competing claims made thicker by disputes over patents and nationalistic bias. Champions of Goodyear assert that he invented vulcanisation and that Thomas Hancock – having laid his hands on the samples that Moulton showed him – reverse-engineered the process to claim credit for himself. Advocates for Hancock insist he was an upright man and an honest dealer; and that, having waited for months in expectation of Goodyear being granted a British patent, he eventually embarked on his own series of experiments, including treating the rubber with sulphur, and at last came up with what he called 'the change'.

Goodyear's difficulty lay in a key requirement of British patent law. Within six months of filing an application, the applicant had to produce a full specification describing the process in sufficient detail 'for a workman to be able to pursue the invention'. He did not, or could not, reach that threshold; Hancock did. In 1843, Hancock was granted the patent, and when he came to write the story – under the catchy title *A Personal Narrative of the Origin and Progress of Caoutchouc or India Rubber* – he did not mention Charles Goodyear.

Goodyear became enmeshed in other troubles. His erstwhile partner, Horace Cutler, had been seduced by a deeply unscrupulous rival, Horace Day, with the promise of untold riches if he would pass on the secrets of vulcanisation. He did not resist the temptation. Horace Day was the embodiment of the fast-talking, big-spending, corner-cutting entrepreneur, and through his India Rubber Co., he swiftly made a fortune off the back of Goodyear's discovery.

Goodyear struck back through the courts. A succession of legal disputes culminated in the notorious Great India Rubber Case of 1852. Goodyear's chief advocate was none other than the great American statesman, Daniel Webster, then close to death and in desperate need of the enormous fee of $10,000 offered if he would take the case, with a win bonus of $6,000. Opposite him, representing Day, was another US congressman and celebrated courtroom performer, Rufus Choate. It was to be Webster's final tour-de-force, and he did not disappoint the cream of New Jersey society, who packed into the courthouse in Trenton.

According to the newspaper accounts, Rufus Choate scaled the heights of eloquence in his account of the wrongs and indignities inflicted on his virtuous and unjustly maligned client. But Webster soared even higher, and prevailed. In his ruling in favour of Goodyear, the judge stated:

'I am entirely satisfied that he is the original inventor of the process of vulcanizing rubber and that he is not only entitled to the relief he asks but all the merits and benefits of that discovery.' It was the triumph he deserved, but profited him little, as the defeated Horace Day resorted to every available subterfuge to avoid paying his dues.

Goodyear decided on one more great venture to promote the cause to which he had given his life. He travelled to Europe, and in Paris met an American businessman, Hiram Hutchinson, to whom he sold the licence to manufacture the rubber. Hutchinson set up a factory in the small town of Châlette-sur-Loing, south of Paris, to make rubber boots, which he sold under the name 'A L'Aigle' (later reduced to l'Aigle and then Aigle, and still selling today). Hutchinson's business boomed, and he soon opened a second manufacturing base in Germany. Typically, Goodyear ended up spending time in a debtors' prison in Paris before returning home to die in 1860, an impoverished invalid.

'Few men,' William Woodruff wrote succinctly in his *History of the British Rubber Industry*, 'have given so much and received so little.' Thirty-eight years after his death, the Goodyear Tire and Rubber Company was named in his honour, a fine acknowledgment of his contribution to the advancement of rubber technology. The man himself had a martyr's philosophy: 'I am not disposed to complain that I have planted and others have gathered the fruits. A man has cause for regret only when he sows and no one reaps.'

A great harvest was indeed reaped in many fields. An anonymous journalist reporting on the Great India Rubber Case for the *Scientific American* journal described in breathless prose the 'countless uses of this singular product':

In the forms of boots and shoes it protects the fairy feet that trip lightly over the wet pavements [. . .] it becomes part of the costume of the rough lumberman or of the Californian miner in the gold diggings [. . .] it forms the powerful but elastic and luxurious spring on which the railroad car loaded with a hundred passengers rushes from city to city [. . .] it is moulded into the delicate billiard cushion on the smooth green table where Phelan [Michael Phelan, the champion US billiards player of the day] bids the rolling balls follow his unerring cue [. . .]

And that was all before the advent of the bicycle and the automobile tyre.

Among those who picked up Charles Goodyear's rubber baton were a New Jersey businessman, Henry Lee Norris, and his partner, Spencer Thomas Parmelee. They bought a Goodyear licence and decided to establish their manufacturing base in Scotland. They found a suitable site on the outskirts of Edinburgh, at Castle Mills on the Union Canal. They called it the North British Rubber Co., and began to make boots, coats, hot-water bottles, combs and golf balls for domestic consumers, as well as tyres and conveyor belts for industry. By 1865, 600 workers were employed at the factory. The company increased its range to include cartridge tubing and gunsight covers for the armaments sector, as well as surgical sheeting, collapsible baths and even a special waterproof suit for ministers wishing to conduct full-immersion baptisms.

But the cornerstone was the black rubber boot. With the outbreak of war in 1914, the War Office commissioned the North British Rubber Co. - by now employing 9,000 workers - to provide a waterproof boot for the soldiers in the trenches. Production was sustained night and day, seven days a week, and almost 1.2 million pairs were dispatched to the battlefields. It was a similar story in the Second World War: eighty per cent of production was war-related, including ground sheets and lifebelts as well as boots. The wellington extended its tread well beyond the arenas of conflict; farm labourers, miners, dockers, navvies, anyone working outside in the wet, all wore the thick-soled, wide-topped black rubber boot branded as the Argyll. Its slogan was: 'Stronger in the leg, tougher in the tread.'

Post-war, the company moved to a new complex near Dumfries, and in 1954 introduced the first green boots, which they called Hunters. The Hunter had the same shape as the Argyll and failed to make much of an impression – until a new, narrower version was launched. This was marketed as a sporting boot and was worn by gamekeepers and beaters and the like. The style was adopted by those higher up the social scale. Queen Elizabeth II and Prince Philip, the Duke of Edinburgh were photographed in them at Balmoral, and Princess Anne commissioned a pair of black Hunters to wear when she was competing at the Olympics.

Then came the Lady Diana moment, and – even though the North British Rubber Co. and its successor, Uniroyal, have long since vanished from the Scottish manufacturing landscape, and Hunter boots are now made in Asia – the green welly's place as part of the look of the countryside remains unchallenged.

CHARLES GOODYEAR was a tragic example of a visionary who – through bad luck, ill health and temperamental issues – strived and failed to gain the recognition and rewards that his genius warranted. Other innovators in other fields have striven and succeeded and become rich and deservedly celebrated. But throughout the history of technological progress there has been the occasional oddity: someone who had a brainwave, an idea that would change everything, who worked long and unflaggingly to realise the idea, but who was content – or seemed content – to remain entirely in the shadows and let others reap the rewards.

'One can, thousands of uses' is the legend attached to the display of WD-40 in our shop. In its familiar yellow and royal blue livery, WD-40 is simply an essential of life. No workshop, no shed, no garage or repair shop, and certainly no hardware shop could function without it. It is universal and indispensable. I spray it in on my bike chain, the blades of my shears, edging and hedge clippers, in the interior of my fishing reels, into my mower engine, onto any nut and bolt that will not come apart. According to the company website, its manifold applications include lubricating locks on dog kennels, and removing shoe polish stains from fabrics, glue from carpets, tree sap from secateurs, and lipstick from anything. Life without WD-40 is literally unthinkable.

But what is it? The company, now a billion-dollar global giant, insists coyly that it is made according to 'the secret formula' devised seventy years ago in a makeshift laboratory over a garage in San Diego, California. But according to the Material Data Sheet registered with the US Occupational Safety and Health Administration Agency, it is composed of fifty per cent aliphatic hydrocarbons (compound of carbon and hydrogen), twenty-five per cent petroleum base oil, twelve to eighteen per cent low-vapour-pressure aliphatic hydrocarbon (which reduces the viscosity so it can be sprayed), two to

three per cent carbon dioxide propellant (to reduce flamma-
bility), and ten per cent 'inert substances' (whatever they may
be). The hydrocarbon makes it possible to squirt WD-40 into
dark corners and tight crevices; it then evaporates, leaving the
lubricant in place. That is the real secret.

But whose secret is it? The particular virtue of WD-40 is
that it is an aerosol, and therefore can be delivered to places
other oils cannot reach. The credit for making it a spray
belongs to Norman B. Larsen, President of the Rocket Chemical Co. of San Diego in the years 1957 and 1958. It was Larsen
who grasped how the aerosol-delivery method would open
up a vast range of potential uses – in effect, anywhere where
rust and damp were a problem. In doing so, he laid the foun-
dations for the company's planet-wide conquest, even though
he himself left the company abruptly to join a competitor. It
is unfortunate from the point of view of clear history that the
name of the man who actually devised the formula several
years earlier should have been Norman Lawson. Inevitably,
the compilers of works of technological reference managed to
mix Lawson with Larsen, so that, over time, Larsen got all the
credit and Lawson was consigned to the shadows of oblivion.

Revisionist history was required to do justice to Norman
Lawson, and it arrived in the form of an article written for
the *Journal of San Diego History* by its editor, Iris Engstrand,
and published in 2014. Under the headline 'WD-40 San
Diego's Marketing Miracle', she elegantly wove together the
story of a man who had one brilliant idea but never profited
much from it and seems to have been unbothered by the
fact that credit went to others. Iver Norman Lawson was a
mechanical engineer who worked in aeronautics until the
early 1950s, when he and others formed the Rocket Chemical

Company. A family friend of Lawson's, a commander in the US Navy, put it to him one day that anyone who could come up with a lubricant that would protect the engines and gear systems of warships would be rendering a signal service to their country.

According to Professor Engstrand, Lawson wrestled with the challenge for long hours in the lab he had fitted out above his garage. He tried formula after formula, until – so the story, or legend, goes – at the fortieth attempt, he succeeded. The lubricant had defeated the water; the Water had been Displaced – at the fortieth go. WD-40 was born.

Lawson handed the formula over to his company to be developed into a commercial proposition. A prototype version was given to the owner of one of the vessels in San Diego's tuna-fishing fleet, who dunked his outboard engine in the sea, applied the WD-40 and then started it first time. Word spread about the healing properties of the wonder substance. Initially, it was sold in cans with a screw top, and one of the first customers to order it in bulk was Convair, which made aircraft for the military and used WD-40 to protect the outer skin of the Atlas missile from rust.

Norman Larsen came on the scene, and his brainwave transformed the fortunes of the Rocket Chemical Co. From being a specialised treatment in a niche part of the aeronautical industry, WD-40 began to spread across America. Wherever tools were being used and engines were being maintained, hands reached for the WD-40 spray can. Sales grew steadily, then surged. Overseas outlets multiplied. The US entry into the Vietnam War in 1964 created a massive new market, as weaponry succumbed to rust like an infectious disease in the dripping jungles of South East Asia. In

1966, the company received orders from the government to supply a quarter of a million canisters of WD-40 and 300 fifty-five-gallon drums.

The bosses decided to change the name of the company to that of its single product. That was the marketing miracle – everyone knew the name, and the more people bought it, the more uses for it were found. Not only did it protect American missiles from corrosion and keep American machine-guns firing, it also unstuck zips, stopped electric fans squeaking, cleaned guitar strings, and removed sticky-tape residue.

Norman Lawson, who had made all this possible, faded quietly from the stage. It may be that he came to find the San Diego Natural History Museum – where he was a long-serving trustee and President of the Board for fourteen years – more congenial than the world of lubrication. Did it worry him that over time he became confused with Norm Larsen? Or that the WD-40 official history overlooked his contribution altogether? According to his family, all he ever got from the Rocket Chemical Co. was a $500 bonus. He died in 1967, and it was not until Professor Engstrand went to work in the archives and produced her model example of local history that he received something of his due.

As we've seen, the unique asset of WD-40 is that it can get lubrication into places beyond the reach of other oils. But a heavier and more viscous oil provides superior protection – if it can be applied where it is needed.

In the 1890s, George William Cole, who had a bicycle shop in Ashbury Park, New Jersey, began selling small bottles containing a mixture of spindle oil, citronella oil and rust inhibitor. It was designed to keep the brakes, gears and chains

of bicycles moving smoothly, and was advertised as being
able to 'clean, lubricate and protect'. Cole gave it a name
derived from the number of components – 3-in-One Oil – and
it dawned on him that it might have commercial possibilities
extending beyond his repair shop. He acquired a partner,
James Noah Slee, who had been born to English parents in
Cape Town, South Africa, and had come to America with his
mother when he was twelve.

Slee was the driving force behind the success of G. W.
Cole Co. He registered 3-in-One as a trademark and began
to market it energetically. It was sold in bottles of various
sizes, and Slee arranged for a tiny green one to be distrib-
uted free with guns, fishing reels, roller skates, bicycles and
other leisure items. He advertised extensively – the display
in the *Boston Post* proclaimed 3-in-One Oil to be 'the ideal
lubricant for bicycles, firearms, typewriters, sewing machines,
hinges, locks, delicate mechanisms of any sort'. A testimonial
from Fred W. Peabody, dealer in pianos and other musical
instruments, was reproduced: 'We have used 3-in-One Oil for
several years with perfect satisfaction.'

Although George Cole remained president of the company for the time being, J. Noah Slee was the well-oiled engine
powering its success. He advertised in as many as eighty different publications, targeting shooting enthusiasts ('For Guns,
3-in-One Oil Has No Equal'), anglers ('Fishing Reel, Rod and
Line All Need 3-in-One'), women ('3-in-One Will Save Any
Housewife Much Hard Work') and boys with mechanical
and outdoor interests. Cole seems to have left the company
in 1904 for unknown reasons, and Slee became president.
He renamed it the 3-in-One Company and remained as president until 1937, by which time it had been taken over. (It was

eventually acquired by Reckitt & Coleman, and subsequently by WD-40, under whose umbrella it still shelters.)

George William Cole retreated into obscurity, dying in 1923. But J. Noah Slee had a considerable influence on American life and morals in a very different sphere. In the early 1920s, as a respected businessman, churchgoer, husband and father, he met and became infatuated with the celebrated – indeed, notorious – birth-control campaigner Margaret Sanger. She and her husband were recently divorced; Slee promptly left his wife for Sanger, and they were married in 1922. She had recently returned from an extended visit to England, in the course of which she had had affairs with the equally notorious social reformer and authority on sexuality Havelock Ellis, the failed novelist and cricket writer Hugh de Selincourt, the literary critic Harold Child, and the novelist H. G. Wells. Sanger made it clear to her sixty-two-year-old husband that marriage would not impinge upon her independent style of life. He – who apparently achieved with her a sexual fulfilment of which he had previously only dreamed – accepted her conditions and made the best of it.

J. Noah Slee had become a very wealthy man as a result of his association with 3-in-One Oil, and he put his wealth at his new wife's disposal. He gave $50,000 to the American Birth Control League, which she founded, and paid its director's salary as well as acting as its assistant treasurer. He also came to the assistance of the clinic she had set up in New York, by procuring rubber-spring diaphragms, which were unavailable in the Unites States but were made in Holland and Germany. Slee had a large consignment sent to one of his factories in Montreal and arranged for them to be smuggled into New York in containers of 3-in-One Oil.

In 1937, he retired with his wife to Tucson, Arizona, where he died in 1943. Sanger continued her campaigning work into old age. She was instrumental in securing funding for Gregory Pincus to develop the first oral contraceptive pill, which may be considered an even more significant contribution to world happiness than her husband's 3-in-One Oil. But no branded version of the pill has come close to matching J. Noah Slee's lubricant as a household name. Rival products, just as good at greasing the wheels and cogs, have come and gone, but in our shop, and in many other hardware shops, 3-in-One continues to hold pride of place. Shro keeps the hand-sized cans with their erect red spouts and little red caps on a shelf above the tools that the oil serves. Sales are steady, and people usually ask for 3-in-One by name. It is more than just a lubricant.

ANOTHER UNFORGETTABLE name completes this tour of hardware shop essentials.

We have pulled on wellington boots. We have been to the shed to get the mower ready for grass-cutting duties by squirting WD-40 into the inaccessible parts of the engine and 3-in-One Oil onto the moving parts. We have scraped off last year's accretions of mud and clippings. We have tenderly wiped the oil rag across and around the cutters, the roller and the basket to get them clean. We have removed the spark plug and vigorously applied the wire brush to banish the carbon. Now it is lunchtime and we need to clean our filthy hands. Where is the tub of Swarfega? And where did it come from?

The answer is Derbyshire. The 'swarf' is a word derived from the Old English for the oily mixture of grit that accumulates at the centre of a wheel axle, or of metal shavings from machining components. The 'ega' was apparently coined by the inventor of the gelatinous green hand-cleaner to suggest an eagerness to get the job done. His name was Audley Bowdler Williamson, which is remembered in the town of Belper, where he lived and had his company, and to which he was an open-handed charitable giver, but should be honoured every time the grimy-handed mechanic thrusts his or her hands into the big red tub and feels the cool, slimy gel slip between the fingers.

Williamson came from a family that operated a haulage business in Heanor, north-east of Derby. He studied chemistry at grammar school and became an assistant at Dalton's, which produced Silkolene lubricating oils at a factory in Belper, to the west of Heaton. In 1941, aged twenty-five, Williamson – known generally as A. B. – set up his own business to make a detergent of his devising to clean silk stockings. The collapse of the silk-stocking market post-war, precipitated by the arrival of nylon, set him working on an adaptation of his formula. He added an emulsifier and combinations of hydrocarbons until it achieved a form suitable for use as a heavy-duty skin cleaner that – unlike paraffin – did not leave the skin sore and cracked.

Launched under the slogan 'Cleans Hands in a Flash', Swarfega was welcomed with open arms and grubby hands by mechanics both professional and amateur. The bright green gel in the green-topped red jar became one of the most recognisable DIY essentials. Like 3-in-One Oil, it inspired many imitations, but succeeded in retaining its pole position in the market, its name metamorphosing into a household name (like Kleenex, Velcro, Biro, Aspirin, Hoover and Escalator, to name but a few to have made the same leap).

A. B. Williamson made a sizeable fortune from his extremely clever concept. Shortly before his death in 2004 at the age of eighty-eight, the family sold the majority stake in the brand for £135 million. He seems to have led a thoroughly upright and admirable life, and left most of his money to local good causes.

And Swarfega lives on, doing its bit to make a dirty world slightly less dirty.

## Chapter Nineteen

# The Cabinet of Death

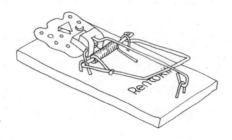

THE BEATING HEART of the shop is the counter, where the transaction that is the reason for its existence starts and finishes. The counter is actually the top of a wooden cabinet with sliding glass doors at the front. The wood is painted black, and a glance through the glass doors reveals that the dominant colour of the packaging of the products inside is also black. The colour of death.

Every hardware shop and store has to deal in death, because every house and garden is a battleground where the legitimate owners – as we see ourselves – are challenged by invaders and usurpers. On our side, we have modern weaponry obtainable from the cabinet of death. On their side, they have many advantages: invisibility, fecundity, versatility, insatiability, agility, an adaptability easily mistaken for low cunning. The war is never won, which is why the shop does such a good, steady trade out of the cabinet. The best we can aspire to is containment. Sooner or later, however numerous their losses, our adversaries regroup and recruit reinforcements through their boundless capacity for breeding; and the gnawing, nibbling, shredding and burrowing resume.

The cabinet of death contains sprays for killing clothes moths, fleas, flies, dust mites, bed bugs, carpet beetles, silverfish, cockroaches and others besides. There are powders to squirt into wasps' nests and ants' nests. There is a 'destroyer foam' for wasps' nests. There are boxes of blocks containing ingredients such as ethoxy hydroxy benzaldehyde, diethanolamine and brodifacoum (described as a 4-hydroxycoumarin vitamin K antagonist anticoagulant poison), which, placed in a trap, are advertised as being capable of killing impressive numbers of rats; although, in fact, they probably kill a few, make some others feel distinctly poorly and are avoided by plenty.

There is a whole range of rat traps and mousetraps, and there are flypapers.

On one occasion, business in the shop was interrupted by the persistent blaring of a car alarm right outside the window. The owner of the car came in, looking flushed and somewhat embarrassed. She had a story to tell, and while she told it, Greg the mower repairman went and lifted the bonnet of the car and disconnected a wire so the alarm fell silent. The woman recounted how a mouse (or mice, because there is never just one mouse) had taken up residence in the engine of the car. There were the usual tell-tale signs of droppings and shreddings and some gnawing of the wiring, hence the alarm problem. She had come to buy a humane mousetrap, one that lures the little creature inside until a door clicks shut, enabling the tender-hearted captor to take it away and release it somewhere beyond its homing range.

She bought the humane trap and went away and came back a while later to report that she had apprehended no fewer than nine mice in her car, all of them safely liberated to resume their activities elsewhere. She is one of a significant proportion of those who come to the shop seeking ways to combat murine infiltrations but are disinclined to pronounce a sentence of death. Most, however, are not so squeamish, and are content with the traditional, very cheap and very effective snap trap.

The problem of rats and mice living, eating, fornicating, defecating, urinating and dying in places we do not want them is one of long standing. A good mouser cat has always been and remains a favoured control and deterrent agent. But for *in loco* destruction, the choice has generally been between poison or a trap (or a combination of the two); although Mick, when he was in charge, used to amuse himself on a summer's evening by sitting out within range of his chicken run, picking off the rats with his air rifle.

The drawback of poison is obvious – it condemns its victims to a horrible and lingering death, and you may end up killing creatures you did not intend to. The drawback with the traps of old was that their ingenuity was rarely, if ever, matched by their efficiency. They caught a few, but never enough. An impressive selection was illustrated in a volume from 1590 entitled *A Booke of Engines and Traps to Take Polecats, Buzardes, Rattes, Mice and All Other Kindes of Vermine*, which was written by Leonard Mascall, a prolific author of what we might now call self-help manuals. The traps are ingenious, but characterised by various degrees of impracticality. One, baited with butter, oatmeal and sugar, had to be placed on the edge of a table with a bowl of water positioned on the floor underneath, so that the mouse plopped into it and drowned. Another, the 'bow trappe', was a kind of guillotine, in which downward pressure on a treadle released a clicket, which in turn released a wooden block in the direction of the mouse's head.

As a predominantly rural life made way for city life and the towns and cities grew, so did the availability of habitat and food sources for rodents. The resulting population explosion set fertile minds working on the challenge of devising a mousetrap that could be easily made and actually worked. There were plenty of false starts. Charles Henert's Improved Animal Trap, patented in the US in 1869, comprised a tiny inverted colander, which would fall and trap the mouse when it took the bait inside; it was then stabbed with a knife suspended from the top of the cage. Another device was patented in which the mouse was supposed to leap upwards at the bait, triggering a number of minute stilettos to spring out and impale it.

Other flights of fancy were even more elaborate. One had a wheel inside a cage that spun as the captive mouse ran on it in vain hope of escape. Another was equipped with a minuscule tricycle and mouse-powered treadmill that propelled it across the floor. Others involved trapping the mice inside to be either released or drowned, according to taste. One of these, the Delusion, sold well – perhaps because of the catchy advertising ditty that came with it:

> The mouse goes in to get the bait
> And shuts the door by its own weight,
> And then he jumps right through a hole

And thinks he's out, but bless his soul,

He's in a cage somehow or other,

And sets the trap to catch another.

The decisive step forward was taken in 1894, when a patent was granted to the first snap trap, designed by William Chauncey Hooker. Hooker lived in Abingdon, Illinois, where he and two partners had established the Animal Trap Company. They had already had some commercial success with Hooker's 'Stop Thief' trap, designed to apprehend rats, skunks, opossums and muskrats, and his 'Out-o-Sight' mole trap. The company prospered for a while, but there seems to have been some sort of divergence between the partners, as a result of which the Animal Trap Co. migrated to Lititz, Pennsylvania, where it merged with the J. M. Mast Manufacturing Company. Hooker remained in Abingdon, where he died in 1909, and it was John Mast who made the snap trap the American mouse destroyer of choice.

In 1899, he submitted a patent application model based on Hooker's design, and it went into production shortly after. The beauty of the snap trap lay in the combination of simplicity with deadliness. Onto a small rectangular base of hardwood were stapled the locking bar, the spring (with one end of the bow – the neck-breaker – inside), the catch for the locking bar and the bait pedal. One mouse step on the pedal was enough to lift it sufficiently to release the spring, and in three millionths of a second, life was terminated.

John Mast's enterprise boomed. A new factory was built and the company was rebranded under its original name, the Animal Trap Co. It made traps to detain or destroy moles, gophers, rats, foxes, mink, squirrels, wolves and even bears, but the bread-and-butter was mousetraps: first the Blizzard, later the Joker, the Gee Whizz, the Peerless, the Devil, the End-o-Mice, the Holdfast and the Victor. 'We are the largest manufacturer of animal traps in the world,' the company boasted in 1905, 'and we ship our products, bearing the name of Lititz, into every country on the globe.' Over time, it was the Victor that secured top spot in consumers' affections, and it is the Victor that is still made in Lititz by Woodstream, the company that grew from John Mast's Animal Trap Co., and that continues to outsell all other US mousetraps combined.

Across the Atlantic, William Hooker's patent and the very clear drawings that accompanied it were receiving close attention from the British mousetrap sector. In the Scottish town of Barrhead, near Glasgow, James Hunter, proprietor of what was known locally as the Mousetrap Factory, already had a profitable line of so-called choker traps, including the Never Fail and the New Never Fail. By 1899, he was making a trap very similar to Hooker's, which he called the Unseen. This was followed by the Hero, the Veto, the Cheapa and others. In Leeds, an ironmonger, James Atkinson, patented a trap similar to Hooker's and Hunter's, but with a significant refinement. The treadle was cut across the whole width of the wooden base, so that the spring was triggered by a mouse anywhere on it. Atkinson called his version the Little Nipper, which was a neat stroke. It was made by Atkinson and advertised and sold by a Leeds firm, Procter Bros., which subsequently moved to Wales and still makes the Little Nipper – with wooden or plastic base – at Bedwas, Gwent.

Ralph Waldo Emerson, one of those nineteenth-century essayists who are often quoted and rarely read, is credited with saying: 'If a man can write a better book, preach a better sermon or make a better mousetrap than his neighbour, though he builds his house in the woods, the world will make a beaten path to his door.' The adage actually appears in a different form in Emerson's journals without any reference to the mousetrap. That indefatigable authority on such matters, quoteinvestigator.com, has tracked down the mousetrap version to a newspaper in Atlanta, which attributed it to Emerson a few months after his death in 1882. Quoteinvestigator.com believes that Emerson must have adapted the original to include the mousetrap in one of his innumerable lectures.

By whatever route it gained its popularity, Emerson's adage – taken to mean that striving to create a good book, a good sermon or a mousetrap that works is a noble endeavour – has been universally embraced. But success with a new mousetrap has proved to be even more elusive than writing a book that people wish to read or composing a sermon that will stir the sinful to seek the path of righteousness. Far more patent applications for mousetraps, more than 4,000, have been granted by the US Patent Office than for any other device or contrivance (with ten times that number rejected). They are divided into thirteen categories, which include live traps, snap traps, crushing traps, spearing traps, exploding traps and electrocuting traps. The criterion for acceptance by the Patent Office is that the invention should do what its inventor claims it should do, not that it should be of any practical use. Of those 4,000-plus, no more than a handful ever achieved commercial production.

Once John Mast's patent expired in the 1920s, imitators flooded the market. The Catchmaster, the Revenge, the Clean Catch, the Quick Kill, the Sure-death, the Exterminator – they all promised to give the consumer the upper hand in the war against mice, but none managed to dent the Victor's dominance. The one technological innovation that gained serious traction in the US was the deeply horrible glue trap, sold under anodyne names such as Holdfast and Mr Stickey. These were, in essence, trays covered in glue and placed on murine travel paths. They were very cheap and did not need to be set with care, as was necessary with the snap trap. In the 1980s, they had thirty per cent of the market, but the upward trend in sales stalled, perhaps reflecting an uneasiness over the fate of the hapless mouse, which was left alive but stuck, thrashing around with its nose, tail and even whiskers caught in the glue, often tearing off sections of its own skin and fur in its efforts to escape, and eventually dying of exhaustion and hypothermia.

What constitutes ethical behaviour towards mice is a tricky matter. I find the idea of the glue trap for mice revolting, as does Shro, and she will not stock it in the shop. But I cannot say that I am seriously bothered by the snap trap, even though I acknowledge that others are. As for other pests, the campaigning group PETA – People for the Ethical Treatment of Animals – would have us treat bluebottles as tenderly as we should mice. One of their campaign slogans is 'Drop the Flyswat'. But while pressure to outlaw the glue trap is persistent (and edging towards legislation in the UK), almost no one cares about the fate of insects. Spray them with poison, flatten them with a swat; they are not deemed to matter. This brings us to the matter of flypapers, which are just glue traps in the air. These the shop does stock, and we also keep them in the house for when the fly issue becomes acute.

The credit for inventing the familiar little cylinders that roll out into sticky strips of flypaper belongs to a quartet of brothers born to a German immigrant, William Thum, in Grand Rapids, Michigan. In Grand Rapids in the 1880s, as in every other town and city, flies were not so much a problem as a curse. The streets were thick with horse dung, rubbish was dumped everywhere, and very few homes had screens fitted to their windows to keep the swarms out. William Thum ran a drug store, where he sold sheets of paper plastered with various tacky substances to mitigate the nuisance. But they were messy to use and did not remain effective for long, so the pharmacist charged his sons with the task of coming up with something better.

The Thum boys – Otto, William, Hugo and Ferdinand – set about experimenting with various formulas. They found that a combination of castor oil, resins and wax lasted well, and, crucially, did not soak into the paper. Their father began to sell the papers in his shop and demand grew rapidly. To meet it, the Thums established a small workshop to make their flypaper. They called the product Tanglefoot, and the company boomed in proportion to the population of flies. The brothers kept their recipe a closely guarded secret, patenting the process in 1889. A few years later came the key breakthrough; they devised and patented a way to produce the flypaper in rolls that could be unfurled and pinned to the ceiling or a beam.

By 1902, O. W. Thum and Co. were shipping the Tanglefoot flypaper – catchphrase 'Catches the Germ as well as the Fly' – all over the fly-afflicted civilised world. The brothers eventually sold up and migrated collectively to the drier and less flyblown climes of California, where Hugo farmed spine-free cactuses, Otto became a property developer in Los Angeles, and William was elected mayor of Pasadena.

The Tanglefoot company diversified into other areas of pest control but continued – and continues – to make the rolls of flypaper.

THE THUM BROTHERS' formula was strictly non-toxic. But long before they went to work, flypapers of a very different kind were widely used in the US, Britain and Europe. Instead of being smeared with sticky substances to attract and trap the insects, these were designed to be soaked in a saucer of water, which was then left out for the fly to drink. The papers would infuse the water with sugar and another ingredient, much favoured in Victorian times for a host of uses: arsenic.

In an article for the *British Medical Journal* published in November 1878 and entitled 'Arsenic in Fly-papers', William Ord, physician to St Thomas's Hospital, described how he had treated an eight-year-old boy who had been poisoned as a result of drinking water in which a flypaper had been soaked. (The lad recovered, but it was a close call.) Dr Ord endorsed a call previously published in the *Pharmaceutical Journal* for chemists to desist from selling flypapers treated with arsenic. The call fell on deaf ears – and it was not until the mass poisoning of more than 6,000 people in Manchester in 1900 and 1901 as a result of drinking ale accidentally contaminated with arsenic that the government brought in controls on its use. But arsenical flypapers continued to be freely sold by pharmacists, enabling them to feature prominently in several of the sensational murder trials that so shocked and delighted the public at that time.

One of the key facts established at the trial in 1889 of Florence Maybrick for the murder of her husband at their home in Liverpool was that she had previously purchased twelve dozen flypapers impregnated with arsenic. In her evidence, she claimed that she extracted the arsenic from the flypapers to improve her complexion (many cosmetics contained arsenic as well as mercury and lead). Furthermore, it was shown that her husband had been treating himself for years for real or imagined ailments with tonics and patent medicines containing strychnine, arsenic and belladonna – all deadly poisons.

The toxicological evidence against Florence was inconclusive; the post-mortem implicated poison, but did not prove it. But there was circumstantial evidence against her that, in the eyes of a brutally and scandalously biased judge, seemed damning. Her husband was twenty years older and had a long-time mistress in London, which was fine for him. But when he discovered that Florence had been having an affair with a young family friend, he told her that he would be seeking a divorce. This would have left her penniless and with her reputation destroyed. Mr Justice Stephen, determined to make it a trial of her morals, convinced the jury that these were sufficient grounds for her to have poisoned him, and they convicted her. But the judge's moral crusade backfired considerably; his conduct of the trial was itself put on trial in the court of public opinion. The outcry led to the death sentence that he pronounced on Florence being commuted to life imprisonment. She served fifteen years before returning to her native US, where she died, an impoverished recluse, in New Milford, Connecticut, in 1941.

There were and remain very strong doubts about Florence Maybrick's guilt, but none whatever concerning Frederick William Seddon, who was hanged at Pentonville Prison in London in April 1912. Again, flypapers played a crucial part in a grim story. It was revealed that shortly before the death of his lodger, Eliza Barrow, Seddon had sent his young daughter, Maggie, to the local chemist in Finsbury Park, London, to buy flypapers. The post-mortem on the wretched Eliza Barrow – whom Seddon had persuaded to hand over most of her worldly wealth and also to name him as executor of her will – was carried out by an up-and-coming Home Office pathologist, Bernard Spilsbury. At the trial of Seddon and his wife, Spilsbury testified clearly and convincingly that the lodger had been poisoned with arsenic. Seddon's celebrated counsel, Marshall Hall, did his utmost to shake Spilsbury's testimony, but in vain.

Marshall Hall also attempted – also in vain – to persuade Seddon not to give evidence on his own behalf. This very bad man made a very bad impression on the jury, and his explanation of Eliza Barrow's death – that she must have drunk the liquid from a saucer in which a flypaper had been soaked – seemed inherently implausible, given the amount of arsenic the pathologist had found in her body. The jury took no more than an hour to convict him – Mrs Seddon was cleared – and the judge put on the black cap to deliver sentence.

Lurid and sensational though these trials were, they paled in comparison with the events that unfolded in a remote village in central southern Hungary between 1914 and 1929. The story of the Angel Makers of Nagyrev has been told in films and books and numerous articles, but remains utterly compelling in its bizarreness. At least forty – and possibly many more – men, elderly women and children of the village and nearby hamlets were murdered by female relatives for whom they had become an irritant or inconvenience. Some of the victims were husbands who returned from fighting in the First World War to wives who had grown used to their absence and were disinclined to put up with the drunken and abusive behaviour that was standard in Hungarian village life. Some were elderly parents whose daughters were tired of looking after them and impatient for their inheritance. Some were illegitimate or unwanted children.

The arsenic and advice on its use were provided initially by a mysterious middle-aged woman, Zsuzsanna Fazekas, who assumed the roles of healer, midwife and abortionist in Nagyrev. She obtained the flypapers, extracted the arsenic, and advised on how it should be administered in food or a medicine. Other women in the village learned from Fazekas and obtained their own flypapers. Sudden death became an accepted feature of village life; murder became almost fashionable. Rumours did spread locally, but Nagyrev was a remote and isolated settlement, lost in the flatness of the floodplain of the River Tisza. Death certificates were signed by a cousin of Zsuzsanna Fazekas, who worked as a clerk for the local administration, and the bodies were quietly buried in the village cemetery.

Finally, the authorities were roused into action. According to the Hungarian historian Bela Bodo, who wrote a book about the case, an anonymous letter was published in a local newspaper drawing attention to the rumours that had by then been swirling for years. The police arrived in force from the provincial capital, Szolnok. Dozens of bodies were exhumed and found to contain traces of arsenic. The nearest and not-so-dearest of the victims were arrested and dragged away to be confined in cells in Szolnok, where they were brutally interrogated and treated like degenerate survivors from a bygone age.

Fazekas took her own life. As the prosecution was prepared, Hungarian newspapers engaged in an orgy of lurid conjecture about the Angel Makers' motives. The story was picked up and spread across Europe. In the end, twenty-six women were put on trial, of whom twenty were convicted, although several convictions were overturned when the verdicts were considered by Hungary's Supreme Court. Two were executed and the remainder served prison sentences.

And, one can assume, sales of flypapers in Szolnok province declined.

RATS BELONG IN horror stories. I remember as a boy reading H. P. Lovecraft's story 'The Rats in the Walls' and having nightmares for weeks. We quite like mice, even if we set traps to snare them, but rats are repulsive. They are also everywhere, but somehow bearable if out of sight. But when they leave their dark haunts and infiltrate our homes, action is needed.

When our girls were little, they would regularly return from school or friends' homes with the results of baking sessions, which were put on the side and sometimes eaten and sometimes not. Early one morning, I came into the kitchen to make coffee before work, and found a batch of fairy cakes devastated and scattered, with tell-tale droppings all around. Mice, I said, nothing to worry about. The next morning, as first light was dawning, I met a rat on the stairs. It scooted at electric speed into the bathroom and vanished behind the boiler. The rodent exterminator was summoned, poison was placed, there was a nasty smell and a lot of bluebottles for a time, and then the rat (rats, because where one rat goes, others always follow) were banished.

The village rat man is Dave. He comes to the shop periodically to chat to Greg, and to put down his little boxes of
poison when Shro feels the rats in the yard are getting above
themselves. Dave also deals with wasps' nests and infesta-
tions of squirrels in attics. He tracked a fox that had been
causing bloody havoc in local chicken pens to its den and did
the necessary. He lays Larsson traps for crows and magpies to
persuade them not eat the songbirds' eggs. And rats, always
rats – Lord knows how many rats he has sent on their way.

For a man whose daily business is dispensing death, Dave
is a gentle soul, slowly and softly spoken. I talk to him about
fishing, because he is a keen angler when he gets the time,
which he rarely does because his services are in constant
demand. I ask him if he has been to the river recently, and
he shakes his head sadly and says it's wasps' nest season,
and he has too many calls to make. He is one of the village
indispensables.

## CHAPTER TWENTY

# 'Would You By Any Chance . . . ?'

THERE IS A MEMBER of staff at the small supermarket in our village who has been spreading good cheer when she is on the till for as long as I can remember. She has round cheeks and sparkling dark eyes, black hair and black spectacles, and a forceful voice that is never quiet. Whatever the age or gender of her customers, she makes them smile and talk, and splashes some colour into their lives.

I have never come across anyone so liberal with their endearments. In the course of a one-minute transaction to buy a loaf of bread and a bunch of bananas, I have been 'sweetheart', 'darling', and 'gorgeous'. Elderly ladies are 'babes', then 'bubbs'. Blokes and girls are 'honey' or 'hon'. Every child is cooed over, every old stick is asked about their wellbeing. A girl who buys flour will be asked what she is baking with her mum. Everyone knows her, and she knows everyone. She has a genius for what she does, and she is treasured in the village for it.

Shro is not as free with the pet terms, although a 'darling' or a 'sweetheart' comes easily to her when she is dealing with female customers of mature years. But, as with the member of staff in the supermarket, Shro's personality fills the space around her. And because space in the shop is so restricted, that means the whole shop. Her strong, warm voice and her throaty, bubbling laugh raise the temperature and energise the air. The bell rings, a customer enters, and they know at once that she is there for them and will have time for them.

Unlike in the supermarket, the interaction between customer and the staff in Heath & Watkins – Shro and Helen, and occasionally our daughter Rosie – is often exploratory in nature:

'I want a pan,' a woman customer states.

Shro: 'A saucepan? A frying pan?'

'You know, a round pan with a lid. And no handle.'

'A stockpot?'

'Could be.'

'I'm afraid we're out of them at the moment. They're on order.'

'Oh no, I really need one.'

'What about a casserole?'

'I really want one with . . . you know . . . enamel.'

'You mean an enamel roaster?'

'That could be it.'

Shro fetches the stepladder, because the enamel roaster is on the highest shelf, next to the electric hair-clippers. She brings it down.

'That's too small.'

'I'm afraid it's the biggest one we have.'

'Can you get a bigger one?'

Shro checks with the supplier. They do not do a bigger one. No sale.

*

Sometimes the customer comes in conscious of a need, but with no more than a very imprecise idea of how it might be met. But they enter in hope, because they know that the shop offers an advisory service as well as items for sale. A woman with backache comes in.

'Strange request, I know, but do you sell inflatable balls?'

Helen: 'I'm afraid not. What do you want one for?'

'I'm a hairdresser and I have a dodgy back, and I need something to work it against, between customers. You know, against the wall.'

'You could try a big ball of garden twine.'

'That might do it.'

On one occasion, a woman came in with a very specific problem requiring targeted solutions. She had a full-size Friesian cow made from fibreglass in her garden, and one of its horns was broken. She had a lengthy consultation with Helen, as a result of which she bought some steel wool and filler to fashion into a replacement horn, and two wooden skewers to support it and keep it in place while the filler dried. I happened to come in at the end of the consultation and remarked that it sounded like quite a tricky and delicate operation. She said she was confident of success. 'I used to be a dentist, you know.'

The good hardware shop acts as a branch of social services. People come in for a light bulb or a nail brush, accompanied by their concerns. 'How are we?' Shro asks. Very often, the answer is a monosyllabic positive, and the transaction is completed in moments. But other times, the invitation is accepted. During the two years when the pandemic was at its worst, that tended to shape the exchanges:

lockdown and the restrictions, musings about whether the vaccines would really work, cancelled holidays, relatives not seen, how bad you felt. But there are other staples: the state of the garden, the behaviour of neighbours, Brexit, Boris, the traffic, the parking. And the weather, always the weather.

Shro and Helen have to be alert to the tone, but they do not necessarily have to listen carefully to the content, because – more often than not – the interaction proceeds along familiar paths, requiring no more from them than the occasional, 'Oh dear', or 'That's terrible', or (with reference to rain) 'Will it ever stop?' What matters is not the substance, but their availability to play their part.

'I NEED A DRILL.' This is a male customer.

Helen goes to the end of the shop and fetches down a Black & Decker.

'No, I've got one of those already. I mean the bit that goes in it.'

'You mean a drill bit?'

'That's what I said. A drill.'

THE AMERICAN POET and author of children's books, Nancy Willard, wrote a poem called 'A Hardware Store as Proof of the Existence of God'. It opens:

> I praise the brightness of hammers pointing east
> like the steel woodpeckers of the future.

It goes on to celebrate 'bins of hooks glittering into bees [. . .] racks of wrenches like the long bones of horses [. . .] mailboxes sowing rows of silver chapels'. The hardware store, she says, belongs to 'a world not perfect, but not bad either'. In the last stanza, she lists more of the store's contents, and the poem ends with the uplifting line: 'In the right hands, they can work wonders.'

Nancy Willard put her finger precisely on one of the key functions of the hardware shop – that it should offer the prospect of making the broken whole again, the imperfect serviceable again. It must give the customer the opportunity to restore a future to things that have, for one reason or another, become useless.

'I love your shop,' a first-time customer said. 'It's so . . .' – she searched for the word – '. . . nourishing.' She bought a funnel, two cotton dishcloths, and a refill bottle of washing-up liquid.

SHRO TOOK A CALL, a male voice. 'I need one of those things with a glass tube and a rubber bulb at the top that you squeeze.'

'Sounds like a baster.'

'That could be it.'

'We have them with a plastic tube.'

'Mine's glass. Was glass. It's broken. That sounds as if it will do the job.'

Later, he came into the shop. 'Guess what I use it for?'

'Basting?'

'Sucking out the water from the rubber seal around the door of the washing machine. I don't like it when there is water in there.'

THE ILLUSION cultivated by the hardware shop is that some-where on the shelves – or the island, or hanging from the hooks, or standing in plastic buckets – is to be found the solution to anything inside or outside the house that is not quite as the householder would want it.

A small girl came in with her father and looked around in wonder as he bought something mundane, and said: 'Daddy, this is the shop of everything.'

Children quite often come in with one parent or another, but rarely on their own. But one day, two brothers entered the shop, and the younger one told Helen he had two pounds to spend and wanted a tool, specifically a knife. Helen looked at him, estimated his age to be maybe eight. She expressed reluctance to sell him a knife and suggested something else.

'What about a screwdriver. They're always useful.' She showed him one that cost £2.15.

'I've only got two pounds.'

His elder brother offered him the fifteen pence.

'But I want to buy sweets as well.'

Helen produced a very small screwdriver costing £1.30. 'That would leave seventy pence for sweets,' she said, helpfully.

The boy pointed to a ball of string. 'What about that? String's always useful, isn't it?' The string was £1.10. The elder brother said their mother, the intended beneficiary of this largesse, already had plenty of string. After further discussion, the elder brother gave the younger a £1 coin, enough for the string and the little screwdriver, with sixty pence left over for the sweetshop.

THE HARDWARE SHOP stands for familiar and reassuring values – reliability, competence, trustworthiness, usefulness, time for others, maintaining things so that they last. These are qualities that many people suspect have become hard to find in the wider world, where their elected leaders display almost none of them. The metrics and algorithms deployed to organise almost every aspect of the working of society have no place in the hardware shop. It is the repudiation of throwaway, the antithesis of the click-of-a-mouse, delivery-van version of consumerism. The hardware shop, in Shro's hands, stands for the traditional, the real, the permanent, the ordinary. It is a rock to hold on to in a sea of threatening currents.

It has, or should have, a timelessness about it. It belongs in the present and the past; you feel that if you had come in through the door as a child rather than the adult you are now, it would have been, in its essentials, the same. Your parents would have come here for the same reasons you are entering now. The smell, the shelving, the fittings, even the conversations – all express a continuity with the past. Even the jokes stand the test of time.

In the 1970s and 1980s, the most popular comedy sketch show on British TV was *The Two Ronnies*, which starred Ronnie Barker and Ronnie Corbett. Each year between 1971 and 1987 a new series was aired, attracting huge and affectionate audiences. Perhaps the most famous sketch they ever performed – it has consistently been voted in the top three of all time – was in a show first aired in 1976 and took place in a traditional hardware shop. Ronnie Corbett, in a brown coat, plays the man behind the counter; Ronnie Barker the uncouth customer who initiates proceedings by grunting his request. Corbett fetches four candles in response. Barker expresses his displeasure. The misunderstanding is resolved by Corbett producing a replacement handle for a garden fork. Later in an escalating farce of homophonic confusion, Barker is presented with a garden hoe and then a role of hose, in response to his request for two letters 'O' with which to spell the name of his house, Mon Repos, on the front gate.

The whole sketch – which was written by Barker under his pseudonym Gerald Wylye – lasts a little more than six minutes. Although it is now almost fifty years old, the sketch is still funny. Comedy often relies on topical or cultural or social contexts that could have been long since forgotten in the intervening years, but that isn't the case here. The premise of this particular sketch is brilliant, and the writing marvellously clever, but the reason it still works is because the setting and the feel of it are so familiar. The shop could be our shop; the candles and fork handle and stick-on lettering and thirteen-amp plug could be our offerings. Almost everything in the retail word has changed beyond recognition since the long, hot summer of 1976, but not the hardware shop.

WHEN RONNIE BARKER came to make a sitcom about shop life, it was set in a small grocer's rather than a hardware shop, which is perhaps a shame, because *Open All Hours* has none of the charm of the Four Candles sketch, and the jokes – sexist, misogynistic and cruel in the style of the times – have not aged well. The hardware shop was the setting for a reasonably successful ITV sitcom, *Hardware*, which ran for two seasons twenty years ago; but, again, the humour – derived largely from talk about sex and girls between the three male assistants in the shop and its male owner, and from mockery of the various (generally male) dimwits who plague them with ridiculous requests – has dated badly.

In the wider cultural context in Britain, the hardware shop has received little attention from writers or artists, and almost none from cultural historians and commentators. But not so in the United States, where the place of the hardware store in national life has been fully explored, documented and honoured.

Much of the credit for this goes to a single man, John McVey, of whom I know nothing beyond the information gleaned from various websites. He comes from Los Angeles, graduated from the University of California, Berkeley, in 1977, did a masters there in the languages and literature of Malaya and Indonesia, worked as a copywriter in Tokyo, did an M.F.A. in design, and finally took up a post at Montserrat College of Art in Beverley, Massachusetts, where he taught design until 2020. His areas of expertise are intriguingly far-flung, and include asphalt, emblematics (I do not know what they are), telegraphic code dictionaries (I do not know what they are, either) and photography. And hardware.

I have not met him or spoken to him, but if I did, I would shake him warmly by the hand and offer him my appreciation and congratulation for a monumental endeavour of research and scholarship in a subject that might otherwise have been left untapped. The treasure trove of reference for which he is responsible is itself like a great hardware store, whose every shelf and space are occupied by something useful or surprising. And it forms just one part of jmcvey.net, which is like a retail park comprising multiple outlets displaying the results of one man's restless curiosity about the more obscure corners of the world around him – and all offered for free.

The hardware section is personal. John McVey's grandfather managed a hardware store and then established his own. His three sons came into the business in Culver City, Los

Angeles County. After ten years there, they relocated to Temple City and became McVey Hardware. John McVey's father, Vic, was still working there a day a week into his eighties, but the next generation had moved on to other occupations, and the store closed its doors for good in 2006, leaving John with memories and impressions that ran very deep.

The hardware department of jmcvey.net is an online equivalent to the commonplace book dear to Milton, Francis Bacon, Coleridge, John Locke, Emerson, Thoreau, Virginia Woolf and many other compulsive hoarders of scraps from old books – a compendium of knowledge, opinion, myth and trivia organised according to principles devised by the proprietor for his or her pleasure and convenience, and likely to be thought arbitrary and confusing by anyone else. I cannot begin to do justice here to the wealth of material that John McVey has tracked down and secured; there is enough there to sustain a three-year degree course and a master's beyond.

Take the memoirs shelf. Here are to be found entries for and links to *The Family Hardware Store: Mirror of a Community* by Mary Love (about A. D. Naylor of Oakland, Maryland, still going strong under the Ace Hardware umbrella after almost 140 years); Charles Everitt's *My Hardware Store: A Memoir of Years Spent in his Family's Store in Concordia, Kansas*; *Fifty Years on the Road: Recollections of a Hardware Salesman* by Lester H. Wand; and Bernard W. Aubuchon's *Aubuchon Hardware*, an account of the birth and growth of a hardware empire that includes more than 100 stores and extends across the north-eastern US. Although the emphasis is understandably on American material, there is a reference to a volume entitled *The Early History of Robert Kelly and Sons Ltd.*, about a well-known Manchester hardware company – a book so obscure that even the British Library does not know it – which records that the founder refused to stock ironmongery and 'hated to be called an ironmonger, finding some ignominy in the word'.

McVey's survey of the hardware store in (mainly American) fiction is epic, running to more than seventy pages with more than 120 entries. Most of the novels and stories and their writers are unknown to me, and it is true that the role of the hardware store in the narrative is generally fleeting and incidental; having a job in a hardware store is a handy way for your protagonist to lay hands on a variety of murder weapons; it can also be used to suggest a character's mundane situation in life, or limited ambitions, or availability for excitement elsewhere. For example, Anastasia Steele, the compliant half of the relationship in E. L. James's supposedly erotic *Fifty Shades of Grey*, is employed part-time in the largest independent hardware store in Portland, Oregon, while studying Thomas Hardy and speculating on the possible use of the cable ties, masking tape and rope that she sells to the smirking Christian Grey.

The title of a British entry, an utterly forgotten 'humorous' novel published in 1908 called *Love and the Ironmonger* and written by Frederick John Randall, suggests a more mainstream part in the proceedings, but a swift skim confirms that ironmongery and hardware are entirely incidental to the footling toings and froings of the plot. Considerably more promising is another British entry: *Sartre's Sink: The Great Writers' Complete Book of DIY* by Mark Crick, a photographer and expert parodist. It is a series of pastiches – Emily Brontë on bleeding a radiator, Dostoevsky on tiling a bathroom, Anaïs Nin on painting a panelled door and so forth. Here is a taste of Hemingway on hanging wallpaper: 'The old man had worked for two days and two nights to strip away the old wallpaper and in the morning of the third day the time to hang the new paper had come and he was tired.'

But it is the poem that offers the ideal literary medium through which to consider the hardware shop with the attention it deserves. A poem can crystallise what the good hardware shop is for, how it smells and sounds and feels, how it affects someone looking in and coming in. John McVey, in a commentary on the old McVey Hardware store that he grew up with, referred to:

> [. . .] the existential condition of the hardware man. To know a little about a lot and be an expert in nothing. To improvise, extemporize, extrapolate. An inclination to philosophize comes with the trade, perhaps because the trade is social. People come in with a problem. There's an encounter, lessons. And too, the hardware man works less with tools, than he thinks about working with tools. Hence philosophy.

A good poet can work with that.

Most startling of the references in the poetry section is Bob Flanagan's 'Why?', performed – not read – by himself. Flanagan was a Los Angeles performance artist much in vogue in the 1980s, whose material was focused on twin preoccupations – his cystic fibrosis, which killed him when he was forty-three, and his obsessive public sado-masochism (a notorious cameo saw him nailing his penis and scrotum to a board while singing 'If I Had a Hammer'.) In the YouTube video of 'Why?' Flanagan explains who he is while a succession of home movies of his childhood are shown. The effect is visceral and moves hardware beyond the everyday and into a formative experience for the artist:

because hardware stores gave me hard-ons

because of hammers, nails, clothespins, wood, padlocks, pullies, eyebolts, thumbtacks, staple guns, sewing needles, wooden spoons, fishing tackle, chains, metal rulers, rubber tubing, spatulas, rope, twine, C-clamps, S-hooks, razor blades, scissors, tweezers, knives, pushpins, two-by-fours, ping-pong paddles, alligator clips, duct tape, broomsticks, barbecue skewers, bungie cords, sawhorses, soldering irons [. . .]

In a poem called 'Quincaillerie' (the mellifluous French word for hardware shop), the French poet, Jean Follain, offered a cool and spare version at the opposite end of the spectrum from Flanagan's hectic S&M outfitters. It ends:

> Ainsi la quincaillerie vogue vers l'éternel
> et vend à satiété
> les grands clous qui fulgurent.

(Thus the hardware store sails towards eternity,
selling the ephemeral brilliance of nails,
satisfying all.)

Inevitably poets tend to concern themselves with the metaphysical rather than the business side of the hardware shop. The need to sell enough to stay in business belongs firmly in the sphere of the prosaic. But if it fails to achieve that, it becomes just another memory, another loss – 'Where have all the hardware shops gone?' People walk past the premises it once occupied, now an estate agent or converted into flats, and pause and ask: 'Do you remember when it was a hardware shop? We used to get everything there. What a shame.' Then they walk on.

That shop did not sell enough of everything to keep it alive. That is the harsh economic truth. The hardware shop is not like the library or the youth club or the charity that organises shopping trips for the elderly. It can't apply for public funds to keep it open. It is not the same as the village shop and post office or village pub, quite a number of which have been saved from extinction by community buy-outs. The hardware shop can only win the battle for survival by providing what people want at prices they are prepared to pay in a volume sufficient to cover the rent and maintenance costs, the purchase of stock and a living income for whoever runs it.

A couple of months before starting to write this book, I resigned from our parish council. I did so partly because of my dismay at having lost a long and draining battle to stop a development company being allowed to build a large 'retirement village' of apartments for the affluent elderly on open countryside at the edge of the village. But also – after twelve years – I had wearied of it.

For a long time, the warm feeling that came from trying to put something back into the community outweighed the boredom that was an inescapable part of attending meetings at which people who had nothing to say would still insist on saying it, and the frustration of engaging with local government bureaucracy at its lowest level. The ratio of time and effort expended to achievement was always hugely disproportionate, but I didn't mind that, because – within the constraints imposed by very limited spending and legal powers – our parish council did manage to do most of the things it usefully could. But, for me, the bruising defeat over the retirement settlement tilted the balance the other way. I put a great deal of effort and time and passion into the battle, and after it had been lost, I felt I had no more to give.

Democracy is an incredibly inefficient means of getting things done. If the parish council were a commercial enterprise (the same applies to the district council, county council, regional assembly and national government), it would go out of business within six months. Fortunately, our shop is a dictatorship; and, fortunately, the dictator is Shro. She certainly regards Helen as a partner in some senses; they discuss challenges and problems together, and often come to joint resolutions on how to meet and tackle them. But the shop is her business, her livelihood. As she says, it is her baby. And it is her personality and way of running it that has made it the success it is.

In a retail and services world in which most of the jobs are held by people who have had no more than cursory training and have no significant personal investment in what they are doing, the hardware shop belongs to an older model. It stands against the cheap, casual-labour template. It challenges what the right-wing neo-liberals term, in their ugly way, 'responsibilisation' – the principle that responsible citizens should manage everything for themselves and not look to others for help. It is there to enable transactions that are generally pretty straightforward, while making itself available to offer other, subtler services, should they be required.

A woman came in for a washing-up liquid refill. While Shro was filling the bottle, her cat Marley – a large, slow-moving animal with multiple health issues whose useful days as a rat- and mouse-catcher are long behind him – padded in, mewing plaintively. The customer asked Shro if Marley was a good eater, which he is, though distinctly choosy. 'The thing is,' the customer said tearfully, 'I had to have my cat put down yesterday, and I've got all this cat food left over and I don't know what to do with it.'

Another time, someone employed by the parish council asked Shro for a peony. 'It's for my stepdad,' he said. 'He's just been diagnosed with cancer.' Shro expressed sympathy. 'Actually, it's for his cat. It died on Saturday, and he wants to put the plant on its grave.'

A very old woman shuffled in to get light bulbs and revealed to Helen that she had bought an ironing board at Heath & Watkins in 1959. She said it was still fine, but at ninety-four, she found it too heavy to put up. 'Thank God for clothes that don't need ironing,' she said, paying £9.94 for the light bulbs and some Sweet Williams that had taken her fancy.

Helen dealt with another woman who needed a new hinge for the door of her bantam coop. 'I don't know why I'm bothering,' she said, with a sigh. 'They're ten years old and I haven't had an egg for two years. But I can't just wring their necks, can I?'

This kind of exchange – almost always inconsequential, very often mundane and banal – is one of the essential elements in the microclimate that sustains the life inside the shop. People have to know without thinking about it that they can share aspects of their lives with Shro and Helen (and Rosie, when she is back from university to do shifts). They also have to know that it doesn't matter how much they spend, or indeed if they decide to spend nothing. The notion that there might be a link between the value of their custom and the amount of time they spend unburdening themselves to the staff must never occur to them. If they spend a pound and go away feeling comfortable at having shared something about themselves or having acquired some useful knowledge, they will come back when the time for the bigger spending project arrives.

Each exchange adds an atom or more to the great store of knowledge and experience vested in the shop. Shro and Helen are the curators of the episteme that Shannon Mattern identified as essential to a good hardware shop, and they are also dispensers of the wisdom. They acquire it themselves in little ways. Helen had a customer whose job was making props for movie sets, and he needed glue. She offered him a glue, but he said he needed solvent, not adhesive glue. Until then, she had not known there was a significant difference. After that she did and was able to offer the next person seeking glue informed advice on what to buy.

This incremental building of the shop's knowledge store is key to its value in the community, and therefore its survival. It requires a strong and enduring investment on the part of those who run it. Shro is never complacent; she endlessly seeks ways to better meet her customers' needs. It visibly distresses her when something she has sold fails to match the expectation, or when she hasn't got something in stock that she feels she ought to, or when her supplier lets her down.

From early spring to autumn, the plants assume a major role in turnover and profit and securing a steady supply of the right ones in top condition is a pressing challenge for her. I know that plants don't qualify as hardware, but they do belong with hardware; they make comfortable stablemates. It helps that both Shro and Helen are knowledgeable and passionate gardeners, and in the season, they are considerable dispensers of that part of the knowledge vested in the shop.

Historically, our village, like most other villages, supported a range of shops that met the residents' basic needs. But in most villages the shops died, squeezed to extinction by supermarkets and big-store competition. Their populations aged and remained static or declined as gradually the flow of new blood weakened and thinned. Picturesque and historic villages suffered worst, because the only way that lifeblood supply can be maintained is by providing somewhere for families with children to live, and those who guarded the old villages were conspicuously resistant to the notion of new housing.

It is the steady increment of new homes that has kept our village alive and our shops in business. The village is reasonably prosperous, and there are other, smaller settlements around whose shoppers prefer to get what they need here rather than fight their way into Reading or Henley. Our shop meets a great variety of everyday needs among a population that is more inclined to shop locally than it once was. Throw in the magic conjured by Shro, with Helen's assistance, and you have a shop that is often referred to as a community asset but asks for no community subsidy to keep it going.

I HAVE JUST come past the shop as dusk gathered. It has been a still winter's afternoon, the day after the shortest day.

It is Christmas week, and the news is all bad news: the virus rampant, family arrangements blown away again, business tottering, retail staggering. In the shop, the lights are bright and welcoming. The Christmas tree in the window sparkles, the coloured bulbs winking at me as I pass. Outside are logs and kindling in bags, a blue plastic toboggan in a wooden half-barrel (not a flake of snow has fallen all winter), primroses and pansies and polyanthas in pots displayed on a stack of pallets. Inside, I can see Rosie (who cares nothing about hardware but likes the money she earns and has a way with her that the customers warm to), frowning in concentration as she taps out the digits on the till. Shro is round the back, potting up unsold bulbs to grow into plants for sale in the summer.

Trade is good. People are buying Christmas lights, decorative wreaths, craft kits for making eco-crackers, wood, light bulbs, always light bulbs. I can see three customers inside, browsing, picking up items, balancing them in the hand, thinking: *Surely this will come in handy for someone someday*. A woman once said to Shro: 'This place is dangerous . . . whenever I come in, I see something I want that I didn't know I wanted.' And it's more dangerous than ever at Christmas, when even the most careful spenders tend to throw off the shackles.

Our shop shines out into the darkness with light and warmth. The American science-fiction writer Ray Bradbury wrote an essay entitled 'The Great American "What am I doing here and why did I buy that?" Hardware Store', in which he suggested that to reassure the potential customer who might be hesitant about identifying what he or she wanted by name, the store should have a sign hanging outside: HARDWARE SPOKEN HERE. Hardware is definitely spoken in our shop, but I'm not sure we need a sign to say so.

\*

AN ELDERLY MAN comes in on occasion, always bringing with him his elderly parrot, Humphrey, in its cage. He said he used to have German Shepherd dogs, but they required a lot of care and exercise and did not live that long, whereas Humphrey was more intelligent, much less demanding in terms of maintenance, and was already nineteen, with the promise – because parrots can live a long time – of being a good companion through the man's old age. Unlike his owner, Humphrey retained something of his youthful good looks, with his ash-grey plumage and orange tail, although some of his feathers looked a trifle ragged.

The man said he took Humphrey everywhere. The bird clearly enjoyed the stimulus of varying surroundings. He was generally silent, but at odd moments had been heard to say in clear tones: 'My name is Humphrey and I am a vulture.'

# Postscript

It is supposedly springtime and the temperature is just above freezing with wet sleet blowing in a bitter north wind. It is distinctly chilly inside the shop and sales of kindling and logs are still lively. Since I finished writing this book there has been a major addition to the shop. A room in the far corner has been opened up by Shro to offer a haven to knitters, sewers, crocheters, dressmakers and other crafters.

It is referred to by the splendidly old-fashioned name The Haberdashery. It was my son Hugh's office but retained a connecting door with the rest of the shop with which it has been reunited (he now works in a cosy, carpeted wooden shed out at the back). Racks of wool of many colours and packets of thread rise to the ceiling either side of the handsome old fireplace. Pins and needles glitter. Drawers hold a multitude of zips as well as decorative paper balls, cats' bells, buckles and other essentials. By the window are the knitting needles, thimbles and pompoms, with the ranks of buttons in the corner.

The opening of The Haberdashery has been greeted appreciatively by the village's significant community of those who love to be busy with their hands. They disappear into it but their presence can be detected by occasional murmurs of appreciation as they discover some precious accessory. Shro – herself an expert with the crochet hook and a prodigious maker of pompoms – is quietly delighted to be able to satisfy this need.

Another very recent and remarkable development in the history of Heath & Watkins concerns Greg's workshop, which I have described in some detail in Chapter Ten. I alluded to its somewhat disorderly state – but this is no more. Greg has tidied his workshop! To say that I was astonished by this news would be an understatement. I have just been inside to marvel at the transformation. The spanners hang from nails in sloping ranks arranged according to size. The shelves are uncluttered, the surfaces clear, the clamps and pliers are gathered in disciplined groups. The effect is amazing and there is plenty of room for Greg and his motorbike.

The first spring plants and vegetables have arrived. The mounds of compost bags are already shrinking. The display of seed potatoes in the window has noticeably diminished. The growing season is almost on us and business is brisk and will get brisker. The shop continues to play its part in keeping this village alive.

# Acknowledgements

First and foremost my thanks go to my daughter-in-law Shro (Sharona) who made this book possible by deciding that running a hardware shop was what she wanted to do, and by showing that she had a genius for doing just that. She also provided the line drawings. Thanks also to my wife Helen for everything – including working two days a week in the shop and keeping alert for enlightening encounters with customers; to our daughter Rosie, an occasional assistant who also provided material; and to Greg Wheadon for allowing me access to his workshop (and for keeping the chain on my chainsaw sharp and various mowers going).

I am grateful to Iain MacGregor for having the good sense to commission the book and for having made important suggestions to improve it. Holly Purdham at Headline has been endlessly patient and helpful in the editing and production process.

Zoe Hendon, at the Museum of Domestic Design and Architecture, was extremely helpful to me in obtaining magazines from the 1950s and 60s, and unearthing other obscure material related to the social history of home improvement. I am grateful to John Brown for insisting that I look into the origins of Swarfega and to Lynn Rosack for providing an image of a beautiful trivert.

Finally I would like to pay a heartfelt tribute to James Watkins. His father was joint founder of the business and James himself ran the shop for twenty years. Living in the street parallel to mine, he was enthusiastic about this book and extremely helpful in providing historical background and checking that I had got my facts right. It was a great shock when he told me he had terminal cancer, and a great sadness that he should have died a few months before publication. I am so grateful to him and his wife Jean.

## Image Credits

*Page 1*   George Mence Smith's hardware shop © The Bexley Archive Image Collection/London Borough of Bexley/Mary Evans Picture Library

Black & Decker – Retro AdArchives/Alamy

2   Practical Householder – Neil Baylis/Alamy

Do It Yourself – Neil Baylis/Alamy

Homemaker – Retro AdArchives/Alamy

3   Barry Bucknell – Evening News/Shutterstock

Toolbox © Tom Fort

B&Q – B&Q Doing It For 30 Years, by kind permission from B&Q Limited

4   Eric Sloane drawing – by kind permission from the Eric Sloane Family Trust

5   RMS *Titanic* – photograph by Robert John Welch/Ian Dagnall/ Alamy

Woman riveting – Ewing Galloway/Alamy

Trivet © Margaret Lynn Rosack

6   Nissen huts – Chronicle/Alamy

Chubb's lock – The History Collection/Alamy

7   Kilner jar – f8 Archive/Alamy

GKN Phillips screw – MichelleBridges/Alamy

Spirit levels © Tom Fort

8   Screwdrivers – Tetra Images/Alamy

The North British Rubber Co. – Chronicle/Alamy

# Bibliography

Alexander, David, *Retailing in England during the Industrial Revolution* (Athlone Press, 1970)

Atkinson, Paul, 'Do It Yourself: Democracy and Design', *Journal of Design History*, 2006

Aubuchon, Bernard W., *Aubuchon Hardware* (Arcadia Publishing, 2008)

Barber, David, *The Spirit Level* (Triquarterly Books, 1995)

Barker, Dennis, 'Obituary of Barry Bucknell', *Guardian*, 2003

Barnett, Le Roy, 'The Tanglefoot Company: Still Sticking with the Business', Michigan History Society, 2011

Basalla, George, *The Evolution of Technology* (Cambridge University Press, 1988)

Beecher, Catharine, and Beecher Stowe, Harriet, *The American Woman's Home* (J. B. Ford & Co, 1869)

*Better Homes and Gardens Handyman's Book* (Meredith Publishing, 1957)

Bigsby, Christopher, *Arthur Miller* (Weidenfeld & Nicolson, 2011)

Blitz, Matt, 'Hobbs and his Lock Picks: The Great Lock Controversy of 1851', www.todayifoundout.com, 2014

Bloom, Loralee J., 'Mining the Archives', Minnesota Historical Society, 2002

Bodo, Bela, *Tiszazug: The Social History of a Murder Epidemic* (East European Monographs, 2002)

Bradbury, Ray, *Yestermorrows: Obvious Answers to Impossible Futures* (Joshua Odell Editions/Capra Press, 1991)

# Bibliography

Brandl, Frances, 'Scott County Memories: Wash Day',
www.scottcountyhistory.org

Brown, Jonathan, 'Obituary of Audley Bowdler Williamson',
*Independent*, 2006

Brown, Peter Jensen, 'The Plunger', Early Sports and Pop
CultureHistory Blog, esnpc.blogspot.com

Bucknell, Barry, *Bucknell's House* (Macdonald & Co, 1964)

Butterworth, Benjamin, *The Growth of Industrial Art* (Government
Printing Office, 1892)

Carlisle, Anne, 'This Is My Work: The Rise of Women in
Woodworking', American Craft Inquiry, 2018

Chesler, Ellen, *Woman of Valor: Margaret Sanger and the Birth Control
Movement in America* (Simon & Schuster, 2007)

Chesterton, G. K., *What's Wrong with the World* (Dodds, Mead, 1912)

Churchill, David, 'Spectacles of Security: Lock-Picking
Competitions and the Emergence of the British Security
Industry in the Mid-Nineteenth Century', History
Workshop Journal, 2015

Cole, David, Browning, Eve, and Schroeder, Fred, *Encyclopedia of
Modern Everyday Inventions* (Greenwood Press, 2003)

Collette, Quentin, 'Riveted Connections in Historical Metal
Structures (1840–1940)', ABC Europe, 2014

Colquhoun, Kate, *Did She Kill Him? A Victorian Tale of Deception,
Adultery and Arsenic* (Little, Brown, 2014)

Crick, Mark, *Sartre's Sink: The Great Writers' Complete Book of DIY*
(Granta, 2008)

Csikszentmihalyi, Mihalyi, *Flow: The Psychology of Optimal
Experience* (Harper Perennial, 1991)

Dagg, Joachim L., 'Exploring Mouse Trap History', Evolution:
Education and Outreach, 2011

# Bibliography

*Dictionary of National Biography* (Oxford University Press, 1917)

Dipman, Carl W., *The Modern Hardware Shop* (Butterick Publishing Co., 1929)

Dresser, Christopher, *The Art of Decorative Design* (Day & Son, 1862)

Drummond, David, *British Mouse Traps and their Makers* (Mouse Trap Books, 2008)

—— 'Unmasking Mascall's Mousetraps', proceedings of the 15th Vertebrate Pest Conference, 1992

—— 'Better Mouse Traps: The History of their Development in the USA', proceedings of the 10th Wildlife Damage Management Conference, 2003

Edwards, Adam, *A Short History of the Wellington Boot* (Hodder & Stoughton, 2006)

Edwards, Clive, 'Home Is Where the Art Is', *Journal of Design History*, 2006

Eichinger, Mike, 'What Are Pop Rivets?', blog.baysupply.com

Engstrand, Iris H. W., 'WD-40, San Diego's Marketing Miracle', *Journal of San Diego History*, 2014

Evans, Charlotte, 'An Anecdotal History of the American Galvanizing Industry', www.galvanizeit.com

Farnsworth, Joshua, woodandshop.com

Fort, Tom, *The Village News* (Simon & Schuster, 2017)

Gauntlett, David, 'Making Is Connecting', Cambridge: Polity, 2018

Gelber, Steven, *Hobbies: Leisure and the Culture of Work in America* (Columbia Press, 1999)

—— 'Do-it-Yourself: Constructing, Repairing and Maintaining Domestic Masculinity', *American Quarterly*, 1997

Goldstein, Carolyn M., *Do It Yourself: Home Improvements in 20th-Century America* (Princeton Architectural Press, 1998)

Hackney, Fiona, 'Use Your Hands for Happiness', *Journal of Design History*, 2006

Hancock, Thomas, *A Personal Narrative of the Origin and Progress of Caoutchouc or India Rubber* (Longman, Brown, Green, Longmans and Roberts, 1857)

Hansluck, Paul (ed.), *The Handyman's Enquire Within*, Cassell & Co., 1908

'Hardware Stores in the UK 2020', www.statista.com

Hargrave, Jocelyn, 'Joseph Moxon: A Re-Fashioned Appraisal', Bulletin of the Bibliographical Society of Australia and New Zealand, 2015

Hewertson, Warren, 'Another Turn of the Woodscrew', *Tools and Trades History Society Newsletter*, 2005

'History of B&Q', www.diy.com

Holly, Henry Hudson, *Modern Dwellings in Town and Country* (Harper & Brothers, New York, 1878)

John Jacob Holtzapffel, *Turning and Mechanical Manipulation*, vols 1–5 (Holtzapffel, 1843–84)

Hooker, James. D., www.lamptech.co.uk

Hope, Jack, 'A Better Mouse Trap', *American Heritage*, 1996

Hunot, Peter, *Man About the House* (Pilot Press, 1946)

Jackson, Andrew, 'Understanding the Experience of the Amateur Maker', doctoral thesis available through research. brighton.ac.uk, 2011

The Thomas Jefferson Encyclopedia, Jefferson's Nailery, www.monticello.org

Jeffreys, James B., *Retail Trading in Britain 1850–1950* (Cambridge University Press, 1954)

Jeykyll, Gertrude, *Old West Surrey: Some Notes and Memories* (Longmans, Green & Co., 1904)

Jones, P. d'A and Simons, E. N., *The Story of the Saw* (N. Neame, 1961)

Kaplan, Abraham, *The Conduct of Inquiry: Methodology for Behavioural Science* (Transaction, 1964)

Kastner, Jeffrey, 'National Insecurity: Alfred C. Hobbs and the Great Lock Controversy of 1851', *Cabinet Magazine*, 2006

Kennedy, Tristan, 'From Brando to Britney: How Denim Became Iconic (and Where it Went Wrong)', vice.com, 2019

Ketley, A. J. (ed.), *Textbook of Ironmongery and Hardware* (National Institute of Hardware, 1949)

Kraybill, Donald, *The Riddle of Amish Culture* (John Hopkins University Press, 2003)

Lilley, Sam, *Men, Machines and History* (Cobbett Press, 1948)

Lockhart, Bill, Schriever, Beau, Lindsay, Bill, and Serr, Carol, 'The Kilner Glass Companies', The Society for Historical Archaeology, available through sha.org

Long, Derek A., *'At the Sign of Atlas': The Life and Work of Joseph Moxon* (Paul Watkins Publishing, 2015)

McCarty, Jennifer Hooper, and Foecke, Tim, *What Really Sank The Titanic: New Forensic Discoveries* (Citadel, 2008)

McCosh, Fred, *Nissen of the Huts: The Biography of Lt. Col. Peter Nissen* (B. D. Publishing 1997)

McCullough, David, *The Great Bridge: The Epic Story of the Building of the Brooklyn Bridge* (Simon & Schuster, 2001)

McLean, Stuart, *The Hardware Store Has All the Answers from The Morningside World of Stuart McLean* (Penguin Canada, 1989)

McVey, John, McVey Hardware, available from jmcvey.net

Marx, Karl, *Capital: A Critical Analysis of Capitalist Production* (Swann Sonneschein, Lowrey and Co., 1887)

Mascall, Leonard, *A Booke of Engines and Traps* (London, 1590)

Maslow, Abraham, *The Psychology of Science: A Reconnaissance* (Chicago Gateway, 1966)

Mattern, Shannon, 'Community Plumbing: How the Hardware Store Orders Things, Neighborhoods and Material Worlds', available through jmcvey.net

Meadows, Cecil A., *The Victorian Ironmonger* (Shire, 1984)

Melchert, Ken, *The Humble Nail – A Key to Unlock the Past*, available through ezeinarticles.com

Melchionne, Kevin, 'Of Bookworms and Busy Bees: Cultural Theory in the Age of Do-It-Yourself', *Journal of Aesthetics and Art Criticism*, 1999

Mercer, Henry C., 'Ancient Carpenter's Tools', Bucks County Historical Society, 1951

Mintel, 'DIY Retailing – UK', Mintel Group, May 2021

Moezzi, Mithra, 'Social Meanings of Electric Light: A Different History of the United States' Lawrence Berkeley National Laboratory

Moxon, Joseph, *Mechanick Exercises or the Doctrine of Handyworks* (London, 1700; available through archive.org)

Munsey, Cecil, 'The Oldest "3-in-One Oil" Container, Bottles and Extras', 2006

Noble, Theophilus Charles, *A Brief History of the Worshipful Company of Ironmongers* (London, 1889)

# Bibliography

O'Dea, William, *The Social History of Lighting* (Routledge & Kegan Paul, 1958)

Petroski, Henry, The Evolution of Useful Things (Alfred A. Knopf, 1992)

Pevsner, Nikolaus, 'Christopher Dresser: Industrial Designer', *Architectural Review*, 1937

Preston, Frank, *A Brief History of the Development of Boring Tools* (Stanley Works Education Service, 1964)

Powell, Helen, 'Time, Television and the Decline of DIY', *Journal of Architecture, Design and Domestic Space*, 2009

Randall, Frederick John, *Love and the Ironmonger* (John Lane/ The Bodley Head, 1908)

Researchpod, 'Get a Grip – The Invention of the Rawlplug', www.design-technology.info

Rocha, Guy, 'Levi's 501 Jeans: A Riveting Story in Early Reno', www.bendavis.com

Roe, John Wickham, *English and American Tool Builders* (Yale University Press/Humphrey Milford, 1916)

Rosack, Lynn, *The A–Z of Collecting Trivets* (Collector Books, 2004)

Rybczynski, Wytold, *One Good Turn: A Natural History of the Screwdriver and the Screw* (Simon & Schuster, 2000)

Sala, George Augustus, *The Battle of the Safes: Or British Invincibles versus Yankee Ironclads* (Tinsley Brothers, 1868)

Sellers, Paul, paulsellers.com

Shove, Elizabeth, and Watson, Matthew, 'Produce, Competence, Project and Practice: DIY and the Dynamics of Craft Consumption', *Journal of Consumer Culture*, 2008

Sjogren, Guy, 'The West Midlands Nail Trade', West Midlands History

Slack, Charles, *Noble Obsession: Charles Goodyear, Thomas Hancock and the Race to Unlock the Greatest Industrial Secret of the 19th century* (Hyperion, 2002)

Sloan, Eric, *A Reverence for Wood* (W. Funk, 1965)

—— *A Museum of Early American Tools* (Ballantine Books, 1974)

Smith, David, 'Under Lock and Key: Securing Privacy and Property in Victorian Fiction and Culture', dissertation available through Vanderbilt Institutional Depository, 2007

Starr, Julian, *Fifty Things to Make for the Home* (McGraw-Hill, 1941)

Stickley, Gustav, 'Home Training in Cabinet Work', *Home Craftsman*, 1905


Thevenot, Melchisedech, *The Art of Swimming* (London, 1789)

Thoreau, Henry, *Walden, or Life in the Woods* (Ticknor and Fields, 1854)

Tolpin, Jim, *The Toolbox Book* (Taunton Press, 1999)

—— *Jim Tolpin's Guide to Becoming a Professional Cabinetmaker* (Popular Woodworking, 2005)

Tomkins, Silvan Solomon, and Messick, Samuel, *Computer Simulation of Personality: Frontiers of Psychological Theory* (Wiley, 1963)

Toulouse, Julian Harrington, *Bottle Makers and their Marks* (Thomas Nelson, 1971)

—— *Fruit Jars: A Collector's Manual* (Thomas Nelson, 1969)

Tromp, Tim, 'Kilkokat's Antique Light Bulb Site', www.bulbcollector.com

Turney, Joanne, 'Here's One I Made Earlier: Making and Living with Home Craft in Contemporary Britain', *Journal of Design History*, 2004

Tweedale, Geoffrey, 'The Ironmonger: The King of Hardware
  Trade Journals', available through eaiainfo.org

Vanderbilt, Tom, 'Alfred C. Hobbs: The American who Shocked
  Victorian England by Picking the World's Strongest Lock',
  slate.com, 2014
Veasey, Christine (ed.), *Pins and Needles Treasure Book of Home
  Making* (Christine Veasey Publications, 1955)

Wakeling, Arthur, *Things to Make in Your Workshop* (Popular Science
  Publishing Co., 1930)
Weil, Marty, The Ephemera Blog, https://ephemera.typepad.com/
Wheeler, James A. (ed.), *The Practical Man's Book of Things to Make
  and Do* (Odhams Press, 1940)
Williams, Donald, *Virtuoso: The Toolbox and Workbench of Henry O.
  Studley* (Lost Art Press, 2015)
Woodruff, William, *The Rise of the British Rubber Industry*
  (Liverpool University Press, 1958)
Woolf Electric Tools Ltd., *The Wolf Cub Book of Profitable Pleasure*
  (London, 1955)

# Index

*ABC of Do It Yourself, The,* ITV series of the 1960s, 84.

*A–Z Guide to Collecting Trivets,* book by Lynn Rosack, 161

*About the Home,* BBC TV show of the 1950s, 80

Abram, Norm, presented of the US show *The Yankee Workshop,* 144

Ace Hardware, chain of American hardware stores
opens first store in 1929, 94
today, 95

Achulean stone tools, 110

Adams, John, US president and friend of Thomas Jefferson, 191

Aigle (formerly A L'Aigle), rubber boot made by Hiram Hutchinson, 237

Allingham, Marjery, detective story writer, 93

*All the Mod Cons,* BBC TV series about home DIY and design, 91

American Birth League, 245

American Screw Co., 227

*American Zinc Lead and Oil Journal,* 180

Amish, traditionalist Anabaptist Christian communities, 206

Angel Makers of Nagyrev, women involved in mass murder in Hungary using flypapers
story told many times, 260
rumours of murders, 261
put on trial, 262

Animal Trap Co., 253

Anne, Princess, commissions black Hunter boots, 239

Archibald Kendrick & Sons, metalware company associated with Christopher Dresser, 164

Archimedes, Greek scientist, inventor of early hydraulic machine, 116

*Architectural Review,* magazine about architecture, 164

Argand, François-Pierre-Amédée, inventor of oil lamp, 202

Argyll, black rubber boot made by the North British Rubber Co., 239

Armstrong, Sir Wlliam, industrialist, instals electric lighting at home, 205

Armstrong Whitworth, British aircraft maker, 155

Artex, textured ceiling coating
popular in 1970s, 98
problematic to remove, 99

*Art of Decorative Design, The,* book by Christopher Dresser, 163

*Art of Swimming,* book by Melchisédech Thévenot, 230

Ascot electric water heater, 179

Ashley wallpaper, 67–8

Atkinson, James, Leeds ironmonger, develops Little Nipper mousetrap, 254

Atkinson, Paul, professor of design and design history at Sheffield Hallam University, 51

Aubuchon, William E., author of book about Aubuchon Hardware, 94

Aubuchon Hardware, chain of hardware stores in north-eastern United States, 94

Ayer, A. J. ('Freddie'), British philosopher married to – among others – Dee Wells, 79

B&Q, chain of hardware stores
  seed sown, 95
  first store, 96
  taken over by Woolworths, 96

Babbage, Charles, Victorian mathematician and theologian, 120

Barber, David, American poet and author of 'The Spirit Level', 231

Barker, Ronnie, British comedian and sketch writer, 270–1

Barrhead, town in Scotland, home of the Mousetrap factory, 254

Barrow, Eliza, murder victim of Frederick Seddon, 260

Batchelor, Denzil, British journalist, cricket writer and *bon viveur*, 93

Bazalgette, Sir Peter, pioneer of reality TV, 145–6

Beatrice Royal art gallery, Eastleigh, 96

Beecher, Catharine, American writer and reformer
  campaigns, 22
  writes *The American Woman's Home* with Harriet Beecher Stowe, 23
  promotes version of domestic life, 36
  cult of domesticity, 55

Beecher, Lyman, father of Catharine Beecher and Harriet Beecher Stove, preacher, 22

Belvoir Castle, country seat of the Duke of Rutland, 202

*Better Homes and Gardens*, American magazine, 56, 72, 94

*Better Homes and Gardens Handyman's Book*, 72

Bigsby, Christopher, biographer of Arthur Miller, 133

Black, Duncan, co-founder of Black & Decker, 54

Black & Decker, manufacturer of power tools
  introduces Homes Utility power tools, 53
  drill makes him five times the man, 59
  tools in Heath & Watkins, 218
  Helen shows customer one, 267

Blair, Edith, home editor of *Woman* magazine and creator of a 'tea waggon', 40

Block, Richard, co-founder of B&Q
  takes lease on premises in Southampton, 96
  starts Beatrice Royal art gallery, 96

Blue, Charles Edwin, American inventor of jar-making machine, 195

Bodo, Bela, Hungarian author of
    book about the Angel Makers
    of Nagyrev, 261
Bogarde, Dirk, British actor, 92
*Booke of Engines and Traps etc, A,*
    book by Leonard Mascall, 251
*Bottle Makers and their Marks*, book
    by Julian Harrison Toulouse,
    195
Boyle's Law, governing relationship
    between volume and pressure
    of a gas, 214
Bradbury, Ray, American writer of
    science fiction and author of
    essay about hardware stores,
    282
Bradman, W. A. G., author of DIY
    books and articles, 93
Brandenburger, Jacques, Swiss
    inventor of cellulose, 209
Brando, Marlon, American film
    actor and wearer of jeans in
    *The Wild One*, 159
Brands, Frances, provider of
    memories about wash day, 178
*British Medical Journal*, 258
British Museum, 211
Brooklyn Bridge, New York
    as symbol of American
        engineering prowess, 172
    use of galvanised steel, 173
Bucknell, Barry, TV DIY expert
    introduces *Do It Yourself* on BBC
        television, 78
    appearance, 78–9
    modesty and simplicity, 78–9
    the challenge of Bucknell's
        House, 80,
    not an innovator, 82
    designs Mirror Dinghy, 83
    later career and life, 84

    unfairly mocked, 87
    legacy, 88
*Bucknell's House*, BBC TV show
    devised, 80
    success, 82,
    last programme, 83
Burns, Horace, American designer
    of trivets, 165
*Business Week*, American magazine,
    54

Cadillac, American automobile
    made using Phillips cross-
    head screws, 227
Calco, British makers of glue, 67
Camm, Frederick J., editor of
    *Practical Householder* and
    pioneer of how-to-do
    journalism, 65
Campbell, Ann Morgan, archivist
    for the Nevada Historical
    Society and historian of Levi
    jeans, 157
Carlyle, Jane, letter writer and wife
    of Thomas Carlyle, 121
Carlyle, Thomas, historian, on the
    importance of tools, 126
Cellophane, packaging material
    invented by Jacques
    Brandenburger, 209
Challenge Nails, made in
    Gloucester, 192
Chamberlain, Joseph, politician and
    partner with Joseph Nettlefold
    in screw-making business,
    122–3
*Changing Rooms*, TV makeover show
    favourite of Shro's, 21
    banter and raucous hilarity, 84
    devised by Peter Bazalgette, 145–6

Chatwood, Samuel, Lancastrian lock
and safe maker involved in the
Battle of the Safes, 187
Chesterton, G. K., novelist, poet and
essayist, 65
Chiochetti, Domenico, Italian
prison-of-war and artist of
Lamb Holm chapel in Orkney,
177
Choate, Rufus, US congressman and
lawyer involved in Great India
Rubber case of 1852, 236
Chubb, Jeremiah, one of the
brothers who founded Chubb
Locks and inventor of the
'detector lock', 182
Chubb, John, nephew of Jeremiah
and boss of Chubb Locks,
challenged Alfred Hobbs to
pick his company's locks 183-4
Church, William Hale, scientist,
creates lacquer to make
cellophane waterproof, 209
Clark, Eugene, president of the
American Screw Co., convert
to Phillips cross-head screws,
209
Clement, Joseph, engineer and
inventor
obtains job with Joseph Bramah,
119
devises lathe to produce screws
of uniform length, 120
Cole, George William, American
inventor of 3-in-One oil, 243-4
*Computer Simulation of Personality:
Frontiers of Psychological Theory,*
book in which one its editors,
Silvan Tomkins, considered
the relationship between
hammers and nails, 221

*Conduct of Inquiry: Methodology for
Behavioral Science,* book by
Abraham Kaplan in which he
also considered the matter of
hammers and nails, 221
Congowall, wall covering, 67
Convair, US aircraft makers, 242
Coope, Octavius E., Conservative
MP and early convert to
electric lighting, 205
Corbett, Ronnie, star with Ronnie
Barker of *The Two Ronnies,* 270
Coronet Tool Co., Derby
toolmaking firm, 67
Corrugated iron
developed by Henry Palmer of
the London Dock Co., 172
used to make rubbish cans, 173
used to make Nissen huts, 174-6
Cotterill, Edwin, Birmingham lock
maker, 185
Crabbe, George, poet and essayist,
201-2
*Craftsman, The,* influential American
magazine founded by Gustav
Stickley, 26
Cragside, mansion in
Northumberland owned by
Sir William Armstrong and lit
by electricity, 205
Craufurd, Cdr. Henry, obtains
patent for process of
galvanising, 172
Crick, Mark, parodist, author of
*Satre's Sink: The Great Writers'
Book of DIY,* 274
Crookes, Sir William, developer of
the Crookes Tube, 203
Cutler, Horace, one-time partner of
Charles Goodyear, 235, 236

Czikszentmihalyi, Mihaly,
    Hungarian-born psychologist
theory of flow, 51
I failed to surrender to flow, 61
specialist woodworkers and flow,
    161

*Daily Mail* Ideal Home Exhibition,
    82, 92
Davis, Jacob W., (born Jacob
    Youphas), tailor in San Reno,
    California
sets up business, 157
fastens jeans pockets with rivets,
    157
adds double arc of orange thread
    to pockets, 157
prospers, 158
Davy, Sir Humphry, chemist, 171
Dawson's, ironmongers in
    Todmorden market, 6
Day, Horace, American
    entrepreneur, attempts to
    cheat Charles Goodyear, 236–7
Day & Newell, New York locksmiths
    and employers of Alfred
    Hobbs, 183
Dean, James, American actor, 65, 159
*Debate of the Carpenter's Tools*,
    anonymous late 15th-century
    poem, 111–2
Decker Jr., Alonzo, instrumental
    in getting Black & Decker to
    manufacture power drills, 54
*Decorating Cents*, American home
    improvement show presented
    by Joan Steffend, 144
Deykin & Sons, Birmingham firm
    making electroplated cutlery
    and other wares, 161

Diana, Princess of Wales, wears
    Hunter wellington boots, 232
*Dictionnaire de la Langue Francaise*,
    224
Difference Machine, early
    mechanical calculator devised
    by Charles Babbage, 120
Dipman, Carl W., author of *The
    Good Hardware Store*, 38–9
Disston & Sons, Philadelphia
    engineering firm specialising
    in saws, 125
DIY, shortened form of Do-It-
    Yourself
term first used, 28
ages of, 37
women and, 40
hierarchy, 49
motives for, 50
as manly pursuit, 55
in post-war Britain, 57–8
growing sector, 68,
incorporated into 'lifestyle', 92
on TV, 143–9
on YouTube, 149
will never die, 150
my patchy DIY life, 212
*DIY SOS*, (later *DIY SOS: The Big
    Build*) TV show, 146–7
*Do It Yourself*, magazine
launch, 68–9
standard front cover, 77
influence on Barry Bucknell, 82
stages exhibitions, 92
*Do It Yourself*, BBC TV show
    presented by Barry Bucknell,
    78, 80
Dresser, Christopher, writer and
    designer
influence as theorist and
    practitioner, 163

Dresser, Christopher (*cont.*)
  embraces mass production, 164
  obscurity and rediscovery, 164
Drew, Richard Gurney, inventor
  of masking tape and Scotch
  adhesive tape, 209–10
Drews Ironmongers, Reading firm,
  42
Durenne, Antoine, French inventor
  of rivet-making machine, 152
Dyer, Joseph, American-born
  industrialist
  sets up nail factory in
    Birmingham, 189
  possible views on Thomas
    Jefferson, 190

Edison, Thomas, American inventor
  and entrepreneur
  demonstrates light bulb, 204
  rivalry with Joseph Swan, 204–5
  expands network in New York,
    205
Edison Swan Electric Light Co.,
  known as Ediswan, 204
Eiffel Tower, Paris, use of 2.5 million
  rivets to hold together, 153
Emerson, Ralph Waldo, American
  essayist, lecturer and
  philosopher, on mousetraps,
  254–5
Empire Level Co., established
  by Henry Ziemann in
  Mukwonago, Wisconsin, to
  make spirit levels, 230
Engstrand, Iris W., historian of
  WD-40, 241, 243
*Evolution of Useful Things, The*, book
  by Henry Petroski, 220

*Expanded A–Z Book of Collecting
  Trivets, The*, book by Lynn
  Rosack, 161, 162

Fairbrother, William Sir, engineer
  and pioneer in using machine
  for punching rivets, 152–3
Fairweather, Sharona ('Shro')
  as hero of the story, 12
  leadership, 14
  takes over Heath & Watkins, 17
  as born DIYer, 21
  customers getting used to, 29–30
  and Helen, 43, 278
  as custodian, 44
  decides to tackle shed, 75
  adapts butcher's hooks, 90
  and Greg, 129
  and rivets, 159–60
  and galvanised tubs, 179
  cuts keys, 181
  attitude to jars, 193
  unforgiving attitude to faulty
    wellington boots, 233
  and 3-in-One oil, 246
  and rats, 263
  talking to customers 264–5
  personality, 265
  as dictator, 278
  her cat, Marley, 279
*Family Handyman, The*, American
  home improvement magazine,
  73, 94
Farnsworth, Joshua, American
  woodworker and host of
  woodandshop.com, 137–8
Fazekas, Zsuzsanna, Hungarian
  dispenser of arsenic and
  advice on how to use it, 261,
  262

*Fifty Shades of Grey*, supposedly
    erotic fiction by E. L. James
    partly set in hardware store,
    274
*Fifty Things to Make for the Home*, DIY
    book by Julian Starr, 54
*Fine Woodworking*, American
    magazine, 138, 139
Fisher, Isaac, patented use of glass
    paper in Springfield, Vermont,
    207
Flanagan, Bob, American
    performance artist, poet and
    self-mutilator, author of *Why?*,
    275–6
Fleming, W. D., author of *Galvanizing
    and Tinning*, 180
flypapers, glue traps for flies
    sold in Heath & Watkins, 256
    invented by Thum brothers in
        Grand Rapids, Michigan, 257
    arsenical, freely sold in
        pharmacies, 258
    alleged use for murder by
        Florence Maybrick, 259
    proven use for murder by
        Frederick Sedden, 260
    used by Angel Makers of Nagyrev
        for mass murder, 260–1
Follain, Jean, French poet, author of
    *Quincaillerie*, 276
Ford, Glenn, American actor and
    woodworker, 74
Ford, Harrison, American actor and
    star of *Witness*, 76
Ford, Henry, American car maker,
    226
Fort, Helen, assistant at Heath &
    Watkins
    knowledge of plants, 43

helping out in early days, 63
    leaves BBC, 75
    as Roof Monkey, 76
    and I move house, 99
Fort, Matthew, *Great British Menu*
    judge, performs ceremony at
    Heath & Watkins, 18
Frank Shaw nails, made in
    Gloucester, 192
*Friday Night Lights*, American TV
    show about a football team,
    139
*Fruit Jars: A Collector's Manual*, book
    by Julian Harrison Toulouse,
    195

Galvani, Luigi, Italian experimental
    scientist
    experiments on frogs' legs, 169
    hopelessly wrong, 170
    gives name to galvanisation, 171
Galvanisation, process of coating
    metals in zinc
    association with Luigi Galvani,
        169
    process invented by Sorel, 171
    and corrugated iron, 172
    Brooklyn Bridge, 172–3
    Nissen Hut, 174–6
    and wash tubs, 177–9
    vain attempts to rename
        'zincization', 180
*Galvanizing and Tinning*, book by
    W. D. Fleming, 180
Gas lighting, in streets, 203
Gavin Diarmuid, Irish garden
    designer and cheerful
    co-presenter of *Home Front*,
    147

General Motors, US maker of
automobiles, 277
Gelber, Professor Steven, American
historian of do-it-yourself
identifies first mention in print,
28
identifies 'non-overlapping
spheres of influence', 36
DIY able to accommodate
masculinity, 73
DIY in Hollywood, 74
Gesner, Abraham, inventor of
kerosene, 202
George Tucker Eyelet Co., makers of
pop rivets, 155
Gilbert, Joan, BBC TV presenter in
the 1950s, 80
Goater, John, chief foreman at
Chubb Locks, 185
*Godey's Lady's Book*, American
magazine for women, 25
Goodyear, Charles, American
inventor of rubber
vulcanisation
attracts misfortune on grand
scale, 234
attempts unsuccessfully to break
into British market, 235
cheated by Horace Day, 236
dies an impoverished invalid, 237
Goodyear Tire and Rubber Co., 237
*Grand Designs*, long-running TV
series about home renovations
presented by Kevin McLeod,
147–8
*Great British Menu*, long-running
BBC TV series about chefs, 18
Great Exhibition, staged at Crystal
Palace, London, in 1851, 182

Great India Rubber Case,
determines Charles
Goodyear did invent rubber
vulcanisation, 236–7
Great Lock Controversy, 185–6
Greg, mechanic
rents workshop at Heath &
Watkins, 11
cylinder grinder, 75
workshop, 127
skill with mowers, 128
love of vintage motorcycles, 128–9
inside workshop, 130–2
Grey, Christian, character in *Fifty
Shades of Grey*, 274
Griffiths, Ira, American
woodworking teacher, 28
*Ground Force*, BBC TV gardening
makeover show originally
presented by Alan Titchmarsh
and Charlie Dimmock, 146
*Groundhog Day*, film starring
Bill Murray and featuring
Punxsutawney Phil, 166
Guest, Keen & Nettlefolds, British
industrial firm, 227

Hackney, Fiona, social historian,
39–40
hammer, tool
origin, 219
multiple varieties according to
Karl Marx, 219
and the Law of the Instrument,
220–2
Hancock, Thomas, pioneer of
rubber
devises machine to press rubber
into blocks, 234

partnership with Charles
Macintosh, 234
fails to give credit to Goodyear,
236
*Handyman's Enquire Within, The,*
book compiled by Paul
Hasluck
covers everything from acetylene
to zinc, 27
severely practical, 28
screwdrivers, 225
spirit levels, 230
Hanging Gardens of Nineveh, 116
hardware, *passim*
origin of term, 6
importance of hardware shops in
community, 43
timelessness, 270
*Hardware,* ITV series about hardware
shop, 271
Harland & Wolff, Belfast shipyard
where the *Titanic* was built, 153
Harmer, John Zimmerman,
American designer and
manufacturer of trivets, 165–6
Hasluck, Paul, Australian-born
journalist, editor of *Work*
magazine and prolific
compiler of books of practical
instruction including *The
Handyman's Enquire Within,*
27–8, 225, 230
Hawley, John Savage, American
inventor and confectioner
invents 'elastic force cup', 216
starts confectionery business
with Herman W. Hoops, 217
turns to writing books about
religion, 217–8

Heaney, Seamus, Irish poet and
author of *The Spirit Level,* 230
Heath, Jack, co-founder of Heath &
Watkins, 4
Heath & Watkins, hardware shop
in Sonning Common,
Oxfordshire, *passim*
Hemingway, Ernest, American
novelist parodied by Mark
Crick, 275
Henley-on-Thames, small town in
south Oxfordshire, 35, 281
Herbert, George, 17th-century poet
and compiler of *Outlandish
Proverbs,* 188
Hero (or Heron), Greek engineer
of 1st-century, devised screw
press, 116
Herring, Silas, unscrupulous
American safe-maker involved
in the Battle of the Safes, 187
*Historic Glass Bottles,* website, 196
*History of the British Rubber Industry,*
book by William Woodruff,
237
Hobbs, Alfred C., American lock-
maker and lock-picker
arrives for Great Exhibition, 182
picks Chubb Detector lock, 183
picks Bramah lock, 184–5
sets up business in Cheapside,
186
Holly, Henry Hudson, American
author of *Modern Dwellings in
Town and Country,* 25
Holtzappfel, John Jacob, member
of London tool-making
family and historian, author
of *Turning and Mechanical
Manipulation,* 119, 207

Homebase, UK chain of DIY stores, 100

Home Depot, US chain of DIY stores, 95

*Home Front*, BBC TV home improvement show, 145, 147

*Homemaker*, DIY magazine launched in 1959, 71, 77

*Homes & Gardens*, magazine, 92–3

*Hometime*, American TV home improvement show presented by Dean Johnson, 144

Hooke, Robert, 17th-century English scientist, 114, 229

Hooker, James D., host of lamptech.co.uk, 199

Hooker, William Chauncey, inventor of early snap-trap for mice, 253, 254

Hoops, Herman, partner of John Savage Hawley in confectionery business, 217

Hukin & Heath, Birmingham silversmiths, employed Christopher Dresser, 164

Hunot, Peter, author of *Man About the House*, 58

Hunter, James, proprietor of the Mousetrap factory in Barrhead, Scotland, 254

Hunter wellington boots worn by Princess Diana, 232 first made, 239

Hutchinson, Hiram, American businessman and manufacturer of Aigle boots, 237

Huxley, Elspeth, English writer brought up in Kenya, 93

Huygens, Christian, 17th-century Dutch scientist with interest in spirit levels, 229

Hyland, Stanley, BBC TV producer possibly responsible for dreaming up *Bucknell's House*, 80

*Ironmonger, The*, magazine tools advertised in 1950, 59 founded by Morgan brothers, 124 expanded reach, 125

James, E. L., author of *Fifty Shades of Grey*, 274

Jefferson, Thomas, US president and slave owner argues against slavery, 190–1 establishes nail factory, 191 dies deep in debt, 192

Jekyll, Gertrude, gardening writer, 201

Johnson, David, founder and editor of *Do It Yourself* magazine, 68, 71

Johnson, Dean, presenter of *Hometime*, long-running US home improvement show, 144

*Journal of Consumer Culture*, 50

*Journal of San Diego History*, 241

Jubilee tea-pot stand, 161

Kane, Andy ('Handy Andy'), regular carpenter on *Changing Rooms*, 21, 146

Kaplan, Abraham, author of *The Conduct of Inquiry: Methodology for Behavioral Science*, 221

keys, cutting, crucial part of shop business, 45

Kier, Samuel Martin, pioneer in
distilling kerosene from
petroleum, 202
Kilner, storage jars
first made by Kilner Brothers,
194
dependent on American-made
machines, 195
status out of proportion to
usefulness, 196–7
Kilokat, antique light bulb website,
200
Kimack, Tim, California
woodworker, 106
Knope, Lesley, character in *Parks and
Recreation*, 140
Koh-i-Noor diamond, shown at
Great Exhibition, 183,
Konovaloff, Tony, US woodworker,
107
Kraybill, Donald, American expert
on Amish, 206

Lady Christl, variety of early potato,
2, 14
Lamb Holm, island in Orkney
used to accommodate Italian
prisoners-of-war during the
Second World War, 177
Lamptech, website featuring British
light bulbs, 199
Lane, Margaret, British journalist,
biographer and novelist, 40
Larsen, Norman B., president of the
Rocket Chemical Co. of San
Diego, 241
Lascaux, caves in south-west France
famous for wall paintings, 201
Law of the Instrument, with
reference to hammers, 220–1

Lawson, Norman, American
engineer
helps form Rocket Chemical Co.,
241
invents WD-40, 242
fades into obscurity, 243
Leche, John, 13th-century owner of
ironmongers in London, 7, 111
Leland, John, 16th-century
chronicler of local history, 189
Levi Strauss, San Francisco makers
of denim
court action against imitators,
156–7
supplies Jacob Davis, 158
prospers from making jeans, 159
Levittown, suburban housing
development in US, 55
Lewis, Jerry, American actor and
woodworker, 74
light bulbs
viewed with boredom in shop,
198
websites illuminating history,
199–200
prototype devised by Joseph
Swan, 203
prototype devised by Thomas
Edison, 204
triumph over gas, 205
technology marches on, 206–7
Lindsay, Bill, creator of Historic
Glass Bottle website, 196
Lititz, Pennsylvania, centre of US
mousetrap manufacture, 253–4
Little Nipper, mousetrap devised
and named by James Atkinson
of Leeds, 254
Llewellyn-Bowen, Laurence, TV
presenter, 21, 146–7

lockdown
  announced, 47
  stimulus to DIY, 48
  making people think about their
    homes, 49
  impact in village, 59–60
*Love and the Ironmonger*, novel by
  Frederick John Randall, 274
Lovecraft, H. P., author of *Rats in the
  Walls* and other horror stories,
  262
Lowe, Lucius Smith, founder of
  Lowe's hardware chain in US,
  95

McCall, Kate Flood, American
  owner of slaves in Virginia, 192
Macintosh, Scottish chemist,
  inventor of waterproofing, 234
McKnight, William L., vice-president
  of the Minnesota Mining and
  manufacturing Co. (later 3M),
  208
McLean, Stuart, Canadian writer
  and broadcaster, 43
McLeod, Kevin, presenter of *Grand
  Designs* on Channel 4, 147–8
McVey, John, American lecturer,
  teacher, expert on asphalt,
  emblematics and hardware,
  curator of jmcvey.net, 272–5
Mallow, Abraham, American author
  of *The Psychology of Science: A
  Reconnaissance*, 222
Malouin, Pierre-Jacques, French
  scientist, devised process to
  protect metals with coating of
  zinc, 170–1
*Man About the House*, DIY book by
  Peter Hunot, 58

*Manchester Guardian*, newspaper, 190
Margaret, Princess, forbidden to
  marry Peter Townsend, 65
Marshall Hall, Edward, barrister,
  260
Marx, Karl, author of *Das Kapital*
  on alienation of workers, 53
  notes proliferation of hammers
    in Birmingham, 219–20
  not much of a DIY man, 220
*Mary Rose*, Henry Vlll's flagship
  sunk in 1545, 112
Mascall, Leonard, author of *A Book
  of Engines and Traps etc*, 251
Mason, John Laudis, tinsmith from
  New Jersey
  developed method to seal fruit
    jars, 195
  work pirated, 196
  dies in poverty, 196
Mast, John, American entrepreneur,
  developed mass-market snap-
    trap for mice, 253
Mattern, Sharon, professor of
  anthropology and author
  of article about hardware
  stores entitled 'Community
  Plumbing', 43, 280
Maudsley, Henry, engineer and
  inventor
  meets Joseph Bramah, 118
  develops advanced lathe, 118–9
  lock made by him and Joseph
    Bramah picked by Alfred
    Hobbs, 184
Maxim, Hiram, inventor of very
  small light bulb, 200
Maybrick, Florence, accused of
  murdering husband using
  arsenic from flypapers, 259

Mays, Laura, Irish-born
  woodworker, 138
Mead Margaret, American
  anthropologist, 73
*Mechanick Exercises on the Doctrine
  of Handy Works*, 17th-century
  DIY book by Joseph Moxon,
  113, 152
*Medieval Housebook*, 15th-century
  German compendium of
  practical knowledge and
  advice, 224
*Mein Kampf*, by Adolf Hitler, 55
Mercer, Henry Chapman, American
  collector and historian of
  early tools, 111
*Metal Worker*, journal featuring
  'elastic force-cup', 217
Miller, Arthur, American playwright
  and woodworker, 132–3
Mintel, marketing analysts, 50
Mirror Dinghy, sailing boat
  designed by Barry Bucknell, 83
*Modern Woman*, magazine, 40
Montgomery, George, American
  actor and woodworker, 74
Monticello, estate in Virginia owned
  by Thomas Jefferson, 191, 192
Morgan, six brothers – William,
  Septimus, Thomas, Walter,
  Octavius, Edward – who
  founded *The Ironmonger*
  magazine, 124
Morris, William, artist, designer,
  writer and inspiration of the
  Arts-and-Crafts movement
principles adopted by Gustav
  Stickley in *Craftsman* journal,
  26
rejects mass production, 164

Moulton, Stephen, sent by Charles
  Goodyear to negotiate sale
  of method for vulcanising
  rubber, 235
Mousetraps
  early models, 251
  intricate devices, 252
  snap trap invented by Hooker,
    253
  thirteen categories, 255
  glue, 256
Moxon, Joseph, author of *Mechanick
  Exercises*
  birth and upbringing, 113
  writes book, 113
  social ascent, 114
  on rivets, 152
*Museum of Early American Tools*, book
  by Eric Sloane, 134–5
Museum of Electric Lamp
  technology, part of lamptech.
  co.uk, 199
Museum of Modern Art, New York,
  55
*Music Trade Review*, journal featuring
  photograph of H. O. Studley,
  107

nails
  origin, 188
  industry in West Midlands, 189
  advent of wire nails, 189
  Thomas Jefferson as nail
    manufacturer, 190–2
National Grid, 206
Nettlefold, Joseph, industrialist
  pays £10,000 for Thomas Sloan's
    screw-making machine, 122
  partnership with Joseph
    Chamberlain, 122–2

Nevada Historical Society, 157
*New Yankee Workshop*, American
    home improvement show
    presented by Norm Abram,
    144
Nicholson, John, author of *The
    Operative Mechanic and British
    Machinist*, 207
Nissen, Peter
    designs Nissen Hut, 174
    made captain, 175
    awarded D.S.O. and cash, 176
Nissen Hut
    principles of construction, 175
    remarkable durability, 176
    on Lamb Holm, Orkney, 177
Norris, Henry Lee, co-founder of
    North British Rubber Co., 238
North British Rubber Co.,
    factory established on outskirts
    of Edinburgh, 238
    producing boots night and day,
    239

Oakey, John, develops early form of
    sandpaper, 207
Offerman, Nick, American actor
    and creator of the part of
    Ron Swanson in *Parks and
    Recreation*
    woodworking scenes in show, 140
    sets up Offerman Workshop in
    Los Angeles, 141
    using nails and planks, 141
    and circle of life, 142
Okie, Francis Gurney, inventor of
    Wet-or-Dry sandpaper and
    author of immense mass
    of poetry composed using

Gematria alphanumerical
    cypher, 208
*Old West Surrey*, book by Gertrude
    Jekyll, 201
Oldowan Industry, prehistoric tools,
    10
O'Leary family, falsely accused by
    Chicago journalist of starting
    destructive fire in 1871, 203
Olmstead, Frederick Law, pioneer of
    suburban building in US, 25
*One Good Turn: A Natural History of
    the Screwdriver and the Screw*,
    book by Witold Rybczynski,
    224
*Open All Hours*, BBC comedy series
    starring Ronnie Barker, 271
*Operative Mechanic and British
    Machinist, The*, book by John
    Nicholson, 207
Ord William, British doctor who
    treated effects of arsenic
    poisoning, 258

Palmer, Henry, developer of
    corrugated iron, 172
*Parks and Recreation*, long-running
    American comedy series,
    139–40
Parmelee, Spencer Thomas,
    co-founder of the North
    British Rubber Co., 238
Parnell, Michael, London locksmith,
    185
Penney, John, 16th-century joiner
    from Eye, Suffolk, 112
PETA (People for the Ethical
    Treatment of Animals),
    urges humane treatment of

bluebottles as well as mice, 256

Petroski, Professor Henry, author of *The Evolution of Useful Things*, 220

Pevsner, Nikolaus, architectural writer and admirer of Christopher Dresser, 164

*Pharmaceutical Journal*, 258

Phillips, Henry Frank, patented cross-head screw and obtained funding for Phillips Screw Co., 227

Phillips cross-head screw
developed by John P. Thompson, 226
taken up by General Motors, 227
'camming out', 228

Pincus, Gregory, developer of first contraceptive pill, 246

*Pins and Needles*, magazine started by Christine Veasey, 90

*Pins and Needles Treasure Book of Home Making*, 91

Piper, Theobald and Co., Norwich ironmonger, 8–9

PITCA (Pressing Irons & Trivet Collectors of America), 166–7

Plungers
in the shop, 214
tackling upstairs basin, 216
invented by John Savage Hawley, 216
acquires current name, 218

*Popular Mechanics*, magazine, 74

Port Townsend, port on coast of Washington State in US, 106

Powell, Dick, American film actor and reputed DIY enthusiast, 74

power drills
introduced by Black & Decker, 53
fifteen million in use in US by 1954, 54

*Practical Householder*, DIY magazine launched in 1955
great demand for first issue, 65
abundance of advertising, 67
field to itself, 68
Barry Bucknell, 82
stages exhibitions, 92

Premier Box Mangle, made by Thomas Bradford & Co., 124

Preston, Frank, DIY journalist and editor of *Homemaker*, 71

*Psychology of Science: A Reconnaissance, The*, book by Abraham Mallow, 222

Punxsutawney Phil, rodent featured in the film *Groundhog Day*, 166

Quayle, David, founder of B&Q with Richard Block, 95

*Quincaillerie*, poem about hardware shops by Jean Follain, 276

Randall, Frederick John, author of *Love and the Ironmonger*, 274

Rate (or Rathe), 15th-century scribe who wrote down the poem *Debate of the Carpenter's Tools*, 111

Rawlbolt, anchor bolt for brick or stone, 212

Rawlings, James Joseph, inventor of the Rawlplug
working at British Museum, 211
brainwave, 211
dies rich man, 212

Rawlplug
  invented, 211
  boon to builders and trade, 211–2
  life for DIYer without
    unthinkable, 212
  some tasks beyond its power, 213
Reading, county town of Berkshire,
  35, 281
*Rebel Without a Cause*, 1955 film
  starring James Dean in jeans,
  65, 159
Recess Screws Ltd., company sets
  up in England by Peter
  Lymburner Robertson, 226
Reed & Prince, company in
  Worcester, Massachusetts
  making Robertson screws, 226
Remsen, Henry, friend of Thomas
  Jefferson, later his secretary,
  191
Rimby, Henry William, master
  maker of trivets in Baltimore,
  162–3
Riverside, suburban community
  created by Olmstead and Vaux
  outside Chicago, 25
rivets
  in the shop
  cold rivet/hot rivet, 152
  use in building *Titanic*, 153
  drawback, 154
  invention of pop rivet, 155
  use in strengthening pockets of
    jeans, 156–8
Robertson, Peter Lymburner,
  Canadian industrialist
  ponders failings of slotted screw
    and screwdriver, 225
  sets up factory in Milton,
    Ontario, 226
  falls out with Henry Ford, 226
  tries in vain to export success to
    England, 226
  screw preferred by connoisseurs,
    228
Rocket Chemical Co., established in
  San Diego, California, makers
  of WD-40, 241–2
Rockwell, Norman, American
  painter and illustrator
  responsible for poster of Rosie
  the Riveter, 55
Roebling, Emily, wife of Brooklyn
  Bridge engineer Washington
  Roebling and driving force
  behind getting bridge built,
  173
Roebling, John Augustus, first
  designer of Brooklyn Bridge
  and first fatality in building
  it, 172
Roebling, Washington, designer of
  Brooklyn Bridge disabled by
  decompression sickness, 172
Rosack, Lynn, American authority
  on trivets and author of two
  books on subject, 161, 166
Rosie the Riveter, American wartime
  poster depicting powerfully
  built woman with rivet gun,
  55
Royal Society, The, association of
  scientists and inventors, 114
rushlight, early form of illumination
  used for centuries, 201
Ruskin, John, 19th-century English
  authority on art and society,
  24

Rutland, Duke of, owner of Belvoir
Castle which was lit by oil
lamps, 202
Ryan, Robert, Hollywood actor said
to be keen on DIY, 74
Rybczynski, Witold, American
academic and amateur
woodworker
author of *One Good Turn:*
*A Natural History of the*
*Screwdriver and the Screw*, 224
on origins of screwdriver, 224
preference for Robertson square-
socket screw, 228

San Diego Natural History
Museum, 243
sandpaper
early versions, 207
Wet-or-Dry invented by Francis
Gurney Oakie, 208
Sanger, Margaret, American birth
control campaigner, 245–6
Sargent, Irene, lecturer at Syracuse
University, New York, and
contributor to early issues of
*The Craftsman* magazine, 26
*Sartre's Sink: The Great Writers'*
*Complete Book of DIY*, book of
parodies by Mark Crick, 274
saw, tool for cutting and major
technological breakthrough,
111
*Scientific American*, magazine, 216, 237
Scotch Brand, masking tape
invented by Richard Gurney
Drew, 209
Scotch Transparent Tape, cellophane
transparent adhesive tape

invented by Richard Gurney
Drew, 209
screwdriver
flat-head v. cross-head, 223
earliest, 224
Phillips v. Robertson, 228
screws
better than nails, 116
all different, 117
lathes for cutting, 118–20
proposals for standardising, 121
first machine for cutting with
pointed ends, 122
Britain clings to Whitworth
standard, 124
early improvements on flat-head,
224–5
Robertson square-socket drive,
225–6
Phillips cross-head, 226–7
Seddon, Frederick, murderer using
arsenic from flypapers, 260
Sellers, Paul, British woodworker
and blogger, 135–6
Sellers, William, American
industrialist and promotor of
new standard screw, 123
Shaw, Tessa, first presenter of *Home*
*Front*, 145
Shorthose, Wood & Co.,
Staffordshire screw
manufacturers, 117
Shove, Elizabeth, British academic
and joint author of article
about DIY motivation, 50
Singleton, Valerie, BBC TV and
radio presenter, 92
*Sixty Minute Makeover*, ITV home
transformation show, 147

Slee, James Noah, businessman
partner of George William Cole
in 3-in-One oil company, 244
energetic marketing techniques,
244
marries Margaret Sanger and
funds birth control campaign,
245
dies in Tucson, Arizona, 246
Sloan, Thomas J., patented machine
to make screws with pointed
ends, 122
Sloane, Eric (born Everard
Hinrichs), American artist
painting for Amish, 134
writes *A Museum of Early
American Tools*, 134–5
loathing of the modern, 135
Smiles Samuel, 19th-century apostle
of self-help and historian of
industry, 117
Smillie, Carol, presenter of *Changing
Rooms*, 21, 146
Smith George Mence, ironmonger,
9
Smith, Robert, engineer credited
with developing rivet-
punching machine, 153
Society for Industrial Archaeology,
195, 196
Sorel, Stanislaw, patented
galvanisation, 171
South Eastern Railway Robbery, 186
South Petherton, village in Somerset
with housing constructed on
Nissen Hut principle, 176
Spilsbury, Bernard, pathologist and
witness for prosecution in
Seddon murder trial, 260

spirit level
satisfying in its function, 228
invention, 229
single vial version invented, 230
celebrated by the poet David
Barber, 232
Sprengel, Herman, inventor of the
vacuum pump, 203
Starr, Julian, author of *Fifty Things to
Make for the Home*, 54
Statista, data provider, 149
Steele, Anastasia, character in *Fifty
Shades of Grey*, 274
Steffend, Joan, American presenter
of long-running home
improvement show *Decorating
Cents*, 144
Stephen, Mr Justice, grossly biased
judge at murder trial of
Florence Maybrick, 259
Stickley Gustav, American Arts and
Crafts pioneer and founder of
*The Craftsman* magazine, 26
Stowe, Harriet Beecher, sister
of Catharine Beecher and
co-author with her of *The
American Woman's Home* as
well as, in her own right, *Uncle
Tom's Cabin*, 22, 23, 26, 55
Studley, H. O., American maker of
famously intricate toolbox,
107–8
Sullivan Gregory F. ('Garson
O'Toole'), curator of
quoteinvestigator.com, 221
Swan, Sir Joseph
creates prototype lightbulb, 203
rivalry with Edison, 204
lighting for grand houses, 205

Swarfega, cleansing gel
  where the name comes from,
    246
  invented by Audley Bowdler
    Williamson, 247
  helping make a dirty world less
    dirty, 248
Szolnok, town in Hungary where
    the Angel Makers of Nagyrev
    were imprisoned, 261

tallow, fat used to make candles, 201
Tanglefoot, trade name for flypapers
    devised by Thum brothers, 25
Thévenot, Melchisédech, French
    inventor of spirit level and
    swimming enthusiast, 229–30
*This Old House*, American home
    improvement show, 143–4
Thom, George, memories of wash
    day in Winnipeg, Canada, 178
Thompson, John P., devised the
    cross-head screw which
    became the Phillips screw,
    226
Thoreau Henry, American nature
    writer, author of *Walden: Or
    Life in the Woods*, carpenter,
    133
3-in-One Oil
  devised by George William Cole,
    243–4
  success, 244
  diaphragms smuggled in
    consignment of, 245
Thum, four brothers – Otto,
    William, Hugo, Ferdinand –
    who invented sticky flypapers,
    257–8

*Time*, magazine, August 1954 cover
    depicts six-armed DIY freak,
    57
*Times, The*, newspaper
  reports Great Lock Controversy,
    186
  publishes letter in praise of
    electric lighting, 205
Tinney, Judge Bill, American
    woodworker, 106–7
Tinsley, Eliza, owner of Midlands
    nail factories known as the
    'Nail Mistress of the Black
    Country', 189
*Titanic*, liner sunk in 1912 after
    hitting iceberg, 153–4
Tolpin, Jim, American woodworker,
    author of *The Toolbox Book*,
    106
Tomkin, Silvan, American
    psychologist and joint
    editor of *Computer Simulation
    of Personality: Frontiers of
    Psychology*, proposed version of
    Law of the Instrument, 221
Toulouse, Julian Harrison, American
    authority on glass jars and
    bottles and author of two
    books on the subject, 195–6
Triumph, maker of motorcycles,
    128–9
trivets
  what it is and is not, 160
  taken seriously by collectors in
    US, 161
  to support sad irons, 162
  made by William Rimby, 162–3
  designed by Christopher Dresser,
    163
  other designers, 165–6
  my own meagre collection, 167

Tromp, Tim, curator of Kilokat
antique light bulb site, 200–1
Twin-tub washing machine, 179
*Two Ronnies*, BBC sketch show
starring Ronnie Barker and
Ronnie Corbett, 270–1

UKASTLE (UK Association of Street
Lighting Enthusiasts), 200
Union Manufacturing Co.,
Boyertown, Pennsylvania,
makes of JZH series of trivets,
165
United Glass, buyers of the Kilner
Jar trademark, 195
Ur of the Chaldees, capital of
ancient Sumeria where saws
were uncovered, 111
US Occupational Safety and Health
Administration, data about
composition of WD-40, 254
US Patent Office, considers tens
of thousands of mousetrap
patent applications, 255

Vanderpump, Wellbelove,
Wellesley-Smith & Co., (now
Vanderpump & Wellbelove),
Reading firm of land and
estate agents, xi
Vaux Calvert, American pioneer of
suburban development, 25
Veasey, Christine, founder of *Pins
and Needles* magazine, 91
'Victor' mousetrap, 254
Village Gardeners, group of
volunteers in Sonning
Common dedicated
to enhancing village's
appearance, x

*Vintage Bike*, magazine featuring
Greg's Triumph Bonneville,
129
Virginia Metalcrafters, American
manufacturers of Ranch
Brand trivets, 165
*Virtuoso: The Tool Cabinet and
Workbench of H. O. Studley*,
book by Donald Williams, 108
Viviani, Vincenzo, 17th-century
Italian scientist interested in
spirit levels, 229
Volta, Alessandro, 17th-century
Italian scientist, rival of
Galvani, devised the Voltaic
Pile to demonstrate electric
current, 170

Wakeling, Arthur, editor of *Popular
Science* and author of *Fifty
Things to Make in Your
Workshop*, 38
Wallis, George, head of
government's School of
Design in Birmingham in
1850s, 122
Watkins, James, takes over Heath &
Watkins from father, 4
Watkins, Ted, joint founder of
Heath & Watkins with Jack
Heath, 4
Watson, Matthew, academic and
joint author of article about
DIY motivation, 50
Watson, Bishop Richard,
18th-century churchman and
theologian, witnessed iron
pots being dipped in melted
zinc, 171

Webster, Daniel, US congressman
    and lawyer, represented
    Charles Goodyear in the Great
    Rubber Case, 236
WD-40, lubricant
    composition, 240
    conversion to spray thanks to
        Norman Larsen, 241
    invention by Norman Lawson,
        241–2
    use in Vietnam War, 242–3
    official history overlooks
        Norman Lawson, 243
Wellington, Duke of, and wellington
    boots, 233
Wells, Dee, American journalist and
    novelist employed by *Daily
    Herald* as TV critic, 79, 82
Wells, Mick, owner of Heath &
    Watkins
    my first encounter, 1
    appearance and inclination to
        chat, 2–3
    previous business as potato
        factor, 3
    takes over Heath & Watkins, 4
    health issues, 5
    fondness for driving forklift, 10
    and workshop, 11
    and polytunnel, 12
    spending less time behind
        counter, 14
    suggests we take over business, 15
    mental agony, 16
    advice to Shro ignored, 19
    beams approval, 30
Welsbeck, Carl Auer von, Austrian
    inventor of the gas mantle,
    205

West Camel, village in Somerset
    where houses were built on
    the principle of the Nissen
    Hut, 176
West Midlands nail industry, 189
Wheeler, James A., editor of *The
    Practical Man's Book of Things to
    Make and Do*
    advice on happiness, 40
    how to make a summerhouse or
        a gramophone, 41,
    central theme, 41–2
    advice on not using electrical
        equipment in bath, 42
Whipple, Clarence, American
    mechanic, develops automated
    machine to make screws, 122
Whitworth, Sir Joseph
    upbringing, 120
    to London to work for Maudsley,
        120
    proposes standardisation of
        screws, 121
    goes to US to promote his
        standard, 121–2
    standard rejected by US
        manufacturers, 123
'Why?', poem performed by Bob
    Flanagan, 275
*Wild One, The*, film starring Marlon
    Brando in jeans, 159
Willard, Nancy, American poet,
    author of poem 'A Hardware
    Store as Proof of the Existence
    of God', 267–8
Willenhall, Midlands centre of lock-
    making, 186, 187–8
Williams, Donald, author of
    *Virtuoso: The Tool Cabinet and
    Workbench of H. O. Studley*, 108

Willamson, Aubrey Bowdler,
    inventor of Swarfega, 247–8
Williamson, Sir Joseph, 17th-century
    President of the Royal Society,
    114
*Witness*, film about Amish
    community starring Harrison
    Ford, 76
Witt, George C., introduces
    corrugated galvanised iron
    rubbish bin, 173–4
woodandshop.com, woodworking
    website curated by Joshua
    Farnsworth, 137
Woodruff, William, author of
    *History of the British Rubber
    Industry*, 237
woodworking
    my own miserable efforts, 132
    Arthur Miller, 132–3
    Henry Thoreau, 133
    Eric Sloane, 134
    early American tools, 134–5

Paul Sellers, 135–7
Joshua Farnsworth, 137–8
male bias in coverage, 138–9
Nick Offerman, 139–42
Woolworth, F.M., chain of retail
    stores
    range of paints, 93
    takes over B&Q, 96
*Work*, magazine edited by Paul
    Hasluck, 26–7
Wyatt, Job and William, brothers,
    set up screw factory at
    Tattenhall, Staffordshire, 117
Wylye, Neil Hamilton, inventor of
    the blind or pop rivet, 155

Yeovil, town in Somerset, location
    of houses built on principle of
    Nissen Hut, 176

Ziemann, Henry, developed
    single vial spirit level in
    Mukwonago, Wisconsin, 230